THE RESILIENCE OF LANGUAGE

ESSAYS IN DEVELOPMENTAL PSYCHOLOGY

North American Editors:
Henry Wellman, University of Michigan at Ann Arbor and
Janet Werker, University of British Columbia

United Kingdom Editor:
Peter Bryant, University of Oxford

Essays in Developmental Psychology is designed to meet the need for rapid publication of brief volumes in developmental psychology. The series defines developmental psychology in its broadest terms and covers such topics as social development, cognitive development, developmental neuropsychology and neuroscience, language development, learning difficulties, developmental psychopathology and applied issues. Each volume in the series makes a conceptual contribution to the topic by reviewing and synthesizing the existing research literature, by advancing theory in the area, or by some combination of these missions. Authors in this series provide an overview of their own highly successful research program, but they must also include an assessment of current knowledge and identification of possible future trends in research. Each book is a self-contained unit supplying the advanced reader with a coherent review of important research as well as its context, theoretical grounding, and implications

IN PREPARATION
Tager-Flusberg: *Autism and William's Syndrome*
Trehub: *Infants and Music*

PUBLISHED TITLES
Byrne: *The Foundation of Literacy*
Cox: *Children's Drawings of the Human Figure*
Forrester: *The Development of Young Children's Social-Cognitive Skills*
Garton: *Social Interaction and the Development of Language*
Goodnow/Collins: *Development According to Parents*
Goswami: *Analogical Reasoning in Children*
Goswami/Bryant: *Phonological Skills and Learning to Read*
Harris: *Language Experience and Early Language Development*
Hobson: *Autism and the Development of Mind*
Howe: *Language Learning*
Inagaki & Hatano: *Young Children's Naive Thinking About the Biological World*
Langford: *The Development of Moral Reasoning*
Meadows: *Parenting Behavior and Children's Cognitive Development*
Meins: *Security of Attachment and Cognitive Development*
Perez-Pereira & Conti-Ramsden: *Language Development and Social Interactions in Blind Children*
Siegal: *Knowing Children (2nd ed.)*
Smith: *Necessary Knowledge and Constructivism*

THE RESILIENCE OF LANGUAGE

What Gesture Creation in Deaf Children Can Tell Us About How All Children Learn Language

Susan Goldin-Meadow

Psychology Press
New York • Hove

Published in 2003 by
Psychology Press, Inc.
29 West 35th Street
New York, NY 10001
www.psypress.com

Published in Great Britain by
Psychology Press, Ltd.
27 Church Road
Hove, East Sussex
BN3 2FA
www.psypress.co.uk

Psychology Press, Inc., is an imprint of the Taylor & Francis Group.
Printed in the United States of America on acid-free paper.

10 9 8 7 6 5 4 3 2 1

Library of Congress Cataloging-in-Publication Data
Goldin, Susan.
    The resilience of language : what gesture creation in deaf children can tell us about how
all children learn language / Susan Goldin-Meadow.
      p. cm. — (Essays in developmental psychology)
    Includes index.
    ISBN 1–84169–026–0
    1. Language acquisition. 2. Gesture. 3. Deaf children—Means of communication.
I. Title. II. Series.

P118 .G57 2003
401'.93—dc21
                                                      2002036719

I lovingly dedicate this book

to the memory of my father, Benjamin J. Goldin,

who was always very proud of me no matter what I did

and to my mother, Mildred Goldin,

for being my mom

CONTENTS

ACKNOWLEDGMENTS

I have always been fascinated by the structure of words—one of those kids who thinks grammar and Latin are fun. I'm not sure where the fascination came from but watching my daughter get hooked on Latin declensions and conjugations this summer (when she took high-school Latin as a middle school student just for fun) and knowing that my mother began her career as a Latin scholar makes me think that I've come by the interest honestly (and down the maternal line). I continued to cultivate the interest at Smith College when I spent my junior year abroad in Geneva at the Piagetian Institute working with Annette Karmiloff-Smith on a project on relative clauses under Mimi Sinclair's direction. Although our discoveries were hardly earth-shaking, this experience convinced me that I wanted to figure out how children learn language and I decided to go to the University of Pennsylvania to do it. I knew I'd find Lila Gleitman at Penn—she was one of the reasons I chose Penn for graduate school. But I didn't know I'd find Heidi Feldman. Heidi was a fellow graduate student in developmental psychology, also interested in language, and together with Lila we began our study of deaf children inventing their own gestures.

The Clark School for the Deaf, one of the best oral schools in the country, is down the road from Smith. I had heard, and observed, that deaf children who are not making progress in oral language nevertheless communicate and use their hands to do so, a titillating observation that resonated with the research program Lila and Henry Gleitman were just beginning. This program of research would result in some of the most interesting research done in the field of language acquisition. The basic idea was to vary the language learner and the language learning environment and observe the effects (or noneffects) of each on child outcomes (Gleitman & Newport, 1995). For example, do the natural variations in how mothers speak to their children result in differences in how those children learn language (Newport, Gleitman, & Gleitman, 1977)? Are children who lack access to vision able to align their sightless worlds with the linguistic inputs they receive so that they too can learn language (Landau & Gleitman, 1985)? Are children whose mental development is delayed able to acquire language following the same trajectory as more cognitively able children (Fowler, Gelman, & Gleitman, 1994)? And our own project—are children lacking access to linguistic input able to develop language nonetheless (Feldman, Goldin-Meadow & Gleitman, 1978)? This was an intellectually exciting research program devoted to exploring *how* children learn language, not just documenting the stages children pass through as they learn language. And our work on the deaf children was a foundational part of the program.

Heidi and I traipsed all over Philadelphia looking for just the right children to study—and we found them. We then spent hours together trying to figure out what we should be looking at and how to write it down. It seems clear in retrospect what we ought to have been focusing on, but it was not at all clear at the time. Heidi was the perfect person for me to work with—we complemented each other beautifully. I continued to observe many of the children long after Heidi and I both graduated (indeed, thanks to NSF, long after I had moved away from Philadelphia). But the seeds of the project were sown in Philadelphia and this book owes its very existence to Lila and to Heidi—and, needless to say, to the deaf children themselves. I am very grateful to the many families who welcomed us and our video equipment into their homes and shared their children and their stories with us.

When I moved to the University of Chicago in 1976, it was an excellent opportunity to ask whether deaf children in the Midwest invent gesture systems that resemble those invented by their East Coast peers. The move also gave me the opportunity to begin new collaborations, the most important of which has been with Carolyn Mylander. Carolyn has run my lab in Chicago for over 20 years. She has a feel for how to code gesture and how to get things done carefully and with just the right attention to detail. Her contributions to this research program are incalculable and, happily, promise to continue—she is currently orchestrating our new studies of deaf children of hearing parents in four cultures (American, Chinese, Spanish, Turkish) with the excellence that is her trademark. I thank her for always making it work.

I also thank Martha Scott who has ably assisted Carolyn in running the lab for as long as I can remember. In addition to making everything in the lab run smoothly, Carolyn and Martha work hard to make sure that people respect one another and have fun together. The healthy attitude in the lab is maintained, in large part, by these two very important people. The weekly meetings that we hold in the lab are to me the heart of the research and educational process. I thank all of the students and colleagues who attend for the hard and constructive thinking they do every Wednesday afternoon. I have learned much from these meetings.

I have been fortunate over the years to have had wonderful collaborations with many students (undergraduate, graduate, and postdoctoral) and colleagues. All of the studies described in this book have been collaborations and much of the credit belongs to my partners: Heidi Feldman, Lila Gleitman, Carolyn Mylander, David McNeill, Peggy Miller, Susan Gelman, Rachel Mayberry, Jenny Singleton, Lisa Gershkoff-Stowe, Jill Morford, Ming-yu Zheng, Xiao-lei Wang, Asli Ozyurek, Cynthia Butcher, Mark Dodge, Jody Saltzman, Sarah Van Deusen Phillips, Elif Yalabik, Amy Hammond, Amy Franklin, and Bari Wieselman Schulman. In addition, my ideas about innateness have developed over the years under the nurturing influence of Martha McClintock and Bill Wimsatt. We have taught the Mind course in the Social Sciences Core at the University of Chicago together since 1977 and have found that our views are strikingly similar despite the vast differences in our fields (Goldin-Meadow, McClintock, & Wimsatt, 2003).

Gesture coding is remarkably labor intensive. We generally spend at least 40 hours coding every hour of videotape, and I have been fortunate to have had a great deal of help over the years. I thank all the many people who spent days and nights coding videotapes, first in Judd Hall and later in Kelly-Beecher-Green, and those who helped collect data in Philadelphia, Chicago, and Taiwan: Tomoko Asano, Ralph Bloom, Sara Broaders, Keeshawna Brooks, Te Chang Chao, Peter Chen, Ruth Breckinridge Church, Susan Duncan, Ellen Eichen, Emily Hammer, Jeff Harlig, Margie Hartfield, Janna Hicks, Monica Ho, Julia (Sae) Kim, Lorraine Kubicek, Tricia Leaky, Simon Li, Lisa Liu, Shuhong Lim, Alexander Meadow, Marolyn Morford, Miriam Rabban, Veronica Sansing, Lisette Tefo, Kristie Wang, Xiao-ping Wang, Rhonda Wodlinger Cohen, and Mitch (Ming Che) Yeh.

My research has flourished under the generous support and attentive eye of Paul Chapin at the National Science Foundation (BNS 8810769 from 1977 to 1992), Tom James at the Spencer Foundation (from 1980 to 1983), and Judith Cooper at the National Institute of Deafness and other Communication Disorders (RO1 DC00491 from 1988 to 2006), and I thank them for their help over the last 25 years. I would also like to thank Irving B. Harris, whose chair I currently hold in the Department of Psychology and Committee on Human Development at the University of Chicago. He has done much over his long career to better the lives of children in our society, and I am grateful for his support and honored to hold a professorship bearing his name.

The book itself got its first breath of life when Henry Wellman convinced me that it would be a good idea to bring all of the studies on the deaf children's gesture systems together in one place and to do it in the Essays in Developmental Psychology series that he was editing with Janet Werker. Having read and greatly enjoyed Carol Dweck's excellent book serving the same function for her research program and published in the Essays in Social Psychology series, I became convinced that this was indeed the right step to take. But it took a sabbatical year funded by a John Simon Guggenheim Fellowship and a James McKeen Cattell Fellowship to get me writing.

The manuscript improved immensely as a result of careful reads from many colleagues and friends. I thank them all for their comments and suggestions: Martha Alibali, Danny Povinelli, Jill Morford, Lila Gleitman, Dan Slobin, Elissa Newport, John Lantos, and Mildred Goldin. I particularly thank my editors, Henry Wellman and Janet Werker, and my reviewer, Virginia Valian, for the detailed and very thoughtful comments they gave me on how to make the book better. I thank Linda Huff for turning videotapes of gestures into lovely line drawings that make it much easier to imagine what an invented gestural language looks like. I thank Amanda Woodward and the students in the graduate and undergraduate courses on language acquisition we taught together in 2002 for reading the book and commenting on how it can (and should) be used in a course. I thank Dedre Gentner for always listening and helping me decide where to publish the book and how to make it useful to teachers and readers. I thank Kathy and Kevin Clougherty for lending me their car phone for several hours so that I could get comments from my readers while working on the revisions on Washington Island. The serenity and peacefulness of the Gibson's cabin on the island (and their hospitality and friendship) made revising the manuscript infinitely easier and greatly improved the final product. I heartily recommend an island for book writing.

And most of all I thank my family, my favorite language learners, Alexander ("Xander"), Nathaniel ("Shmug"), and Jacqueline ("Beanie") whose linguistic accomplishments I chose to revel in rather than document. I am also grateful to my favorite language teacher, my mother, Mildred Goldin, whose attention to language form stemming from her own interest in Latin and Greek sowed the seeds of my curiosity about words. And, of course, I must mention the family dogs, Rugeleh, Knish, Kugel (there's a theme here), and Metro Goldin-Meadow, none of whom came close to inventing a language despite hours of some of the best "motherese" I could muster. Finally, I thank my husband, Bill Meadow, who has read every word of this book several times over, and improved on most of them. He has been totally supportive of me and my interests since our early days together in undergraduate and graduate school. Our marriage has been my most productive and deeply satisfying collaboration. I cannot thank him enough.

Susan Goldin-Meadow
Chicago
November 2002

☐ References

Feldman, H., Goldin-Meadow, S., & Gleitman, L. (1978). Beyond Herodotus: The creation of a language by linguistically deprived deaf children. In A. Lock (Ed.), *Action, symbol, and gesture: The emergence of language* (pp. 351–414). New York: Academic.

Fowler, A. E., Gelman, R., & Gleitman, L. R. (1994). The course of language learning in children with Down Syndrome: Longitudinal and language level comparisons with young normally developing children (pp. 91–140). In H. Tager-Flusberg (Ed.), *Constraints on language acquisition: Studies of atypical children* (pp. 75–90). Hillsdale, NJ: Erlbaum.

Gleitman. L. R. & Newport, E. L. (1995). The invention of language by children: Environmental and biological influences on the acquisition of language. In L. R. Gleitman & M. Liberman (Eds.), *Language, Vol. 1, Invitation to Cognitive Science Series* (pp. 1–24). Cambridge, MA: MIT Press.

Goldin-Meadow, S., McClintock, M. K., & Wimsatt, W. (2003). Solving psychological problems in four dimensions: Heuristics for the social and biological sciences (under review).

Landau, B., & Gleitman, L. R. (1985). *Language and experience: Evidence from the blind child.* Cambridge, MA: Harvard University Press.

Newport, E. L., Gleitman, H., & Gleitman, L. R. (1977). Mother I'd rather do it myself: Some effects and non-effects of maternal speech style. In C. E. Snow & C. A. Ferguson (Eds.), *Talking to children* (pp. 109–150). New York: Cambridge University Press.

ACCOMPANYING WEBSITE OF VIDEO CLIPS

In order to bring the gestures that are described in this book to life, there is an accompanying website of video clips gathered from the tapes that Heidi Feldman, Lila Gleitman, and I collected many years ago (which explains their blurriness). If the book is used as part of a course (see *How the Book Can Be Used in a Course on Language Acquisition,* page xix in the Introduction), the clips will be particularly important in making the phenomenon of gesture creation real. I thank Zachary Johnson and Carolyn Mylander for their help in preparing the clips. And I thank the children and their families for sharing their lives first with us and now with the readers of this book. The video clips, which are listed in the table below, can be viewed at:

www.psypress.com/goldinmeadow

Page in Book	Short Name	Description
59	Shovels	Combining gestures into sentences to talk about shovels
73	Dad-Sleep	Pointing at a chair in the room to indicate dad who is sleeping in another room (Figure 1 in book)
75	Break	An emblem meaning "break" (Figure 2A in book)
75	Give	An emblem meaning "give" (Figure 2B in book)
77	Flutter-Fall	Communicating about manner (snow flutters) and path (snow falls) in two separate gestures (Figure 3 in book)
79	Headshakes & Nods	Incorporating headshakes and headnods into a gesture sentence to negate ("Lisa is not eating") and affirm ("but I am eating")
79	Wait	A modulating gesture "wait" used to signal the immediate future (Figure 4A in book)

INTRODUCTION

☐ The Goal of the Book

With each of my three children, I waited with some amount of trepidation for the first signs of language—the first word, the first sentence, the first story. Being a nervous sort, I was concerned that maybe they wouldn't be able to do it—that they wouldn't be able to master the complex and intricate system that we use effortlessly and without thinking.

I needn't have worried. Language-learning is a remarkably robust and resilient process, one that comes naturally to the vast majority of children (including my own). This book explores the resilience of the language-learning process.

For the last 25 years, I have been studying children who are growing up in language-learning circumstances that are not typical. The children are deaf with hearing losses so severe that they cannot acquire the spoken language that surrounds them. In addition, they are born to hearing parents who have not exposed them to a conventional sign language (e.g., American Sign Language). The children thus lack access to a usable model of language. Under such inopportune circumstances, these deaf children might be expected to fail to communicate.

Yet the children do communicate. Not surprisingly, they use their hands to do so—they gesture. What is surprising, however, is that the gestures the deaf children use to communicate are structured in language-like ways. The children are inventing their own, simple language. My goal in this book is to situate the study of deaf children who invent a gesture system within the phenomenon of language-learning—to make it clear why a study of deaf children who do not have access to a usable model for language is important, and what such a study can tell us about how all children learn language.

☐ The Organization of the Book

The book is divided into three sections. The first section, "The Problem of Language-Learning," lays out the challenges language-learning presents both to the child trying to figure out how language works and to the experimenter trying to figure out how the child is figuring out how language works. In these five chapters, I provide an overview of what we know about the steps children take as they acquire language, a description of current attempts to explain language-learning, and a brief summary of what we've learned from studying language-learning under varying circumstances—in children exposed to different languages in various cultures across the globe, in children exposed to conventional sign language, and in children exposed to varying amounts of linguistic input within a single culture.

The second section of the book, "Language Development Without a Language Model," explores in depth a situation in which children are lacking input from a language model yet in all other respects are experiencing normal social environments—deaf children inventing their own gesture systems. In these ten chapters, I first provide background on deafness and language-learning, background that is crucial for understanding the unique circumstances in which deaf children of hearing parents find themselves. I then describe properties of the deaf children's gesture systems—how gestures function as words, how they are combined to form sentences, and how they are used to describe situations beyond the here-and-now. Finally, I consider where the deaf children's gesture systems might come from. I first entertain the most obvious hypothesis, that the children's hearing parents provide a gesture model which the deaf children adopt. I explore this hypothesis by examining the gestures of hearing parents of American deaf children, and also by studying the invented gesture systems of deaf children of hearing parents in another culture (a Chinese culture). The striking finding is that the American deaf children's gestures do not resemble those of their mothers—indeed they look much more like the gestures of the Chinese deaf children halfway across the globe than the gestures of their hearing parents in their own living room. The gestures that the hearing parents produce do not appear to serve as a model for the deaf children's gestures.

The properties that appear in the deaf children's gesture systems are resilient—they appear in the children's communications even though the children do not have a usable conventional language to guide their development. If these properties are so fundamental to human communication, why then do they not appear in the gestures of the deaf children's hearing parents? What is it about either the circumstances of acquisition, or the nature of the acquirer, that seems to lead inevitably to this type of structured communication system in the child?

I tackle these questions in the final section, "The Conditions That Foster Language and Language-Learning." I begin by considering what the phenomenon of gesture-creation in deaf children can tell us about language-learning in all children—how do the resilient properties of language help children, deaf or hearing, learn language? I then explore the conditions under which gesture becomes language using an experimental approach with hearing adults. We put hearing adults in situations that simulate some of the conditions under which the deaf children find themselves, and ask whether those conditions lead adults to develop a gesture system that has some of the resilient properties of language. In the third chapter in this section, I consider what we learn from the deaf children about the age-old question: Is language innate? I suggest that, although tired and worn, the word "innate" has not yet outlived its usefulness. What it needs is to be freed from genetics and tied to developmental resilience. I end by reviewing the resilient properties of language with an eye toward what we learn from them about how all children learn language.

☐ How the Book Can Be Used in a Course on Language Acquisition

This book is not a stand-alone textbook, that is, it was not intended to be used as the sole text in a course on language acquisition. However, I did write it with students of language in mind. I believe that the phenomenon of children creating language can be used as an excellent teaching device to get students to think hard about what communication is and what "counts" as language. Ask your students to imagine what it would be like if there were no language to learn and they wanted to make their wants, desires, and thoughts known to others. What would they do? It's an exercise that forces students to think about what is essential to human language.

Because the phenomenon of language creation is so compelling, the book can be used as an extended case study that supplements a traditional text in both upper level undergraduate courses and introductory graduate courses. I have used it along with readings from primary sources, each week supplementing the readings on how children learn a piece of conventional language, say syntax, with the chapters of this book describing what children can do in the syntactic domain without a conventional language—and it has worked remarkably well.

I realize, however, that there may not be time in a course to read the whole book. As a result, I have tried to write the book so that pieces can be assigned on their own. And I have some recommendations for how the book can best be used in this way.

The first five chapters offer an overview of the problem of language-learning and can be used for this purpose. Because my focus is on the properties of language that are resilient, I have reviewed literature and highlighted topics that are often treated peripherally in traditional texts. For example, to my knowledge, no text on language acquisition has a chapter on how children learn different languages across the globe—traditionally, cross-linguistic facts are scattered throughout the text where relevant. But I think something very important can be learned by thinking about the learning problems children face when acquiring different languages—and, of course, by figuring out what's resilient across these variations and what's not. As another example, learning sign language in most texts is relegated to a chapter near the end of the book on atypical language-learning. Its lessons are rarely integrated into the main story of how children learn language. My focus on resilience makes a chapter of this sort central to the enterprise. So the first five chapters provide a short introduction to language acquisition taking a perspective that is slightly different from, but clearly complementary to, the perspective typically taken in textbooks on how children learn language.

How then can the rest of the book be used in a course on language acquisition? I suggest to prospective teachers that Chapter 6 be used to introduce the communication problem that faces these deaf children and that the other chapters in Part 2 be assigned according to the particular emphasis of the course. For example, if it's methods and the problems of description that you'd like to emphasize, Chapter 7 describes how to go about analyzing an unknown system that may not even be there, and thus presents the "how to" problem in an unusual and instructive light. If you'd like to focus on words and their composition, Chapters 8 and 9 form the basics, supplemented by Chapter 12 which is where nouns and verbs are discussed and Chapter 13 which is where you'll find a discussion of generics. If the focus of the course is syntax, Chapters 10 and 11 describe the structures children impose on the sentences they create and Chapter 12 describes how this system develops over time. If you'd like to focus on the functions of language, Chapter 13 describes the uses that the children's invented language serve, uses that go well beyond making requests in the here-and-now—to talking about past, future, and hypothetical events; to making generic statements about classes of objects; to telling stories; to talking to oneself; and even to talking about talk. Finally, if you'd like to focus on the role that environmental input plays in language-learning, Chapter 14 describes the unconventional input that these language-creating children receive from their parents and Chapter 15 takes a different approach to the same problem by looking at language-creating across the globe (on the assumption, which turns out to be correct, that the children are doing their creating in very different worlds).

Another possibility is to skip Part 2 entirely and assign Chapter 16 which summarizes the resilient properties of language described in Part 2 and speculates about how these properties help children learn conventional languages. Chapter 16 is the heart of the book and indeed provides a roadmap of Part 2. Chapter 17 explores what happens when adults who already have language are forced to create a gesture language, and again encourages students to think about what language is and why it looks the way it does. Chapter 18 is a discussion of innateness and language-learning and therefore can be assigned along with Chapters 14 and 15 to continue the discussion of the importance (and nonimportance) of linguistic input in language-learning (it can even be used to foster discussions of innateness independent of language acquisition in the context of a broader course on developmental psychology). Chapter 19 is a brief summary of what the phenomenon of gesture creation tells us about how all children learn language.

Because I think the phenomenon of gesture creation is instructive not only for experts in the field, but also for people who do not routinely think about language, I have tried to make the book accessible to readers who have no knowledge of language or linguistics. However, in order to make a convincing case that the deaf children in our studies really have invented a system that looks like language, I have to show you that their gestures can be described in the terms that work so well to describe natural languages. So I do have to use some linguistic terminology. But I've described the children's structural patterns minimizing linguistic jargon whenever possible and explaining technical terms when it has not been possible to avoid them. My goal has been to give you a feel for language as it comes out the hands of a child.

Throughout the book, I use the term "we." It is not the royal "we" to which I refer, but rather the collaborative "we." All of the studies on the deaf children, from the earliest studies with Lila Gleitman and Heidi Feldman to the latest with Susan Gelman, Carolyn Mylander, Ming-yu Zheng, and Lisa Gershkoff-Stowe, were done working closely with others. It is my good fortune that I have had so many smart and insightful colleagues and students with whom to think. Whatever insights about language-learning have been gained by studying deaf children of hearing parents were achieved through endless hours of watching and thinking with others. I offer this book as another step in the process of collaboration, in the hope that others will find the questions raised here worthy of continued probing and thinking.

THE PROBLEM
OF LANGUAGE-LEARNING

Out of the Mouths of Babes

The fact that children learn language so effortlessly at a time when tying their shoes is a real hurdle makes language-learning appear miraculous. Children are faced with the seemingly difficult task of learning a complex symbolic system, one that varies from culture to culture in seemingly arbitrary ways. We have all had the experience of listening to a foreign language fluently spoken by a native speaker—it feels to us, although not to the speaker, that there are no breaks in the flow. Where are the words? Where do the sentences stop and start? This is the first task that faces young children, discovering the units of the language they are to learn.

In addition, children must learn how the units of their language are combined. When children produce utterances that they have never heard before, and that follow the patterns of the language they are witnessing, we know that they have learned something about the underlying regularities that make English English, Swahili Swahili, or American Sign Language American Sign Language. Children hear particular sentences, yet they acquire rules. Moreover, every child hears a different set of particular sentences, yet they all acquire the same rules and in approximately the same sequence. This is the wonder of language acquisition.

To begin to understand this miraculous process, we will take a brief tour through the steps children follow in acquiring language, beginning with their discovery of the sounds of language.

☐ Discovering the Units of Sound

When we speak, we run words together without reliable pauses between them, which is what gives listeners who don't know the language the feeling

3

that there are no breaks in the stream. How then do native language-users parse the language they hear into recognizable units? Adult listeners use their knowledge of regularities in the sound structure of the language to predict the boundaries of units like words. Since sound structure differs across language, knowledge of regularities in one language may not be useful in identifying boundaries in another language. Infants thus need to learn the particular features of the sound structure of *their* native language in order to be able to find words in the stream of talk that is addressed to them. When do they accomplish this feat?

Much to everyone's surprise, infants know something about the language they are to learn on the day they are born. Newborn babies born to French-speaking mothers listened to tapes of French and Russian speech and sucked on a wired nipple while doing so. The babies sucked more—and, by inference, were more aroused—when they listened to the French tapes than when they listened to the Russian tapes. Babies who had not heard French during their prenatal months showed no such effect (Mehler, Jusczyk, Lambertz, Halsted, Bertoncini, & Amiel-Tison, 1988). What the babies appear to have learned about French during those months in the womb was its prosodic structure (its intonation contours, or "music"); when the speech samples were filtered so that *only* the prosodic cues remained, the findings were unchanged. Thus, babies are already attuned to the music of their mother's tongue on day 1.

However, babies do not become sensitive to the particular sounds of their native language until the second half of their first year. Babies start out ready to learn any language—an essential characteristic since, in principle, they could be exposed to any of the world's languages, present or future. Babies are able to make essentially all the discriminations in sound contrasts that languages across the globe require. But sometime during the latter part of the first year, the ability to discriminate between contrasts *not* found in the infant's native language fades. (Adults are only able to hear those contrasts used in their particular language and can no longer hear the rest.) For example, Hindi and Salish have consonant contrasts not found in English. Surprising those who believe that adults always know more than children, infants learning English are able to make these Hindi and Salish discriminations, adult English-speakers are not. However, the infants are only able to do so during their first year—by 12 months the ability fades and they begin to listen like adult English-speakers. Importantly, the ability to discriminate these contrasts does *not* fade if the infant is exposed to input that makes use of the contrasts—infants learning Hindi or Salish are still able to make the discriminations in their respective languages at 12 months (Werker & Tees, 1984). Babies start to fail to make discriminations among vowels (as opposed to consonants) that are not found in their language even earlier (perhaps as early as 6 months; Kuhl, Williams, Lacerda, Stevens, & Lindblom, 1992).

By 9 months, infants can recognize words in their language independent of prosodic cues. English and Dutch have very similar prosodic characteristics. They differ, however, in phonetic and phonotactic structure (that is, in which sounds are produced in the language and how those sounds combine). For example, the [r] in English words is very different from the [r] found in Dutch words (a phonetic difference). English allows [d] to occur at the end of a syllable while Dutch doesn't, and Dutch allows [kn] or [zw] to begin syllables while English doesn't (phonotactic differences). When presented with a spoken list of English and Dutch words, 9-month-old English-learners listen longer to the English than the Dutch words. In contrast, 6-month-old English-learners show no preferences (Jusczyk, 1993). By 9 months, babies have learned enough about the sound structure of their language to prefer their own language to others, even those that have the same "music."

While learning to listen to sounds, infants are also learning to produce them. Infants do not produce what we might recognize as words until they are approximately 1 year old. However, long before then they use their voices in changing ways. They begin by using their voices to cry reflexively and to make vegetative sounds; they then coo, laugh, and begin to play with sound. Sometime around 6 to 9 months, infants begin to babble (Oller & Lynch, 1992)—they produce true syllables, often in a reduplicated series of the same consonant-vowel combination, for example, [dada] or [mamama]. Later still, infants begin to produce variegated babbling in which the range of consonants and vowels expands and sounds no longer need to be reduplicated (Stark, 1986). The child is now adding prosody to strings of babbles and, as a result, begins to sound like a native speaker (as long as you're not listening too closely).

Indeed, it is at this point (around 8 months) that native listeners can begin to identify an infant as one who is learning their language. For example, when they heard tapes of 8-month-old babbling, French speakers were able to tell the difference between French babies' babbling and Arabic or Chinese babies' babbling (deBoysson-Bardies, Sagart, & Durand, 1984). When the infants' babbles were closely examined by trained linguists, the French babies were found to display lengthenings and softer modulations than the Arabic and Chinese babies, who exhibited other characteristics that were found in the languages they had been hearing for 8 months (deBoysson-Bardies, 1999). Thus, by the end of the first year, children are beginning to speak, and listen, like native users of their language.

☐ Starting With the Word

All natural languages, spoken or signed, are structured at many levels. Meaningless units (phonemes) combine to create morphemes, the smallest meaningful units of a language, which in turn combine to form words, phrases, and sentences. Having made significant progress in learning the sound system underlying their language in the first several months of life, children are then free to tackle larger units. Regardless of the language learned, children tend to enter the system of larger units at the level of the word, rather than the morpheme or sentence. Between 10 and 15 months, children produce their first words, typically using each word as an isolated unit. Children then proceed in two directions, learning (1) that the word can be composed of smaller, meaningful parts (morphology), and (2) that the word is a building block for larger, meaningful phrases and sentences (syntax).

What is a word? Consider a child who wants a jar opened and whines while attempting to do the deed herself. This child has conveyed her desires to those around her, but has she produced a word? A word does more than communicate information—it stands for something; it's a symbol. Moreover, the mapping between a word and what it stands for is arbitrary—"dog" is the term we use in English for furry four-legged canines, but the term is "chien" in French and "perro" in Spanish. There is nothing about the form of each of these three words that makes it a good label for a furry creature— the word works to refer to the creature only because speakers of each language act as though they agree that this is what it stands for.

At the earliest stages of development, children may use a sequence of sounds consistently for a particular meaning, but the sequence bears no resemblance to the sound of any word in their language. These "proto-words" (Bates, 1976) are transitional forms that are often tied to particular contexts. For example, a child uses the sound sequence "brmm-brmm" every time he plays with or sees his toy truck. In fact, a child's proto-word need not be verbal at all—gesture works quite well. For example, a child smacks her lips every time she feeds her fish, or flaps her arms when she sees a picture of a butterfly (Acredolo & Goodwyn, 1985, 1988; Iverson, Capirci, & Caselli, 1994). Indeed, some children rely heavily on gestural "words" to communicate with others at the early stages.

Sometime around 18 months, children's vocabularies reach 50 words (Nelson, 1973), and they continue to add an average of nine words a day throughout the preschool years (Carey, 1978). Children's most common words are names for people and pets ("mama," "Metro"), objects ("bottle"), and substances ("milk"). These nominal terms are among the earliest terms children learn, along with social words ("want," "no," "bye-bye"). Adjectives ("hot") and verbs ("go," "up") are part of a young child's repertoire, but tend to be rare relative to nouns (Gentner, 1982; Goldin-Meadow, Seligman, & Gelman, 1976; although children learning languages other than English may show the noun bias less than English-learners, e.g., Korean; Gopnik & Choi, 1995; Mandarin; Tardif, 1996).

It is, of course, not trivial for the child to figure out exactly what adults mean when they use a word like "dog" or "run" (let alone abstract terms like "liberty" and "conjecture"). "Dog" could refer to the furry creature in its entirety, its paws, its tail, its fur, and so forth. "Run" could refer to the trajectory of the motion, the manner in which it is carried out, its direction, and so on. An infinite number of hypotheses are logically possible for the meaning of a word in a given adult utterance (Quine, 1960). Yet children are able to zero in on adult meanings of the words they hear. How? It would certainly be easier for children to settle on the meaning of a word if they were constrained to consider only a subset of the possibilities as candidate word meanings—if, for example, they were biased to assume that labels refer to wholes instead of parts (the creature, not the tail) and to classes instead of particular items (all dogs, not one dog). Constraints of this sort have, in fact, been proposed as part of the equipment that children bring to the language-learning situation (Markman, 1991, 1994), although others are equally convinced that inherent constraints are not needed to explain how children learn the meanings of words (Bloom, 2000).

Constraints on what a word means can also come from the discourse context in which the word is used. An adult may, for example, label an object when the child is directing full attention to that object, effectively making a set of meanings particularly salient to the child. More constraining still, the linguistic frame in which a word appears narrows down the meanings that the word can have (Gleitman, 1990). For example, English sentence structure conveys who does what to whom and, in this way, provides clues as to the meaning of the verb in the sentence. A 2-year-old child who hears "the rabbit is gorping the duck," will look longer at a scene in which the rabbit is acting on the duck than at a scene in which both the rabbit and the duck are circling their arms. The child correctly assumes that "gorp" must refer to an action on an object, in this case, the duck (Naigles, 1990). This is an impressive inference, particularly since the same child when hearing "the rabbit and the duck are gorping" will look longer at the scene in which the rabbit and the duck are each circling their arms. Now the child correctly assumes that "gorp" refers to the arm-circling action. Thus, the clues that children exploit to determine the meaning of a word come not only from how that word is used in relation to the world of objects and actions, but also from how it is used in sentences—children use language itself to bootstrap their way into word meanings (Fisher, Hall, Rakowitz, & Gleitman, 1994; Landau & Gleitman, 1985).

☐ Learning That Words Are Made of Parts

Words in English, and in all languages, can be broken down into parts. For example, the word "dogs" refers to more than one furry creature, but it does so quite systematically—"dog" stands for the animal, while "s" stands for many-ness. We know this because we know that words like "cats," "shoes," and "books" all refer to more than one cat, shoe, or book. We have extracted (albeit not consciously) what the words have in common—the "-s" ending in their forms and "plural" in their meanings—to form what is called a morpheme, a consistent pairing between a form and a meaning.

At the earliest stages, children learn morphologically complex words as unanalyzed wholes, "amalgams" (MacWhinney, 1978). For example, "shoes" may not, in the child's mind, be composed of the stem "shoe" plus the plural "-s," particularly if the child never produces the form "shoe" and uses "shoes" to refer to footwear in singles and in pairs. At some point, English-learning children discover that "shoes" is composed of parts ("shoe", "-s") and that each part has a meaning (footwear, plural). It is often not easy to tell when this analysis has taken place, particularly since it is not likely to have been done consciously.

One key piece of evidence, possible only when the pattern in the language the child is learning is not completely regular, comes from children's overregularizations—errors in which children make exceptions to the adult pattern (e.g., feet) conform to the regular pattern (e.g., foots). Children who produce the incorrect form "foots" must have extracted the plural morpheme "-s" from a variety of other regular forms in their system, and added it to the noun "foot." Similarly, children who produce "eated" must have extracted the past tense morpheme "-ed" from verbs like "walked" and "stopped" and added it to the verb "eat" (Marcus, 1995). Creative errors of this sort also indicate that children know the differences between nouns and verbs; children add the "-ed" ending to verbs like "eat" or "walk" but rarely to nouns like "foot" or "shoe." In addition to waiting for creative errors to occur, experimenters can give older children nonsense words and ask them to generate novel forms for different sentence frames, as Jean Berko (1958) did in her well-known "wug" test. Berko showed children a picture of two unknown creatures and said, "This is a wug. Now there are two of them. There are two _____". The child who knows about plural endings should supply the word "wugs."

The "wug" test gives children the sentence frame ("There are two _____") and a referent (a picture with two items) and asks them to supply the *form* of the appropriate grammatical morpheme ("-s"). In a clever study, Brown (1957) turned the question around and gave children the form of the grammatical morpheme and asked them to supply the *meaning*. For example, Brown showed children a picture of hands acting on a confetti-like substance in a pail and told them that this was "sibbing." They were then asked to identify sibbing in a set of three pictures showing just the acting hands, just the substance, or just the pail. They correctly pointed to the acting hands, indicating that they knew the grammatical morpheme "-ing" attaches to words for actions, not objects. Importantly, when they were told that the original picture contained "some sib," they pointed to the substance picture, and when they heard it contained "the sib," they pointed to the pail picture.

Thus, at a young age, children know that forms and meanings are *paired* in a grammatical morpheme and can approach the morpheme from either direction; if given the meaning of the morpheme (as in the "wug" test), they can provide the form, and if given the form of the morpheme (as in Brown's test), they can provide the meaning.

English does not have a very rich morphological system—words in English typically contain relatively few morphemes, unlike languages like Hebrew whose words tend to contain many morphemes. It turns out that children learning languages rich in morphology (like Hebrew) learn the parts of words earlier in the course of language development than do children acquiring morphologically impoverished languages (like English; Berman, 1985). Moreover, a morphological system that is regular is particularly easy to master. For example, children acquiring Turkish, which has a rich, predictable and perceptually salient inflectional system, produce words with grammatical morphemes even before they combine words (Aksu-Koc & Slobin, 1985). In contrast, children acquiring English generally do not begin to learn the morphemes of their language until after they begin to combine words into sentences.

□ Combining Words Into Sentences

At about age 18 months, children begin to produce two-word strings. The two-word combinations children produce are highly similar in two respects (Bloom, 1970; Bowerman, 1973a; Brown, 1973). First, the content is the same. Children note the appearance and disappearance of objects, their properties, locations, and owners, and comment on the actions done to and by objects and people. Second, the words in these short sentences are consistently ordered (Braine, 1976). The particular orders that children use mirror the orders provided by the language models they experience. Even when the language children are learning has relatively free word order, children tend to follow a consistent pattern (based on a frequently occurring adult order; Slobin, 1966).

Young children produce words in consistent orders as soon as they combine them and, in this sense, adhere to a syntax (Bloom, 1970). But is it the syntax of adults? Adult regularities are formulated in terms of syntactic categories—subject, object, noun phrase, verb phrase, and so on—rather than semantic categories, categories that focus on the role that the object is playing in an action, for example, the role of doer (agent) or the role of done-to (patient). Is there evidence for syntactic categories in the young child's language?

In fact, the earliest orders that children produce can all be described at a semantic level and thus do not *require* a syntactic analysis (although they do not violate one either). For example, the sentence "baby drink" can be described as agent-action, as opposed to subject-verb. Indeed, the fact that young children often interpret sentences like "babies are pushed by dogs" to mean the babies are the *pushers* (not the *pushees*) suggests that, for these children, the first word is an agent, not a subject (i.e., it's defined in terms of its role in the action rather than its role in the syntactic structure of the sentence). A subject-verb description is needed when the words that fill the first position are no longer restricted to a single semantic category (Bowerman, 1973b; e.g., "bottle falls"—bottle is not affecting an object and thus is not an agent) and when other aspects of the sentence depend on this nonsemantic category (e.g., subject-verb agreement—one says "bottle falls" about a single bottle but "bottles fall" about several). It is not until children begin to fill in their telegraphic utterances with grammatical morphemes (e.g., tense endings on verbs that must agree in number with the subject—bottle falls vs. bottles fall) that clear evidence for syntactic categories can be found. However, the fact that children use their grammatical morphemes appropriately *as soon as* they appear in their repertoires suggests that the groundwork for syntactic categories may have been laid quite early, perhaps from the start (cf. Valian, 1986).

Word order is an important device used by languages to convey who did what to whom. Importantly, even before children produce two-word combinations, they have some knowledge of this device. Children who produce single words only, when shown two scenes (Big Bird washing Cookie Monster vs. Cookie Monster washing Big Bird), will look reliably longer at the scene that matches the sentence they are listening to—the first scene for the sentence "Big Bird is washing Cookie Monster" and the second for "Cookie Monster is washing Big Bird" (Hirsh-Pasek & Golinkoff, 1991). The order of words must be conveying information to the child about who is the doer (agent) and who is the done-to (patient) of the action.

Moreover, children who are limited to two words per sentence in their talk appear to know something about the larger predicate frames underlying their short sentences. They produce, at times, all of the appropriate arguments that a given predicate allows (essentially all of the slots that nouns fill, e.g., they produce "*baby* drink" and "drink *juice*" when talking about drinking the juice, or "*mommy* give," "give *juice*," and "give *me*" when talking about giving the juice). Indeed, for children at the two-word stage, the rate at which a semantic element (like juice) is put into words depends on the predicate frame underlying the sentence (Bloom, Miller, & Hood, 1975). If a predicate frame underlying a two-word sentence is small, an element in that structure will be more likely to be produced as one of the two words in the sentence than will an element that is part of a larger predicate frame: There's less competition for one of the two word slots in a sentence with a smaller versus a larger predicate frame. Thus, for example, children are more likely to produce "juice" in a two-word sentence with a two-argument predicate frame (x drinks y, where x and y are the two arguments) than in a two-word sentence with a three-argument predicate frame (x gives y to z); that is, "juice" is more likely to appear with "drink" than with "give" simply because there is less competition for one of the two word slots in a sentence with two versus three underlying arguments (Goldin-Meadow, 1985; Goldin-Meadow & Mylander, 1984). The fact that the child's rate of production of a given element in a sentence varies systematically according to the size of the predicate frame underlying that sentence is evidence for the existence of the predicate frame itself.

At some implicit level, the child seems to know how many arguments there ought to be in each frame. Moreover, when provided with sentences that differ in their argument structures, children can make the appropriate inferences about the type of action described. For example, children will look longer at a scene in which Cookie Monster is making Big Bird turn (as opposed to one in which each is turning independently) when they hear the two-argument sentence, "*Cookie Monster* is turning *Big Bird*," than when they hear the one-argument sentence "*Cookie Monster* is turning with Big Bird" (Hirsh-Pasek, Golinkoff, & Naigles, 1996).

☐ Elaborating Sentences

Although from the outset, children are able to say "no," ask questions, and make demands (they do so gesturally or through simple lexical devices), with the advent of grammatical morphemes, they can begin to accomplish these goals using sentential forms expressing these various functions. Negatives and questions are not, however, completely adultlike even after grammatical morphemes appear. For example, they deviate from the adult form in that children often omit subjects and auxiliary verbs (do, is, have). From the few within-child analyses that have been done, subjects and auxiliaries appear to be introduced into both negatives and questions at about the same time (Klima & Bellugi, 1966). Negative markers are placed between the auxiliary and the verb ("baby is *not* drinking"); however, some period of time is needed before children consistently invert the subject and the auxiliary in questions ("is baby drinking?").

Children also build their sentences by elaborating one element of a single proposition ("baby drinking big bottle"), and by combining sentences to express complex or compound propositions (Bowerman, 1979; Limber, 1973). For example, English-learning children produce object complements ("I hope I don't hurt it"), embedded clauses ("that a box that they put it in"), coordinate clauses ("maybe you can carry that and I can carry this"), and subordinate clauses ("I gave him some so he won't cry").

The advent of two-proposition constructions brings with it the problem of appropriately relating the propositions, not only in production but also in comprehension. Children can show some remarkably subtle behaviors in this regard. For example, consider a child who is told that a little girl fell and ripped her dress in the afternoon and reported the event to her mother later that night. When 3-year-olds are asked "when did the girl say she ripped her dress?" they will provide one of two possible answers (in the afternoon, or at night), but when asked "when did the girl say how she ripped her dress?" they will correctly provide only one (at night) (deVilliers, Roeper, & Vainikka, 1990). The reason for this interpretive pattern has to do with how the two propositions ("say," and "rip") are linked in the probe question (that is, their constituent structure). The important point is that, at the young age of 3, children appreciate this subtlety that would, in fact, be difficult to teach.

However, children do make errors in interpreting complex sentences that adults find easy. When asked to act out the sentence, "the lion tells the bear to climb up the ladder," they appropriately make the bear do the climbing. But when asked to act out the sentence, "the lion pushes the bear after climbing up the ladder," many children incorrectly make the bear climb rather than the lion (Hsu, Cairns, Eisenberg, & Schlisselberg, 1989). The reason the climber differs in the two sentences again has to do the with the structural relations between the constituents in each sentence. Here, however, children have not yet achieved an adult performance level (although even this complexity will be mastered by age 8 and typically by 6½).

☐ In Sum

We have looked at the steps children take when learning language, but our brief tour has not really made the process appear any less miraculous. There is a great deal for children to learn, and they do it in a remarkably short period of time. Some have even suggested that the task is so great, and the constraints imposed by the input so few, that children must be coming to the language-learning situation with preconceptions about what language is—good guesses as to what the right units in a natural language are, and how those units are allowed to combine with one another. In the next chapter, we review the kinds of explanations that have been offered for how children learn language, and consider how this question can best be studied.

How Do Children Learn Language?

To study the process of language-learning, the most common technique is to do nothing more than watch and listen as children talk. In the earliest studies, researcher-parents made diaries of their own child's utterances (Stern & Stern, 1907; Leopold, 1939–49). The diarist's goal was to write down all of the new utterances that the child produced. Diary studies were later replaced by audio and video samples of talk from a number of children, usually over a period of years. The most famous of these "modern" studies is Roger Brown's longitudinal recordings of Adam, Eve, and Sarah (Brown, 1973).

Because transcribing and analyzing child talk is so labor-intensive, each individual language acquisition study typically focuses on a small number of children, often interacting with their primary caregiver at home. However, advances in computer technology have made it possible for researchers to share their transcripts of child talk via the computerized Child Language Data Exchange System (CHILDES; MacWhinney, 1995). A single researcher can now call upon data collected from spontaneous interactions in naturally occurring situations across a wide range of languages, and thus test the robustness of descriptions based on a small sample. In addition, naturalistic observations of children's talk can always be, and often are, supplemented with experimental probes that are used with a larger number of subjects (e.g., Berko's "wug" test, 1958).

Thus, although time-consuming, it is possible to describe what children do when they acquire language. The harder task is to figure out *how* they do it. This is the question that drives this book.

Many theories have been offered to explain how children go about the process of language-learning. I begin by briefly reviewing the major accounts. We will find that, although there is disagreement among the theories in the details, all modern day accounts accept the fact that children come to the language-learning situation prepared to learn. The disagreement lies in what each theory assumes the child is prepared with—a general outline of what language is? a set of processes which will lead to the acquisition of language (and language alone)? a set of processes which will lead to the acquisition of any skill, including language?

In the final section of this chapter, I describe an agenda for an empirical program of research that is designed to discover what children are prepared with when they come to language-learning. Children learn language in a variety of different environments. If, despite these differences in environmental input, the outcome of the language-learning process is the same, it begins to look like the children themselves are prepared to learn language in a particular way. In the remaining chapters of this section (Chapters 3 through 5), we discover what we can learn about a child's preparation for language-learning from the variations in language-learning environments that occur routinely—learning language in different cultures, in different modalities, with varying amounts of input. The rest of the book focuses on language development in an environment that is an extreme variation from the typical—developing language without any linguistic input at all.

Children are typically exposed to language and, in response, learn language. But what if a child were able to develop the same linguistic properties when not exposed to a language model? These properties of language would be *resilient* in the sense that they do not require a language model to be developed. Conversely, properties of language that a child is unable to develop without a language model would be *fragile*, requiring a language model to be developed. The goal of this book is to discover the resilient properties of language.

☐ Theoretical Accounts of Language-Learning

Behaviorist Accounts

Consistent with the psychological theories of the day, prior to the late 1950s language was considered just another behavior, governed not by its own rules and constraints but by the general laws of learning. Mechanisms of imitation and reinforcement were considered adequate to produce the grammatical habits that made up language. This behaviorist account of language was dealt a devastating blow with the publication of Noam Chomsky's review (1959) of B.F. Skinner's *Verbal Behavior*. Chomsky argued that adult language use cannot be adequately described in terms of sequences of behaviors or responses. A system of abstract rules underlies each individual's knowledge and use of language, and it is these rules that children acquire when they learn language. When viewed in this way, the language acquisition problem requires an entirely different sort of solution.

Nativist Accounts

The premise of the Chomskian perspective is that children are learning a linguistic system governed by subtle and abstract principles without explicit instruction and, indeed, without enough information from the input to support induction of these particular principles (as opposed to other principles)—"Plato's problem" or the poverty of the stimulus argument (Chomsky, 1999). If there is not enough information in the input to explain how children learn language, the process must be supported by innate syntactic knowledge and language-specific learning procedures. The theory of *Universal Grammar* (UG) formulates this *a priori* knowledge in terms of principles and parameters that determine the set of possible human languages. UG is assumed to be part of the innately endowed knowledge of humans. The principles of UG provide a framework for properties of language, often leaving several (constrained) options open to be decided by the data the child comes in contact with. For example, word order freedom is a parameter of variation. Some languages (English) mandate strict word orders; others (Russian, Japanese) list a small set of admissible orders; still others (Walpiri, an Australian aboriginal language) allow almost total scrambling of word order within a clause. Input from a given language is needed for learners to "set" the parameters of that language.

One important aspect of this theory is that setting a single parameter can cause a cluster of superficially unrelated grammatical properties to appear in the language. For example, the "null-subject" parameter involves a number of properties (Hyams, 1986): whether overt subjects are required in all declarative sentences (*yes* in English, *no* in Italian); whether expletive elements such as "it" in "it seems" or "there" in "there is" are exhibited (*yes* in English, *no* in Italian); whether free inversion of subjects is allowed in simple sentences (*no* in English, *yes* in Italian), and so forth. The prediction is that the input necessary to set the "null-subject" parameter results in the simultaneous alignment of all of these aspects within a child's grammar. There is, at present, controversy over whether predictions of this sort are supported by the child language data (e.g., Valian, 1991).

Innate knowledge of the principles underlying language is, however, not sufficient to account for how children acquire language. How are children to know what a noun or a subject is in the specific language they are learning? They need to identify subjects and verbs in their language before they can determine whether the two are strictly ordered in that language, and before they can engage whatever innate knowledge they might have about how language is structured. Thus, in addition to innate syntactic knowledge, children also need learning procedures, which may themselves be language-specific. One example is a set of rules *linking* semantic and syntactic categories (Pinker, 1984, 1989). Children are assumed to know innately that agents are likely to be subjects, objects affected by action are likely to be direct objects, and so on. All they need do is identify (using context) the agent in a scene; the linking rules allow them to infer that the term used to refer to that agent is the subject of the sentence. Their innate knowledge about how these elements are allowed to be structured can then take over. Again, controversies exist over whether child language data support these assumptions (e.g., "ergative" languages do not straightforwardly link agents with subjects and yet are easily acquired by young children; Ochs, 1982; see Chapter 3).

Social/Cognitive Accounts

The nativist position entails two claims: (1) at least some of the principles of organization underlying language are language-specific and not shared with other cognitive systems, and (2) the procedures that guide the implementation of these principles are themselves innate. Note that, while these two claims often go hand-in-hand, they need not. One can imagine that the principles underlying linguistic knowledge might be specific to language and, at the same time, implemented through general, all-purpose learning mechanisms (although such mechanisms must be more complex than the mechanisms behaviorist accounts have offered). This constitutes the position that has come to be known as a social or cognitive account of language-learning.

Children do not sound like adults when they begin to speak; there clearly is developmental work that needs to be done. The question is what type of work is required? One possibility, favored by some nativists, is that children have in place all of the grammatical categories and syntactic principles they need; they just lack the "operating systems" that will allow those principles to run. The developmental work to be done does not, under this view, involve a changing grammatical system.

In contrast, the child's language may change dramatically during development, transforming from a system based on semantic categories to one based on syntactic categories. This transformation could be maturationally determined (Wexler, 1999) or guided by innate linking rules, preserving a nativist account. However, the transformation could also result from an inductive leap children make on the basis of the linguistic data available to them, in conjunction with the cognitive and/or social skills they bring to the task—this inductive leap is at the heart of all social or cognitive accounts.

Cognitive underpinnings may be necessary but they are rarely sufficient for the onset of linguistic skills. For example, the onset of gesture-speech combinations that convey two elements of a proposition ("open" + point at box) precedes the onset of two-word combinations ("open box") by several months, suggesting that the cognitive ability to express two semantic elements is not the final stumbling block (Butcher & Goldin-Meadow, 2000; Goldin-Meadow & Butcher, 2003). More than likely, it is extracting linguistic patterns from the input that presents the largest problem.

Social and cognitive accounts claim that there is, in fact, enough information in the linguistic input children hear, particularly in the context of the supportive social environments in which they live, to induce a grammatical system. Ample research indicates that adults alter the speech they direct to their children. Speech to children (often called *motherese;* Newport, Gleitman, & Gleitman, 1977) is slower, shorter, higher pitched, more exaggerated in intonation, more grammatically well formed, and more directed in content to the present situation than speech addressed to adults (Snow, 1972). And children pay particular attention to this fine-tuned input, interpreting it in terms of their own biases or "operating principles" (e.g., paying attention to the ends of words, Slobin, 1985b). One problem that arises with postulating motherese as an engine of child language-learning, however, is that child-directed speech may not be universal. In many cultures, children participate in communicative interactions as overhearers (rather than as addressees) and the speech they hear is not likely to be simplified in the same ways (Ochs & Schieffelin, 1984; see Chapter 14). Nevertheless, children in these cultures become competent users of their grammatical systems in roughly comparable time frames, suggesting that there may be many developmental routes to the same end, a reasonable conjecture given the robustness of language.

One very interesting possibility that skirts the problem of children not universally getting simplified input is that the children themselves may do their own simplifying. For example, young children's memory limitations may make them less able to recall entire strings of words or morphemes. They would, as a result, be doing the analytic work required to abstract linguistic regularities on a smaller, filtered data base ("less is more"; Newport, 1991). This filtering may be just what children require to arrive at their linguistic systems. Moreover, it is a general process that children across the globe presumably bring, in equal measure, to the language-learning situation.

Connectionist Accounts

In a sense, connectionism is more of a technique for exploring language-learning than an explanatory account. But connectionism does come with some theoretical baggage. For example, most connectionist models are based on the assumption that language (like all other cognitive skills) can be explained without recourse to rules. And, of course, you have to buy the assumptions of the theory in order to find the technique useful.

In a connectionist account, behavior is produced by a network of interconnected units. Language development is a process of continuously adjusting the relative strengths of the connections in the network until they produce an output that resembles the input. As a result, connectionism can offer a tool for examining the trade-off between the three components central to all theories of language learning (Plunkett, 1995)—input, structures the child brings to the learning situation (architectures of the artificial system), and learning mechanisms (learning algorithms). The latter two are considered innate on the nativist account and specific to language. Connectionism provides a technique for determining the innate structures and learning processes that must be present, given the input children typically receive, to achieve learning. As an example, networks have been shown to arrive at appropriate generalizations from strings of sentences *only if* the memory span of the network for previously processed words begins small and gradually increases (reminiscent of Newport's "less is more" hypothesis described above, 1991; Elman, 1993).

☐ Studying Language-Learning by Manipulating Environments

All theoretical accounts agree that human children are prepared to learn language. The question is—what are they prepared with? Do children come to the learning situation with specific hypotheses about how language ought to be structured? Or do they come with general biases to process information in a particular way? Under this second view, the strong inclination that children have to structure communication in language-like patterns falls out of their general processing biases coming into contact with a natural language.

One obvious way to explore the nature of the biases children bring to the learning situation is to observe language-learning in varying circumstances, circumstances that vary in how much linguistic structure the child is bathed in. The assumption is that children bring the same processing biases to whatever circumstances they encounter. To the extent that child outcome remains the same across these various input situations, we have strong evidence that the child's processing biases are themselves important in determining the language the child develops—that the child's developmental trajectory is buffered from vagaries in the input. However, to the extent that each varying input situation results in a different child outcome, we not only have evidence that input matters, but we can begin to explore the patterns between input and child outcome to make inferences about the child's biases and processing strategies.

In other scientific domains, when we are interested in understanding the mechanisms that underlie developmental change, we attempt to experimentally manipulate the situation, altering circumstances of acquisition and observing the effects of those alterations on child outcome. But for obvious ethical reasons, we cannot tamper with the circumstances under which children learn language. The alternative is to take advantage of the varied circumstances that children find themselves in when they attempt to learn language. In the next three chapters (Chapters 3 through 5), I consider different input conditions that could, in principle, alter the language-learning task for the child.

Children who grow up in Taipei face the task of learning Mandarin. The task for children who grow up in Philadelphia is to learn English. Children across the globe are thus exposed to very different models of language, each of which could dramatically alter the acquisition task. As a result, we have a naturalistic "experiment" in which we can observe how child output is affected by the input they receive. The "results" of this experiment will be described in Chapter 3, with a focus on the commonalities in acquisition patterns found across languages.

Children born to deaf parents who use sign language to communicate with them are exposed to a language system that differs dramatically from the typical. It is language by hand and eye, rather than by mouth and ear. We could ask whether language-learning takes a different course when it is conducted in a different modality. The answer, which will be described in Chapter 4, is that for the most part it does not—children learn language in the manual modality as easily and on the same time table as children learning language in the oral modality.

Across linguistic communities, children are exposed to very different kinds of input. Within a community, however, children also experience variations in input, since some parents talk often to their children and use a wide variety of constructions, and others talk less. Does this variability in amount of input affect child acquisition? There have been many studies of the effect of natural variation in linguistic input on child language-learning. Moreover, there have been attempts to extend the range of variation children experience within ethical limits—that is, to increase the amount of input a child receives and determine whether that increase affects child output. I describe the results of these studies in Chapter 5.

☐ The Resilient and Fragile Properties of Language

What I am proposing is a research program for studying language-learning and, more importantly, a way to think about the findings of such a program. Any particular manipulation of the environmental conditions under which language-learning takes place has the potential to alter the language-learning outcome. To the extent that a property of language is *unaffected* by a given manipulation, it can be said to be developmentally *resilient*—its developmental course is impervious to the change in input conditions. Of course, the more radical the manipulation is—that is, the more different the conditions are from the conditions that surround the typical language-learning situation—the more impressive it is that a given property of language continues to crop up.

My goal in the next three chapters is to identify the properties of language that are resilient when children learn different languages, when children learn language in a different modality, and when children get different amounts of input in their language. I also explore whether there is convergence across these manipulations in the properties identified as resilient. It is an empirical question as to whether the same property of language will survive a variety of input manipulations—that is, whether it will be resilient across a range of learning conditions. If so, we can be that much more certain that this particular property of language is fundamental to human communication, one whose development is not beholden to the vagaries of environmental input but is, instead, robustly overdetermined.

Finally, it is likely that some properties of language will *not* survive a particular manipulation and may, in fact, not survive a variety of manipulations. I call such properties of language *fragile* for it is these properties whose development is sensitive to changes in input conditions. Note that when we use the manipulation strategy to identify a resilient property of language, we look for the *presence* of the property under changed conditions. In contrast, when seeking a fragile property of language, we are, in effect, looking for the property's *absence* under the changed conditions—that is, we are seeking negative evidence. Relying on negative evidence is always a relatively shaky enterprise. As a result, we are on firmer ground when we use the manipulations described in the next three chapters, and in the second section of the book, to identify the resilient properties of language than to identify the fragile properties of language.

3 CHAPTER

Language-Learning Across the Globe

Languages vary across the globe. The question we ask in this chapter is whether the differences across languages make a difference to the language-learning child. Is it easier to learn a language in which verbs are positioned in the middle of the sentence? What about a language in which nouns are placed before adjectives? Or a language that has both properties?

Conveniently, the world has supplied us with just the right "experiments" to answer questions of this sort. Some languages, like English, Polish, Hebrew, and Sesotho, tend to order verbs in the middle of simple declarative sentences, between subjects and objects. Others, like Japanese, Georgian, Walpiri, and Greenlandic, place verbs at the end of sentences. And others still, Samoan and K'iche' Mayan, place verbs at the beginning of sentences. Moreover, some languages of each ordering type place nouns before adjectives (verb-medial English and Polish; verb-final Japanese and Georgian; verb-initial K'iche' Mayan) while others place nouns after adjectives (verb-medial Hebrew and Sesotho; verb-final Walpiri and Greenlandic; verb-initial Samoan; Slobin, 1992).

These different types of languages pose different types of acquisition problems for learners. By observing children who are exposed to languages that vary systematically along one or more dimensions, we can get some sense of which types of languages, if any, present stumbling blocks to the language-learner. For example, children might find it difficult to learn sentences that begin with verbs, and might find ways of avoiding the troublesome construction. To the extent that we see children *change* the input they receive, we get a sense of the role children themselves play in shaping the language they learn—the child as "language-maker" (Slobin, 1985b).

☐   Children Learn the Particulars of Their Language

In 1985, Dan Slobin encouraged the field of language acquisition to take advantage of the "experiments of nature" offered by the world's languages. He did so by pointing out the kinds of questions that could only be addressed by cross-linguistic studies (Slobin, 1985a), and by publishing the first two volumes of *The cross-linguistic study of language acquisition*.

The encouragement was wildly successful. Language acquisition researchers, who up until this point had been narrowly focused on English, began expanding their horizons and their languages. As an example, during the 1970s, 80% of the data-oriented articles in the *Journal of Child Language* examined language-learning exclusively in English. But by 1990, the number had dropped to 57% (Slobin, 1992). Moreover, completely new languages were being added to the list every year, so that by 1990, some aspect of acquisition had been explored in 36 different languages. And as of 1997, there were five volumes in Slobin's cross-linguistic series exploring acquisition in 28 different languages.

What have we learned from these studies? When we look carefully at children learning vastly different languages, we find that, overall, children accept the differences graciously. They learn the particular properties that their language presents, and they do so from the earliest stages.

For example, English and Korean languages present children with very different ways of talking about joining objects. In English, placing a videocassette in its case or an apple in a bowl would both be described as putting one object "in" another. However, in Korean, a distinction is made according to the fit of the objects—a videocassette placed in a tight-fitting case would be described by the verb "kkita," whereas an apple placed in a loose-fitting bowl would be described by the verb "nehta." Indeed, in Korean, the notion of fit seems more important than the notion of containment. Unlike English-speakers who say that the ring is placed "on" the finger and that the finger is placed "in" the ring, Korean-speakers use "kkita" to describe both situations since both involve a tight-fitting relation between the objects. As it turns out, children have no trouble learning to talk about joining objects in terms of containment in English, or in terms of fit in Korean (Choi & Bowerman, 1991), as early as 17 to 20 months. Not only do distinctions made in each language draw children's attention to different facets of spatial relationships, but children appear to be perfectly comfortable being drawn to either set of distinctions.

The way in which a distinction is expressed in a language might also affect the speed with which a child expresses that distinction. In other words, the form of expression that a language uses for a meaning can either facilitate, or hinder, early expression of that meaning. For example, Slobin (1985b) has argued that children pay particular attention to the ends of words, a strategy which makes postpositions and suffixes more salient than prepositions and prefixes. And indeed, children acquire simple locatives like "in" and "on" earlier in postpositional languages like Hungarian and Turkish (where they occur at the end of a word) than in prepositional languages like English and Serbo-Croatian (where they occur before the word; Slobin, 1973). As Slobin points out, comparisons of this sort can only be carried out cross-linguistically since it is essential to hold meaning (and, if possible, frequency of use) constant while "contrasting" how the meaning is expressed.

In general, languages offer children different patterns for structuring communication (i.e., different typologies, cf. Slobin, 1997a), and those patterns can have widespread effects throughout the child's language. For example, English is principally a right-branching language, whereas Japanese is left-branching. The principal branching direction of a language refers to the direction in which major recursive devices, such as relative clauses and other forms of sentence complementation, are positioned (Lust, 1981; 1983). The generation of recursive terms in English tends to occur to the *right* of the term that is elaborated (e.g., "the friend *who came from Tokyo*"); in Japanese the generation of recursive terms tends to occur to the *left* of the elaborated term (e.g., "*Tokyo kara kita* tomodachi" [= *Tokyo from came* the friend]; see Smith, 1978).

Early in development, children notice this fact about their language, which affects not only their initial sentence complements, but also how they deal with redundancy—in particular, whether they prefer sentences in which the reduced or null element (θ) is to the *right* of the expressed element (e.g., "*frogs* jump and θ catch flies," where θ follows "frogs") or to the *left* of the expressed element (e.g., "frogs θ and kangaroos *jump*," where θ precedes "jump"). English-learning children produce and imitate complex sentences in which redundancy is reduced in a rightward direction (in keeping with their right-branching language; Lust, 1977; Lust & Mervis, 1980), whereas Japanese-learning children prefer complex sentences in which redundancy is reduced in a leftward direction (in keeping with their left-branching language, Lust & Wakayama, 1979). Thus, languages differ in the global patterns they present to children, and children pay attention to those patterns.

☐ When Children Change the Input They Receive

We have just seen that children are able to learn the particulars of the language to which they are exposed. However, there are times when children seem to ignore or perhaps override the linguistic input they receive. It is these instances that are of particular interest in our search for the biases that children themselves bring to language-learning.

One of the most obvious ways in which children alter the input they receive is that their utterances are short even though all of the adults around them produce long sentences. Adults (and older children) in many cultures do shorten their utterances when they talk to young children; however, these utterances are never as short as the ones young learners themselves produce. Moreover, not only are children's first utterances short, but they are also simple and lack the grammatical morphemes required in adult talk. There may well be processing constraints operating in all cross-linguistic situations that limit the child's earliest productions to single words.

Over time, children across the globe gradually enlarge their productions to two-word or, in some cases (e.g., Greenlandic; Fortescue & Olsen, 1992), two-morpheme constructions. Do children's initial grammatical encodings of meanings in these early two-unit constructions have anything in common? We might expect that they would *not*, simply because, as we have seen, languages use different forms to express the same meaning. Surprisingly, however, there are cases where children across the globe all express a common meaning apparently without regard for the varied forms it takes across the world's languages. Whenever this happens, we begin to suspect that the meaning is part of the baggage children themselves bring to language-learning—a meaning that children might attempt to express even if they received no linguistic input whatsoever. We begin by examining these privileged meanings, which could serve as the conceptual starting point for all children learning language (cf. Slobin, 1985a).

Privileged Meanings

At times, children across the globe begin to express a set of meanings in precisely the same order despite wide variations in the forms their individual languages use for those meanings. In these cases, we are inclined to believe that the children themselves had a hand in guiding their own developmental trajectory (although, of course, the frequency with which meanings are used across cultures, if universal, could also have a hand in creating uniform developmental patterns). For example, when children begin to talk about locations, there is a common order of emergence across languages. Children learning English, Italian, Serbo-Croatian, and Turkish all follow the same pattern—"in" and "on" precede "under" and "beside,". which precede "between," "back," and "front" for objects that have an inherent front-back orientation (e.g., cars, houses), which precede "back" and "front" for objects that don't have an inherent orientation (e.g., plates, blocks; Johnston & Slobin, 1979). Importantly, the forms used to express these meanings differ across the languages—prepositions (English, Italian), prepositions and case inflections (Serbo-Croatian), and postpositions and case inflections (Turkish). In addition, the absolute ages for these developments differ across children learning each language. However, the order remains the same, perhaps reflecting the child's growing ability to deal first with two-dimensional topological relations and only later with more complex projective relations that add the third dimension of depth.

There are two other ways in which children can convince us that they play an active role in constructing their language. The range of meanings children express with a given form may be *narrower* than the adult range—children are thus using the form for a subset of the meanings expressed with the adult form. Or, the range of meanings children express with a given form may be *broader* than the adult range—here, children are using the form for a wider group of meanings than are expressed with the adult form. We find instances of both types.

Children across the globe begin by grammatically marking agent-patient (that is, doer-done to) relations in basic causal events. These are events in which an agent carries out a physical and perceptible change of state in a patient, either by means of direct body contact or an instrument—for example, mother pours milk (Slobin, 1985a)—what Hopper and Thompson (1980) call "highly transitive" events. As an example, in Russian, a particular linguistic marker called an accusative inflection must be placed on all words that fill the syntactic slot *direct object*, regardless of the type of event conveyed. However, children acquiring Russian first use the accusative inflection *only* for direct objects in sentences describing manipulative physical actions (giving, putting, throwing). In sentences describing actions that are less obviously operating on an object (e.g., seeing), young children use a noun without any inflection at all (Gvozdev, 1949, as described in Slobin, 1985a).

We find a similar pattern of *underextension* in ergative languages, languages in which the inflection is placed on the agent (as opposed to the patient) of a transitive event (e.g., Kaluli). This ergative inflection is first used by Kaluli-learning children to mark agents in sentences describing concrete, manipulative actions—giving, grabbing, taking, hitting. It is *not* used to mark agents of less physical actions (e.g., saying, seeing; Schieffelin, 1985). Interestingly, Kaluli-learning children correctly use the ergative marker for doers of transitive events and not for doers of intransitive actions (actions that do not involve objects, e.g., running). Intuitively, we might think it reasonable to treat all doers alike, as we do in English—"he runs" vs. "he hits her"—the boy is doing the running and the hitting, and is referred to with the same term ("he") placed in the same position (before the verb). However, this is not what Kaluli-learning children do—they follow the ergative pattern set forth in their language, that is, they use the ergative marker on *he* in "he hits her" but not on *he* in "he runs." But, Kaluli learners, like Russian learners, first grammaticize the participants of highly transitive manipulative activities like hitting, pouring, or eating. Slobin (1985a, 7) suggests that such highly transitive activities constitute a "central semantic organizing point for grammatical marking", a starting point for the language-learning child.

Children's initial use of tense reflects the same focus on events that bring about visible change of state. Children first use past-tense, perfect, or perfective verb inflections to comment on an event that was just completed and that results in a visible change of state or location of an object—that is, on verbs like "drop," "break," and "spill" (Bloom, Lifter, & Hafitz, 1980; Slobin, 1985a). Only later do children develop a more general past tense. Moreover, the focus on results may bring with it a tendency to concentrate on marking patients at the expense of agents. For example, Italian-learning children will make the past participle of transitive verbs agree in number and gender with the direct object-patient, not the subject-agent—despite the fact that, in the input language, the participle agrees with *neither* object nor subject of a transitive verb, and agrees with the *subject* (actor) of an intransitive verb (Antinucci & Miller, 1976). The close relation between objects and *results* in the real world may encourage the child to create grammatical structure where there is none.

These are all examples of children *narrowing* the meaning of a particular grammatical marking to focus on, what we assume are, for the child, conceptually salient events. There are, however, also examples of how children *broaden* the meaning of an adult grammatical form. For example, children often use the same grammatical form for both animate and inanimate reference points in a locative relation, despite the fact that a distinction is made in adult talk. German-learning children incorrectly generalize "zu," the preposition used to express location (a relation involving an inanimate recipient), to express possession (a relation involving an animate recipient and conveyed by the preposition "von" in adult talk; Mills, 1985). As another example, English-learning children at times confuse "give," which adults use to refer to moving objects toward a person, and "put," which adults use to refer to moving objects to a place (e.g., "give some ice in here, mommy," and "can I go put it to her?"; Bowerman, 1982a). The children are effectively *ignoring animacy* distinctions that are present in the adult language to which they are exposed.

In addition to *meanings* that appear to be privileged in the early stages of child language, there are *forms* that children apparently find easy to incorporate into their language. We turn next to those forms.

Privileged Forms

Across the globe, children combine words into strings. Even the earliest strings that children produce are characterized by two properties: (1) Words in a string are not combined in haphazard order, but rather follow particular ordering patterns. (2) A string is characterized by a frame which dictates how the words in that string are interpreted (Gleitman & Newport, 1995).

Turning first to *word order* within sentence strings, we find that when a language uses word order consistently, children learning that language also use word order consistently, even in two-word strings. As we might expect, the ordering patterns that children produce in their two-word strings reflect the ordering patterns in the input language. For example, an English-learning child will produce the sentence "baby milk" when the baby is drinking the milk, but the sentence "milk baby" when putting the milk on top of the baby's head—thus closely following the typical patterns English-speaking adults would use in these two situations (Bloom, 1970).

Even more impressive is the fact that children use consistent word order when the language they are learning has relatively free word order. Some languages, like Russian, are much more forgiving than English with respect to word order: a word can be placed in a variety of positions within the sentence, as long as it carries the appropriate marking. Children learning these languages choose among the many sentence orders in their input, and produce a much narrower range of orders than they hear (Bates, 1976; MacWhinney, 1977; Slobin, 1966).

What about *predicate frames* underlying sentence strings? We saw in Chapter 1 that very young English-learning children are able to use the predicate frame of a sentence to figure out what the verb in that sentence means (e.g., the fact that "x gorps y" has two slots for nouns tells the child that "gorp" refers to an action on an object). In their own talk, children put verbs in unusual sentence frames (unusual from an adult's point of view), as though expecting the verb to take on the meaning appropriate to that frame. For example, an English-learning child said "Kendall fall that toy" to mean that she dropped the toy (Bowerman, 1982a). She had, up until this point, always used "fall" appropriately to indicate the downward descent of an object on its own (i.e., she used it in an x ____ frame). By placing "fall" in an "y ____ x" frame rather than the correct "x ____" frame, Kendall is giving the word a transitive meaning (action on an object) rather than an intransitive meaning (action with no object). Comparable examples have been reported in children learning French, Portuguese, Polish, Hebrew, Hungarian, and Turkish—and even in languages where the input does not model this possibility (Slobin, 1985a).

Children are not only sensitive to regularities of form within sentences but also across sentences. They detect regularities across word sets called *paradigms*. As an example of a paradigm, the various forms that verbs can take (*walk—walks—walked*) constitute a verb paradigm. We saw in Chapter 1 that English-learning children detect regularities within paradigms, and often attempt to "regularize" any ill-fitting forms they find; for example, children alter the past tense form for "eat" so that it conforms to the paradigm constructed on the basis of the regular verbs in their language (*eat—eats—eated* rather than *eat—eats—ate*).

Verb paradigms in English are rather simple compared to paradigms in other languages (e.g., Romance languages like French or Spanish, or Latin which is said to have at least 100 inflectional forms; Akmajian, Demers, Farmer, & Harnish, 1995). Children are capable of learning, and indeed improving upon, rather complex systems. For example, in Spanish, nouns that are masculine take the indefinite article *un* and the definite article *el* and generally end in –*o*; in contrast, nouns that are feminine take the articles *una* and *la* and generally end in –*a*. Spanish-learning children acquire these regularities early, as is evident from the fact that they will attempt to "clean up" any nouns that happen to violate this paradigm, e.g., they produce "una mana" rather than the irregular, but correct, form, "una mano" (= hand, feminine), and "un papelo" rather than irregular correct form, "un papel" (= paper, masculine; Montes Giraldo, 1976, as described in Clark, 1985).

Thus, children do not learn words as isolated units, but as elements in sets. The child's focus, then, is not only on how a word maps onto the world (i.e., word-world relations), but also how that word relates to other words in the system (word-word relations; Karmiloff-Smith, 1979; Newport, 1981).

Children are learning ordering patterns for words within a sentence at the same time as they are learning the markings appropriate to each word's paradigm. Under certain circumstances, the two processes can exhibit a trade-off. Children learn inflectional markings early in development if the inflectional system of their language is completely regular and exceptionless, as in Turkish (Slobin, 1982). However, in the absence of a clear and fully reliable inflectional system, as in Serbo-Croatian, children begin by relying heavily on word order (Slobin, 1982). Moreover, if the inflectional system (although regular) is not adequately represented in the speech children actually hear, children will again resort to word order. For example, when Samoan-speaking adults talk to other adults, they use an ergative inflection to mark the agent in a transitive sentence. The marker serves to distinguish agents from patients in transitive sentences (e.g., the eater from the eaten) and also from actors in intransitive sentences (e.g., the eater from the runner). However, adults rarely produce this ergative inflection when they talk to young children. As we might expect given their input, young Samoan-learning children rarely express this marker in their own speech. But the children do exhibit an ergative pattern in their early language—through word order. They produce words for both patients (the eaten) and intransitive actors (the runner) after the verb, and don't produce words for transitive agents (the eater) in this postverbal position—an ergative alignment of the cases, one which is *not* found in adult speech to Samoan-learning children (Ochs, 1982).

☐ Taking Cross-Linguistic Universals to Another Level

We find that children do exhibit some commonalities in the early steps they take in the language-learning process despite wide differences in the languages to which they are exposed. These commonalities could well constitute "conceptual starting points for grammaticized notions" (Slobin, 1997b).

Starting points are just that—a place to begin. In the longer term, children are clearly able to cope with the wide diversity across languages, learning whatever system is put before them. And, indeed, the job of any theory of language acquisition is to account for the developmental progression that takes children from their starting point to such very different endpoints.

If the endpoint language matches the child's starting point in a particular domain, that domain is likely to be relatively easy to learn. If, however, the endpoint language uses categories that are wider, or narrower, than the categories with which the child starts the language-learning process in a domain, that domain is likely to be more difficult to learn. Where the rough and easy spots are in the developmental process may thus depend on how the particular language a child is learning overlaps with the child's starting point.

But what would happen if a child were exposed to no language whatsoever? Under such unusual circumstances, we might expect nothing at all—after all, a language model might be *essential* to catalyze children into applying their starting points to the task of communication.

On the other hand, it is possible that a language model is *not* essential for a child to engage in communication. Under this scenario, we would expect that children who are not exposed to a learnable language model might well display just those commonalities that we find in cross-linguistic learning situations—that is, the conceptual starting points for grammaticized notions.

Thus, for example, we might expect model-less children, not only to communicate about highly transitive events, but also to begin to construct a grammatical system around these events. Similarly, we might look for burgeoning grammatical systems in representations of the results of events, with perhaps little focus on animacy. Moreover, we would expect such children to construct grammatical systems that have structure within sentences (e.g., ordering patterns, underlying predicate frames), as well as structure across sentences (e.g., word sets or paradigms).

The cross-linguistic universals described in this chapter, in effect, constitute a set of hypotheses as to how children might be expected to communicate in the absence of usable linguistic input. We will put these "hypotheses" to the test in the second section of this book. But before doing so, we explore a completely different set of input conditions that might, in principle, be expected to alter the language-learning task for the child.

4

CHAPTER

Language-Learning by Hand

How do deaf children acquire sign language? The first point to stress is that the sign system they are acquiring is a formal language in the full sense of the word. Deaf individuals across the globe use sign languages as their primary means of communication. These sign languages assume all of the functions of spoken languages. They are used to communicate about the here-and-now, but also about worlds that are not present. They are used to direct, to advise, to declare, to joke, to pun—any functions that spoken language serves can be, and are, filled by sign language.

Equally striking, sign languages assume the structural properties characteristic of spoken languages. At one point in their history, sign languages were thought to be nothing more than pantomimic systems lacking all linguistic structure. In 1960, William Stokoe set the wheels in motion to change this view with the publication of *Sign Language Structure*. Stokoe argued that the signs of American Sign Language (ASL) are *not* global pantomimic wholes, but rather are composed of discrete meaningless units, akin to phonemes. The next 40 years brought a steady stream of research on the structure of sign language, with a very clear conclusion: Sign languages are fully grammaticized languages.

Like spoken languages, sign languages have structure at the sentence level (i.e., syntactic structure; Klima & Bellugi, 1979; Liddell, 1980; Lillo-Martin, 1986), at the word or sign level (i.e., morphological structure; Klima & Bellugi, 1979; Padden, 1983; T. Supalla, 1982), and at the level of meaningless units (i.e., "phonological" structure, Brentari, 1998; Coulter, 1986; Klima & Bullugi, 1979; Lane, Boyes-Braem, & Bellugi 1976; Liddell, 1984; Liddell & Johnson 1986; Sandler, 1986; Wilbur 1986). Although all sign languages are structured, they (like spoken languages) differ in the particular structures they display. For example, ASL is structured differently from Finnish Sign Language, which in turn is structured differently from Japanese Sign Language.

Thus, the manual modality is as good a medium for language as the oral modality, suggesting that the capacity for creating and learning a linguistic system is modality-independent. Language assumes certain kinds of structure whether it comes out of the mouth or the hands—a remarkable fact given how differently the ears and eyes process information.

The question we address in this chapter is whether deaf children exposed to a sign language from birth acquire that language in the same way that hearing children acquire spoken language. Why might they not?

Sign languages are autonomous systems which are *not* based on the spoken languages of hearing cultures (Bellugi & Studdert-Kennedy, 1980; Klima & Bellugi, 1979; Lane & Grosjean, 1980). Thus, the structure of ASL is distinct from the structure of English. Indeed, the structure of *American* Sign Language is distinct from the structure of *British* Sign Language—a fact which dramatically underscores the point that sign languages are not derivatives of spoken languages. ASL is a morphologically complex language, closer in structure to Navajo (a polysynthetic language) than to English. However, ASL (and all sign languages studied thus far) look different from spoken languages—even languages like Navajo—in two respects.

First, many signs in ASL are "iconic"—the visual form of the sign resembles its referent. For example, in the sign for "bird," the index finger and thumb are held at the mouth and are moved together and apart several times. The sign looks like a bird's beak as it opens and closes, and therefore might be relatively easy to learn. Of course, many signs in ASL are not at all iconically motivated—they are as arbitrarily related to their referents as the word "bird" is to its feathery referent. However, the iconicity that does exist in the system could play a role in easing the child's entry into the language. If so, deaf children learning ASL might be expected to acquire the iconic aspects of their language earlier than the non-iconic. Indeed, children might find it easier overall to acquire a partially iconic sign language than an arbitrary spoken language.

Second, unlike morphemes in spoken language which are produced in sequence within a word, morphemes within a sign are often produced simultaneously. For example, to indicate that an activity is ongoing in English, we add "-ing" to the *end* of the verb, thus creating the form "eating." In ASL, however, the affix is produced *at the same time as* the verb. In its uninflected form, "eat" is produced with the hand jabbing repeatedly toward the mouth; to indicate that the activity is ongoing, the hand continues to move repeatedly toward the mouth but along a small circular path with even rhythm (Wilbur, 1987). The inflectional marker is therefore incorporated into the verb itself. The fact that inflections cannot easily be separated from word stems might make it particularly difficult for children to figure out what constitutes a unit in sign language. Thus, there are reasons to believe that some aspects of language might be harder to learn in sign language than in spoken language.

In addition, it is striking that no hearing culture has developed a sign language in preference to a spoken language—despite the fact that sign languages work perfectly well, and that hearing individuals can process language in either modality. Given this imbalance, we might have guessed that sign languages are harder to learn than spoken languages. But they aren't.

Deaf children born to deaf parents, and therefore exposed from birth to a sign language like ASL, acquire that language as easily as hearing children acquire spoken language. Moreover, deaf children learning sign languages progress through the same stages as hearing children learning spoken languages (Lillo-Martin, 1999; Newport & Meier, 1985; Petitto, 2000). Remarkably, the differences that we find between signed and spoken languages do not appreciably alter the language-learning task for the young child. In the next sections, we examine the steps deaf children take as they acquire sign language from their deaf parents.

☐ First Signs

Prior to producing their first recognizable signs, deaf children who are exposed to a sign language from birth "babble" manually in much the same way that hearing children babble orally. Moreover, deaf children begin their manual babbling at around the same age as hearing children begin their oral babbling (Masataka, 2000; Meier & Willerman, 1995; Petitto & Marentette, 1991). Children thus begin the language-learning process by playing with the units of the language they are to learn, whether those units are sounds or signs.

Manual babbling develops into first signs, just as vocal babbling develops into first words. Deaf children produce their first recognizable signs slightly earlier in development than hearing children produce their first recognizable words (Bonvillian & Folven, 1993; Meier & Newport, 1990), presumably because sign production requires less fine motor control than word production. However, these early signs do not appear to be used referentially (Bonvillian & Folven, 1993; Lillo-Martin, 1999; but see Meier & Newport, 1990). It is not until approximately 12 months that deaf children clearly use their signs in referential contexts (i.e., to name or indicate objects and actions in their worlds)—precisely the age at which hearing children produce their first recognizable words in referential contexts (Petitto, 1988).

Thus, although it may be easier to produce signs than words, it is not easier to use those signs symbolically. This important step in the language-learning process is taken at the same developmental moment, whether the child is learning a signed or spoken language.

Once children begin to learn signs in earnest, do they acquire iconic signs first? Surprisingly, they don't. When hearing adults learn ASL as a second language, they are often captivated by the iconicity of the language. Signs like "drink" (a cupped hand moved up at the mouth) or "tree" (the forearm extended vertically) are easy to remember and are very often the first signs these adult learners acquire. However, children don't seem to notice—or, at least, they fail to take advantage of—the iconicity in the signs they are learning. Only one-third of the first signs that children produce are iconic (Bonvillian & Folven, 1993), and those signs refer to objects and actions that all young children talk about. Indeed, the meanings of the early signs that deaf children produce are no different from the words used by one-word speakers in other languages (e.g., "milk," "mommy," "daddy," etc.; Newport & Meier, 1985).

Another striking example of how deaf children seem to be unaware of the iconicity in their language comes from their acquisition of pronouns. Pronouns for *me* and *you* are produced in ASL by pointing either at oneself or the addressee. Note that these signs are no different from the gestures that hearing individuals produce along with their speech, and are indeed quite iconic. As a result, we might expect deaf children to acquire these first- and second-person pronouns early and effortlessly. But again, they don't. In fact, they seem to be caught by the same stumbling block that interferes with the acquisition of first- and second-person pronouns in hearing children acquiring English.

Many hearing children when they first produce "me" and "you" actually reverse the terms, saying "me carry you" to mean "you carry me." Presumably, this pronoun reversal occurs because the meanings of "me" and "you" shift in discourse according to who is doing the speaking (I call myself "me" but you too call yourself "me"). Interestingly, this same pronoun reversal takes place in deaf children acquiring ASL, despite the fact that the ASL pronouns look just like gestures (Petitto, 1987). Between 6 and 12 months, deaf children (like hearing children) point to people (including themselves) and objects as a way to investigate and explore their surroundings. However, between 12 and 18 months, deaf children will often stop pointing at people (the points to objects continue). Following this period, the children may go through a phase in which they use the sign "you" to refer to themselves. They point away from themselves and toward their addressee when they want to refer to themselves, presumably because they've made the wrong generalization from the fact that others point away from their bodies when they want to refer to the child. By 25 to 27 months of age, deaf children (like hearing children) resolve these difficulties and no longer reverse their pronouns.

It looks as though deaf children begin by using pointing just as hearing children do—as a gesture. At some moment in development, they discover that the point plays a *linguistic* role in their language (Petitto, 1987). They may then stop using the point entirely to refer to people. When they begin using it again, the point is no longer a prelinguistic gesture—it has become a linguistic unit and, like other linguistic units, it is learned as an arbitrary rather than iconic representation. As such, it is susceptible to pronoun reversals, just as spoken pronouns are in English.

Thus, deaf children seem to discover the linguistic role that points play in sign language relatively early in development. In addition to displaying pronoun reversals, they combine their pointing signs syntactically with lexical signs—unlike hearing children who rarely combine their pointing gestures with other gestures (Goldin-Meadow & Morford, 1985). Thus, even as transparent a sign as the point is interpreted, not as an iconic gesture, but as part of a linguistic system.

☐ The Parts of Signs

As mentioned earlier, American Sign Language is comparable to spoken languages that are morphologically quite complex. There are two classes of signs in ASL—"frozen" signs whose stems are unanalyzable, each containing only one morpheme; and "productive" signs whose stems are constructed by combining several morphemes. Both types of stems can then be further modified with, for example, inflectional markers for aspect, number, and so on. We begin by looking at how stems are formed in the productive lexicon, and the steps children take in acquiring this lexicon. We then turn to the acquisition of inflectional processes.

Morphology of Stems

The productive signs of ASL are highly mimetic in form. These mimetic signs were originally thought to be built on an analog use of movement and space in which movement is mapped in a continuous, rather than discrete, fashion (Cohen, Namir, & Schlesinger, 1977; DeMatteo, 1977). In other words, mimetic signs were thought not to be divisible into component parts, but rather were considered unanalyzable lexical items that mapped, as wholes, onto events in the world. However, subsequent research found these mimetic signs to be composed of combinations of a limited set of discrete morphemes (McDonald, 1982; Newport, 1981; Schick, 1987; Supalla, 1982). For example, to describe a drunk's weaving walk down a path, an ASL signer would *not* represent the idiosyncrasies of the drunk's particular meanderings, but would instead use a conventional morpheme representing random movement (i.e., a side-to-side motion) in conjunction with a conventional morpheme representing change of location. Mimetic signs in ASL include, at a minimum, a motion morpheme combined with a handshape morpheme (called "classifiers"; Supalla, 1982).

Even though these productive signs in ASL are *not* analog representations of real-world motions, many of them do resemble the events they represent. Children might then guess wrong and assume that these signs are essentially pictures, with no internal structure. If so, then we might expect children to acquire these complex multi-morphemic forms relatively early. If, however, children do not make use of the iconicity that underlies these multi-morphemic forms, we might expect them to treat these signs, from the start, as complex combinations of smaller units. The signs should then be acquired relatively late.

As we have now come to expect, at no point during the acquisition process do deaf children acquiring ASL consider multi-morphemic signs to be unanalyzed pictorial representations. Rather, they treat multi-morphemic signs as just that—combinations of discrete and separable morphemes (Newport, 1981; Supalla, 1982). At the earliest stages, children are unable to produce several morphemes within a single sign. Their strategy is either to substitute a frozen (mono-morphemic) sign, or to produce only one of the morphemes that comprise the multi-morphemic sign, typically the motion morpheme (e.g., "linear path"). Morphemes for manner (e.g., "bounce") are often omitted, and classifier morphemes for the moving object (e.g., "round") tend to be incorrect. Between ages 3 and 3½, children begin to produce correct handshape classifiers for objects in combination with either a path movement ("round + linear path") or a manner movement ("round + bounce"), but not both. Indeed, at this point, children will demonstrate their knowledge of the component parts of a multi-morphemic sign by sometimes producing its parts sequentially rather than simultaneously, as is required in the adult form (e.g., "bounce" followed by "linear path," rather than "bounce + linear path").

With increasing age, the number of correctly combined morphemes increases. But even by age 5, deaf children produce large numbers of complex signs which do not contain all of the morphemes that would be required in an adult form. As in hearing children's acquisition of morphologically complex spoken languages, morpheme acquisition continues in deaf children until at least age 6 (Kantor, 1980; Supalla, 1982).

Morphemes in sign are simultaneously produced and are thus not easy to separate from one another. Nevertheless, deaf children appear to have no problem seeing the units in their language and learning them as such.

Inflectional Morphology

Many verbs in ASL are inflected to agree with their noun arguments. For example, the ASL verb "give" agrees with the nouns filling the x and z slots in the frame "x gives y to z." What does it mean for an ASL verb to "agree" with a noun? Inflections modify a verb's location, orientation, and/or direction of movement so that the spatial locus of the relevant noun is incorporated into the verb. If the noun arguments refer to real-world objects in the immediate context, the verb incorporates their real-world locations. For example, the sign "give" in its uninflected form is produced in neutral space (at chest level), with a short outward movement. To indicate "I give to you," the signer moves the sign from herself toward the addressee. To indicate "you give to me," the signer reverses the movement, beginning the sign at the addressee and moving it toward herself (Padden, 1983).

But what if the noun arguments refer to objects that are not in the room? Under these circumstances, the signer establishes an arbitrary location in the signing space that stands for the non-present object, and positions her verb to agree with that location. Thus, to indicate "I give to Elmer" (if Elmer is not in the room), the signer first sets up a location in the signing space that stands for Elmer and then moves the sign "give" from herself toward that space. Note that the way a verb is modified to agree with its arguments is precisely the same whether those arguments refer to present or non-present objects—the only difference is in how the spatial location is established for a present versus non-present object. Interestingly, children first acquire the verb agreement system in relation to present objects, and only later apply the system to the cognitively taxing task of representing non-present objects (Lillo-Martin, 1999; Newport & Meier, 1985).

Iconicity could play a role in the deaf child's acquisition of verb agreement system. After all, the sign "I-give-you" is largely identical to the motor act children actually perform when they give a small object to an addressee. This type of iconicity, which Meier (1981, 1982) calls "mime," could facilitate the acquisition of agreement forms. Other parts of the agreement system do not mirror the child's actions, but do map neatly onto real-world motions. For example, the sign "you-give-him" involves a trajectory moving from the addressee to a third party, precisely the route that would be followed if the addressee were to perform the giving act. Do these iconic aspects of the agreement system help acquisition?

The agreement system should be relatively easy to acquire if iconicity is playing a role. However, if children are treating a sign like "I-give-you" not as a holistic representation of the giving act, but as a verb with markings for two arguments (the giver and the givee), the sign should be a relatively late acquisition. As we saw in the acquisition of spoken language, it takes some time for children to be able to produce a full complement of inflections on a verb.

As it turns out, the verb agreement system is *not* an early acquisition. Initially, children fail to produce verbs that require agreement markers (not all verbs in ASL demand agreement)—they just leave these agreement-requiring verbs out of their repertoires entirely even though, at first glance, these verbs seem particularly easy to produce (Meier, 1981, 1982). Beginning at age 2, children produce verbs that require agreement, but they produce them in their uninflected citation forms, that is, without any agreement markers. When they finally do begin to use agreement, children do so on only a small number of verbs, and in only a small number of agreement forms. This restricted use suggests that the children are not yet using agreement productively—the few inflected signs they do use are likely to be unanalyzed rote forms, akin to the amalgams MacWhinney (1978) describes in the acquisition of morphology in spoken language.

It is not until between 3 and 3½ years that deaf children use agreement widely and consistently, and thus can be said to have productive control over the system (Meier, 1982). Moreover, the path of acquisition children follow seems to adhere to morphological principles rather than iconic ones. As would be expected if children are approaching the problem as a morphological one, signs that agree with two arguments (e.g., "give") are acquired *later* than signs that agree with only one argument. Any iconic hypothesis ought to predict that "give" would be an early acquisition. Thus, the verb agreement system in ASL is not acquired as early as we would expect if iconicity were playing a role.

☐ Combining Signs Into Sentences

As in the acquisition of spoken languages, children progress from producing one word at a time to two-word (two-sign) productions. Children learning sign begin to produce two-word utterances around the middle of the second year—approximately the same time as children learning spoken language.

Despite the differences in the modality of the languages they are learning, sign-learning children express approximately the same range of semantic relations in their early two-word utterances as children learning spoken languages. Children sign about the existence and nonexistence of objects, actions on objects, possession of objects, and location of objects. Moreover, within this set, particular semantic relations emerge in about the same order as they do for English-learning children: existence relations appear early, followed by action and state relations, then locative relations, and finally datives, instruments, causes, and manners of action (Newport & Ashbrook, 1977; Newport & Meier, 1985).

When hearing children produce their early two-word sentences, those sentences tend to follow a consistent word order. Do the early two-sign sentences produced by deaf children also follow a consistent word order? We might expect that they would not simply because sentences produced by adult signers do not always adhere to a consistent sign order.

As in spoken languages, adult signers can use inflections to indicate who does what to whom, or they can convey this information by placing their signs in particular orders within the sentence. Subject-Verb-Object (SVO) is the unmarked order for ASL—that is, the order signers use when they do not use inflections to mark semantic roles. However, other orders are allowable when one of the constituents is moved to the beginning of the sentence and marked for topic (Fischer & Gough, 1978; Liddell, 1980; Padden, 1983). In fact, it turns out that adult signers frequently use inflections to mark role relations in their sentences, using order to mark topic. As a result, they display considerable flexibility in the word orders they use in their sentences.

Despite the word order flexibility in the sign input they receive, deaf children learning ASL from their deaf parents use consistent word order as a syntactic device for marking role early in development (Hoffmeister, 1978; Newport & Meier, 1985). Thus, for example, whereas an adult would sign "I-give-you" by moving the sign from herself toward the addressee, a sign-learning child produces three separate signs, and produces them in a consistent order (point at self—give—point at addressee; Newport & Ashbrook, 1977).

As in children learning spoken languages, children pick up the least marked or pragmatically most neutral orders in the sign languages they are learning. ASL-learning children use the SVO order that appears in unmarked sentences in adult ASL (Hoffmeister, 1978). However, children who are learning the Sign Language of the Netherlands (SLN) use Subject-Object-Verb (SOV), the unmarked order in adult SLN (Coerts, 2000).

☐ Relating Signs to the World or to Other Signs

All of the evidence thus far suggests that learning a sign language is no harder—and no easier—than learning a spoken language. It is particularly striking that children are not taking advantage of the iconic properties of sign. The pictorial aspects that make it easy for adult learners to comprehend and remember signs and their structure seem to make no difference to the young child. The question is "why"?

One possibility is that children are unable to make use of the iconicity found in sign. Although apparent to adult learners, the iconic features of conventional sign languages may not be obvious to child learners.

Another possibility, however, is that children see the iconicity and would be happy to exploit it, but are biased in other directions. In particular, they are biased to approach the language-learning problem as a formal system (cf. Karmiloff-Smith, 1992), one in which pieces of the language not only need to be related to the world, but also to other pieces within the language itself (Meier, 1982; Newport & Meier, 1985). In other words, children not only need to consider how a sign represents aspects of the real world (representations that, in sign, often have iconic components), but they also need to consider how that sign fits into, and contrasts with, other signs in the system. Under this scenario, children could incorporate iconicity into the systems they are developing, but only if that iconicity does not conflict with the formal system they are constructing.

What if a child were not learning a particular sign language, but were creating one *de novo*? Such a child might, despite the lack of a language model, display a strong bias to pay attention to how the pieces of the created language fit together as a system. However, a child in such circumstances is also likely to take advantage of whatever iconic properties the manual modality offers. How does the bias to treat language as a formal system interact with a need to create an iconic system that can be understood? It is questions of this sort that we explore in the second part of this book.

For now, we conclude this chapter by noting that, when exposed from birth to a sign language, deaf children learn that language as easily and effortlessly as hearing children learn spoken language. Children are sufficiently flexible that, if presented with a language system processed by hand and eye, they will not only learn that system, but they will do so without a hitch. Children appear to be completely equi-potential with respect to language-learning—ready to learn either sign or speech. Whatever biases children bring to the task of language-learning, they must be broad enough to work in the manual or the oral modality.

Does More or Less Input Matter?

Although we cannot tamper with the circumstances under which children learn language, we can take advantage of the real-world variation that surrounds language-learning. We have looked thus far at children exposed to very different types of language models, including models in the manual modality. Children are remarkably open to learning all languages, even those processed by hand. Moreover, children learn many of the particulars of the language model to which they are exposed from the very start. However, there are places in the learning process where children appear to be asserting themselves—places where children override the input they receive, and thus provide clear evidence of the biases they themselves bring to language-learning.

Another way to explore the effect of language input on child output is to hold type of language constant and observe whether differences in the amount of input children receive affect how those children learn the language. Some children learning English hear a lot of talk, others hear much less. Do differences of this sort make a difference? To address this question, we need to observe variations in how a particular language, English, for example, is used across families, and then explore whether those variations have an impact on child language-learning—in other words, we need to examine differences across individuals within a culture. Before turning to these within-culture studies of individual differences, we need to acknowledge that, as a group, children tend to be treated as special listeners, and that this special treatment is characteristic of all cultures.

☐ Children Receive Special Input in All Cultures

Across the globe, adults appear to speak to their children in special ways. Indeed, even adult signers adjust their language when signing to young children (Masataka, 1992). There are differences, however, in the form that this special register takes across cultures (Ochs & Schieffelin, 1995). In some communities, adults simplify the sounds and the structural forms of the talk they address to young children, and alter how they use that talk in discourse. Simplification takes place at all of these levels among the Tamil, (Williamson, 1979), Inuit (Crago, 1988), and middle-class European-Americans (Newport, Gleitman, & Gleitman, 1977; Snow, 1972). In other communities, adults limit their simplifications to discourse, leaving the sounds and structures of their talk unchanged. Thus, for example, parents in Samoan (Ochs, 1988), Kaluli (Schieffelin, 1990), and working-class African-American (Heath, 1983) communities may repeat parts of an earlier utterance when young children are around, but will make no phonological or grammatical adjustments.

Note that this second strategy for simplification preserves the integrity of the adult form of an utterance, while the first distorts it (Ochs & Schieffelin, 1995). These different strategies are not unlike strategies that can be used to teach a child any conventional act—for example, teaching a child a dance by breaking the dance into components versus repeating the dance over and over again in its entirety. The "breaking-down" strategy guides children's participation in the act, but has the effect of deforming the conventional shape and execution of the dance as a whole (Rogoff, 1990).

Why do cultures vary so much in how they present language to children? The differences are likely to have little to do with attitudes toward language-teaching per se, but may instead reflect deep cultural attitudes toward children as conversational partners (Ochs & Schieffelin, 1995). Cultures that simplify at all levels of linguistic structure tend to put children in the role of conversational partner—children are expected to be full-fledged participants in conversations despite their minimal linguistic skills. Indeed, American parents often respond to the burps and sneezes of their tiny infants as though they were legitimate turns in the conversation (Snow, 1988). In contrast, cultures that simplify primarily through repetition do not consider young children to be full-fledged participants in a conversation until they have mastered some language skills. As a result, young children in these cultures participate in conversations, not as active speakers or listeners, but as overhearers of adult conversation.

The question for us, of course, is whether any of these adjustments affects how children learn language. We know that children in all cultures acquire the language to which they are exposed, suggesting that no one type of adjustment is essential for language-learning. But do the different types of adjustments result in different language-learning trajectories? At the moment, we don't know. It is possible that children who participate in conversations as overhearers and receive discourse (but not grammatical and morphological) simplifications go about the process of learning language in a different way from children who participate in conversations as full-fledged partners and receive simplifications at all levels. For example, children who learn language from the speech they overhear may be more likely to learn grammar by first producing large rote-learned chunks of talk, only later analyzing those chunks into smaller units (Lieven, 1994). A great deal of work needs to be done before we can say whether language-learning is affected by cross-cultural differences in the adjustments adults make in their talk to children.

What about the adjustments adults make within a culture? Do they have an impact on language-learning? Here we know more, although most of what we know pertains to English. Two types of studies have been done, those exploring the natural range of variation in input that English-learning children receive, and those extending the range of variation. We take a look at each in turn.

☐ The Natural Variation in Language Input That Children Receive Within a Culture

The sentences spoken to English-learning children are, by and large, short, usually consisting of a single clause; they are clearly spoken and therefore intelligible; they almost never contain grammatical errors; and they tend to focus on events that are taking place in the here-and-now and involve objects that are visible (Hoff-Ginsberg & Shatz, 1982; Newport, 1977; Snow, 1972). All English-speaking adults—and even older children (Shatz & Gelman, 1973)—simplify their speech in these ways when addressing younger children. However, adults vary in how much they simplify their speech, and in how much they talk at all. The question is whether this variability in input is related in any way to child language-learning.

One obvious problem in addressing this question is that *a priori* we don't know which properties of parental speech ought to promote language-learning. Is it good to hear simplified speech, and is more better than less? Can the input to a child be too simple? A question such as "Are Bert and Ernie on the boat?" involves moving the subject and thus seems more complex than the declarative statement "Bert and Ernie are on the boat." But it might be important for children to have these relatively complex forms in their input simply because questions can focus children on the units in their language ("Bert and Ernie" is moved in its entirety, changing positions with "are," and thus pops out as a unit). Moreover, simple sentences alone will not display all aspects of syntactic structure. How will children who hear only single-clause sentences (e.g., "Ernie is hitting Bert") be able to figure out which auxiliary verb ought to be moved when forming questions in a two-clause sentence? For example, in the sentence "Ernie who is quite a bruiser is hitting Bert," which "is" should be inverted with the subject "Ernie" to make the sentence into a question—the first "is" in the subordinate clause

("Is Ernie who quite a bruiser is hitting Bert?") or the second in the main clause ("Is Ernie who is quite a bruiser hitting Bert?")? Even more troublesome, it is not clear what we mean by "simple" input. What makes us think that statements are, in fact, simpler than questions? There is no theory-neutral way of rank ordering constructions from simple to complex.

Studies that have explored the impact of linguistic variation on child language-learning have effectively avoided these problems by taking large numbers of measures of parental input at Time 1, and relating these measures to changes in child language from Time 1 to a later time (Newport, Gleitman, & Gleitman, 1977, conducted the first of these studies). Measures of parental speech include sensible items, for example, the average length of utterances; counts of different types of sentences (declaratives, imperatives, questions); counts of different parts of speech (verbs, pronouns); and counts of parental expansions of their children's utterances or repetitions of their own utterances. In many cases, frequency of use is the way parental variables are measured. There is, of course, no firm reason to believe that frequency is the right measure to take. After all, the appearance of a construction (even once) under interpretable conditions might be much more important for learning than its frequency overall. Nevertheless, there is some plausibility to the idea that children will notice, and therefore profit from, constructions that occur frequently in their input.

Measures of child language also often involve frequency of use, and typically include average length of utterance, and numbers of verbs per utterance, noun phrases per utterance, auxiliaries per verb phrase, noun inflections per noun phrase, and so on. Here again, frequency measures could be problematic. It is not clear that a child who produces a small number of complex sentences (i.e., sentences with more than one verb) is any less knowledgeable about how to form complex sentences than a child who produces many. Again, however, there is plausibility to the idea that a child who produces many constructions of the same type has *productive* mastery over that construction, and more so than a child who produces few.

It is clear that frequency in the input a child receives does matter, at least for vocabulary-learning. The amount of talk mothers address to their children is related to the number of words the children acquire (i.e., vocabulary size)—the more a mother talks, the larger the child's vocabulary (Huttenlocher, Haight, Bryk, Seltzer, & Lyons, 1991). Thus, the number of word-learning "trials" to which a child is exposed is an important factor in predicting how large that child's vocabulary will be. Frequency of particular words plays a role as well. The more often a verb appears in a mother's talk, the more often that verb is used by her child some weeks later (Naigles & Hoff-Ginsberg, 1998). Interestingly, the range of syntactic environments in which a verb appears in a mother's talk also has an effect (over and above the effect of frequency) on how often her child uses that verb—the more different syntactic contexts in which a verb appears in mother's talk, the more often that verb is later used by the child (Naigles & Hoff-Ginsberg, 1998).

Frequency may play a role in syntax-learning as well (Huttenlocher, Vasilyeva, Cymerman, & Levine, 2002). The more an adult talks to children, the greater gains they make, in particular, the longer and more semantically complex their utterances (Barnes, Gutfreund, Satterly, & Wells, 1983). However, unmitigated frequency is not the whole story. The most robust finding across a variety of studies (although some question the robustness of even this finding; see Valian, 1999) is that the development of auxiliaries (e.g., *can, do, will, is*) appears to be related to adult speech (Barnes et al., 1983; Furrow, Nelson, & Benedict, 1979; Gleitman, Newport, & Gleitman, 1984; Hoff-Ginsberg, 1985; Newport et al., 1977; Richards, 1990). But the relation in not a straightforward one.

Newport and colleagues (1977) found that the rate at which adults (in their study, mothers) use auxiliaries is *not* related to the child's use of auxiliaries. What does predict child use of auxiliaries is mothers' use of *yes/no* questions—questions in which the auxiliary appears at the front of the sentence in a particularly salient position (*"Will* you tie your shoes?" *"Are* you coming over here?"*). Mothers who frequently produce sentences with auxiliaries at the beginnings of their sentences have children who make great progress in acquiring auxiliaries. Moreover, mothers who frequently produce sentences that do *not* have auxiliaries (i.e., imperative sentences, such as "tie your shoes," "come over here") have children who make slow progress in acquiring auxiliaries.

Thus, it is not just how often mothers produce auxiliaries that matters, it is how often auxiliaries are produced in salient positions in the sentence that matters. Note that "salient" is defined here in terms of the child. We assume that children find it relatively easy to process and pay attention to words that appear at the beginning of the sentence. Thus, there are "learning filters" (Newport et al., 1977) that children bring to linguistic input, and that determine whether input becomes "uptake" (Harris, 1992).

To make the story even more complicated, children are not merely "copying" (Valian, 1999) the input they receive. The fast auxiliary learners tend to hear auxiliaries in first position of sentences addressed to them. However, they first produce auxiliaries in the *middle* of sentences, even for questions (e.g., "this *can't* write a flower?" "what he *can* ride in?" "how he *can* be a doctor?" Klima & Bellugi, 1966). Thus, what the linguistic input does is provide opportunities for learning the language system—but it is up to the child to do the inductive work to figure out what that system is. Input is most effective when it matches the processing biases of the learner. In a sense, we need to think about simplicity, not in terms of simplicity of grammar, but in terms of simplicity for learning (Gleitman et al., 1984).

Newport and colleagues (1977) argue that it is no accident that the auxiliary effect is the most robust finding in these studies. Auxiliaries are closed-class morphemes, that is, members of a class that is small and does not readily accept additions (e.g., determiners like "the," "a," or "an"; or pronouns like "he," she," or "it"). They contrast with open-class morphemes whose set is large and constantly growing. Closed-class morphemes turn out to be particularly susceptible to variations in learning conditions. For example, a child who was prevented from learning language until age 13 had little trouble learning the open-class items of her language, but had difficulty with the closed-class items (Curtiss, 1977; Goldin-Meadow, 1978). As a result, it may not be surprising that we find effects of adult talk on child learning of auxiliaries. These properties may be particularly sensitive to variations in linguistic input.

But what about the properties of child language that were *not* affected by variations in linguistic input? These properties are good candidates for what we might call "environment-insensitive" properties of language (Newport et al., 1977)—properties whose development is relatively unaffected by variations in linguistic input. The problem, however, is that we are making this inference on the basis of a negative result. It is the *absence* of an effect of adult input on a particular property in child output that would lead us to nominate the property as environment-insensitive. As Newport and colleagues (1977) point out, we might not see an effect of adult input on child output simply because the range of variation in adult input is too narrow to see such an effect. After all, adults all use the same special speech register when they address children. Linguistic input could play an important role in the development of these properties, but the natural variation that exists in the talk parents use with children might not be great enough for us to find this out. To combat this problem, we turn to studies that extend the range of variation.

☐ Enriching the Input to Children

An alternative approach to the input question is to increase the range of variation in the input children receive by providing either richer or poorer linguistic environments than those found in nature. In enrichment studies, experimenters provide children with additional input in a particular construction, often constructions that involve the predicate (and thus auxiliaries). For example, a child says, "You can't get in!" and the experimenter replies "No, I can't get in, can I?" Or, the child asks, "Where it go?" and the experimenter replies, "It will go there" (Nelson, 1977). The goal is for experimenters to focus their responses on a particular aspect of the child's language, and to fit those responses seamlessly into the conversation.

Overall, enrichment works—at least when it comes to auxiliaries. Moreover, enrichment works selectively. When children are provided with enriched input in predicate constructions, their predicates (including auxiliaries) become more complex, but the average length of their utterances and their noun phrases don't change at all (Nelson, 1977; Nelson, Carskaddon, & Bonvillian, 1973). In addition, if children are provided with enrichment utterances containing an auxiliary at the beginning of the sentence ("Could the girl slide down?"), they make more progress in auxiliaries than children who hear the auxiliary in the middle of the sentence ("This one could roll") or in both positions (Shatz, Hoff-Ginsberg, & MacIver, 1989).

Enrichment studies can provide clear data on the positive effects of linguistic input on language acquisition, that is, on properties of language that are *sensitive* to the effects of environment. However, enrichment studies cannot provide unequivocal data on the negative effects of linguistic input on acquisition, that is, on the environment-*insensitive* properties of language. If the language children naturally hear already provides enough input for a given language property to develop, enriching their input is not likely to have a further effect on the development of that property.

As an analogy, say we are interested in discovering whether cornstarch thickens soups. Once the thickening process begins—that is, once a threshold has been reached—continuing to add spoonfuls of cornstarch has no effect on the thickness of the pot. If we were to investigate the effect of cornstarch on soup thickness *only* after the threshold had been reached, we would come to the incorrect conclusion that cornstarch has no effect on soup thickness.

Similarly, if we provide additional input in a particular language property only after the threshold for that property has been reached, we may come to the incorrect conclusion that linguistic input has no effect on the development of that property. However, the property might very well be sensitive to linguistic input but only *below* the threshold—that is, it may be sensitive only to a *reduction* in input more drastic than is usually observed in nature.

☐ Degrading the Input to Children

It is, in principle, possible to remove the language input children receive. If there is a threshold level of linguistic input necessary for certain language properties to develop, these properties should *not* develop in a child who lacks linguistic input. If, however, linguistic input is not necessary for a set of language properties to develop, these properties ought to emerge in the communications of a child without input. Note that, in studies of speech in natural and enriched environments, non-effects of linguistic input must be inferred from negative results: A property is assumed to be environment-insensitive if input *does not* affect its development. In contrast, in a deprivation study, the presence of a particular property in a child's language is positive evidence for environment-insensitive properties of language—a property is assumed to be environment-insensitive if it *does* appear in the deprived child's repertoire. These are language properties whose development is not affected by linguistic input. They therefore might be properties that children themselves are able to introduce into linguistic systems.

Of course, we cannot deliberately remove a child's language input. Nevertheless, circumstances arise in which children have been inadvertently deprived of linguistic input. There are reports of children who have been raised by animals with no human contact at all (Brown, 1958; Lane 1977) or raised by humans who have treated the children inhumanely, depriving them of physical, social, and linguistic stimulation (Curtiss, 1977; Fromkin, Krashen, Curtiss, Rigler, & Rigler, 1974; Kulochova, 1972; Skuse, 1988). For example, a young girl was discovered at age 13, after having been isolated and confined to a small room with no freedom of movement and no human companionship. This child, called "Genie," did not develop language or any other form of communication during her years of isolation and deprivation (Curtiss, 1977; Fromkin et al., 1974). Perhaps not surprisingly, children do not develop human language under developmental conditions this extreme.

Thus, there appear to be limits on the resilience of language. Human contact seems to be essential for children to develop language—and those humans, at a minimum, must be humane. But contact with humans involves many factors, only one of which is exposure to a model for language. The radical deprivation studies say little about the effect of linguistic isolation per se on language development—language was only one of the many human factors missing in these circumstances.

There are, however, a few studies of children experiencing normal environments except for their impoverished linguistic input. For example, consider Jim, a hearing child whose deaf parents exposed him neither to conventional oral nor to conventional manual linguistic input, and who had heard English only from the television and briefly at nursery school (Sachs, Bard, & Johnson, 1981). Unlike Genie and the "wild children" raised by animals, Jim did develop some properties of spoken language (e.g., the recursive concatenation of propositions) during his period of limited exposure to conventional language. However, he did not develop all of the properties found in child language (e.g., the auxiliary and certain movement rules). Although Jim's speech was impoverished, it was not uniformly impoverished, suggesting that Jim's dearth of linguistic input had differential effects on various aspects of his language development. Thus, without the benefit of repeated exposure to linguistic input in an interactional setting, children are able to develop certain properties of language, but not others.

Creole genesis is another context in which children receive degraded linguistic input (although, unlike Jim, this input is used in interaction with others). Here too children go well beyond their input. Creole languages develop out of pidgin languages. Pidgins typically arise in colonial or trade situations when two groups who need to communicate with one another do not share a language. Pidgin languages are simple, having little structure. Creoles have a more expanded vocabulary than the pidgin out of which they grow and a more complex grammatical structure. Bickerton (1990, 1999) claims that, across the globe, all creoles have the same grammatical structure (different vocabulary, of course). This is striking because the creoles of the world have evolved out of very different pidgins. Bickerton argues that the commonalities across creoles reflect the influence of child learners who transform pidgins into creoles by adding structures that are basic to human communication according to a "bioprogram."

Bickerton's proposal is controversial, in part because questions have been raised about the historical accuracy of the data upon which his claims are based (e.g., Goodman 1984; Samarin 1984; Seuren 1984). There is, however, a well-documented example of the sort of process Bickerton hypothesizes for creoles. A case study, based on developmental data in a single individual, suggests that a child can introduce complexity into the language system he receives from his parents. Singleton and Newport (2003) have described the language of a deaf child whose deaf parents were late-learners of sign and thus produced signs that provided an incomplete model of the morphological structure in American Sign Language (ASL). The child, exposed only to this imperfect model of ASL, nevertheless developed a sign language with morphological structure more complex than that of his parents, and comparable in many respects to the morphological structure developed by other deaf children exposed to complete models of ASL.

The newly developing Nicaraguan Sign Language is another creole-like situation in which we can explore the role children play in generating linguistic structure. Opening the first school for the deaf in Managua in the late 1970s created an opportunity for deaf children to interact with one another and form a sign language. This system, which resembled a pidgin language in some respects, was then learned by a second generation of young signers who introduced new linguistic structures into the language (Kegl, Senghas, & Coppola, 1999; Senghas, 1995, 2000; Senghas & Coppola, 2001; Senghas, Coppola, Newport, & Supalla, 1997).

We find comparable creativity when deaf children are not exposed to a naturally evolving sign language such as ASL, but rather to a sign system invented by educators. Manually Coded English (MCE) is the name for a set of sign systems which map English surface structure onto the visual-gestural modality. MCE was invented to teach English to deaf children and, as such, is not a "natural" language system spontaneously developed by language users. Unlike ASL, which uses simultaneous spatial devices to mark morphology, MCE uses invented signs which attempt to follow in a one-to-one mapping the morphologic structure of English. English-like sequential structure within a sign is apparently very difficult to process. Indeed, deaf children exposed only to MCE alter the input they receive, innovating forms that systematically use space to convey meaning, as do many of the grammatical devices of ASL (Gee & Goodhart, 1985; Goodhart, 1984; Livingston, 1983; S. Supalla, 1991; Suty & Friel-Patti, 1982). Thus, when provided with an input that may be difficult to process, children are capable of altering that input and constructing a rule-governed system of their own.

An even more remarkable example of children's ability to go beyond their input comes from our work on children who lack input from a language model yet in all other respects experience normal social environments. The children are deaf with hearing losses so severe that they cannot acquire spoken language. Moreover, the children are born to hearing parents who have not exposed them to a model of a sign language, either ASL or MCE. Such children are, for all intents and purposes, deprived of a usable model for language—although, importantly, they are not deprived of other aspects of human social interaction. Despite their lack of linguistic input, the children use gesture to communicate. The interesting point is that these gestures assume the form of a rudimentary linguistic system, a system that displays structure at both word and sentence levels and that is used for many of the functions served by conventional language. This gesture system is the focus of Part 2 of this book.

☐ Where Are We?

We have now set the stage for looking at the gesture systems that deaf children create without benefit of linguistic input. We have seen that, when provided with linguistic input, children take advantage of that input, moving seamlessly through the stages of language-learning—discovering words, breaking those words into morphemes and combining them into structured sentences. Children accomplish this feat whether the input they receive is spoken or signed. Moreover, when exposed to the languages of the world— languages that vary in the learning problems they present to young children—children respond with aplomb. They figure out early on which type of language they are acquiring and let the characteristics of that language guide their learning.

However, there also seem to be privileged meanings and forms that children acquire early in development regardless of the language they are learning. For example, children across the globe construct their early grammatical systems around highly transitive events and focus on the results of events with little attention to animacy. They also construct grammatical systems that have structure within sentences (e.g., ordering patterns, underlying predicate frames), as well as structure across sentences (e.g., word sets or paradigms). It is these forms and meanings that children themselves seem to have a hand in developing, and that are likely to be resilient properties of language. We might therefore expect to find these particular properties in the gesture systems created by children who do not have access to linguistic input—and indeed we do, as we will see in the second section of this book.

It is also important to point out as we begin our tour of the gesture systems created by deaf children that these gesture systems offer a special kind of evidence for the resilient properties of language. In most studies of the effect of variation in input on child language-learning, the evidence for a resilient property of language is a *non-effect*—the child's failure to develop a particular property of language in the face of variation in environmental input constitutes (negative) evidence for the resilience of that property in these studies. In contrast, in studies of deaf children who lack input from a conventional language yet develop gesture systems nevertheless, the evidence for a resilient property of language is a positive effect—the child's ability to develop a property of language without benefit of linguistic input constitutes (positive) evidence for the resilience of that property in studies of the deaf children's gesture systems. It is, of course, easier (and more reliable) to generate hypotheses from positive than negative data. As a result, our studies of the deaf children's gesture systems offer us a unique and powerful way to isolate properties of language that are resilient, properties whose robustness can then be confirmed through other types of studies. Part 2 of the book begins with background on deafness and language-learning, background that is necessary to understand the unusual language-learning circumstances in which our deaf children find themselves.

LANGUAGE DEVELOPMENT WITHOUT A LANGUAGE MODEL

6

Background on Deafness and Language-Learning

The worlds in which deaf children develop language are different from typical linguistic environments for both physical and social reasons. Physical limitations prevent deaf children from making use of the auditory input that surrounds them. We saw in Chapter 4 that this makes little difference in terms of the child's ability to learn language—deaf children who are exposed from birth to visual input from a sign language learn that language as easily as hearing children learn spoken language. However, it is deaf children's social circumstances that determine whether they have access to sign language input—some are first exposed to sign language at a young age, others not until much later in life.

My goal in this second part of the book is to ask whether children must experience input from a conventional language (be it signed or spoken) in order to communicate in language-like ways. To address this question, my collaborators and I have explored language development in deaf children who were not able to make use of input from spoken language, and who were not exposed to sign language input until late in the language-learning process. In this chapter, I first describe circumstances for spoken and sign language-learning in deaf children in general. I then describe characteristics of the particular deaf children whom we studied.

☐ Learning Spoken Language

One in 1,000 children born in the United States is profoundly deaf (Ruben, 1972). Ninety percent of these children are born to hearing parents (Hoffmeister & Wilbur, 1980) who, not surprisingly, would like their children to learn to speak. Unfortunately, however, although surrounded by spoken English, children with severe hearing losses cannot learn it unless provided with specialized instruction. Oral methods of education advocate intense training in sound sensitivity, lipreading (or speechreading), and speech production. On the assumption that learning a sign language interferes with learning a spoken system, many of these programs discourage the use of conventional sign language with the child. Oral methods for instructing deaf children were first introduced into the United States around 1860 and continued to gain in popularity. These methods completely dominated American deaf education between 1900 and 1960 (Lou, 1988). But many children have not achieved linguistic competence through these methods.

Sound is essentially inaccessible to children who have severe to profound hearing losses. A child with a *severe* hearing loss (70- to 90-decibel) is unable to hear even shouted conversation and thus cannot learn speech as a hearing child would. A child with a *profound* loss ($\geq$ 90-decibel) hears only occasional loud sounds and these sounds may be perceived as vibrations rather than sound patterns. The child's limited hearing abilities can, of course, be augmented with hearing aids. Amplification via a hearing aid does increase a child's awareness of sound. However, for many children, hearing aids do not alter the clarity of those sound patterns (Mindel & Vernon, 1971; Moores, 1982). The cochlear implant is a relatively new device designed to improve upon the hearing aid. Unlike a hearing aid which is removable, the cochlear implant is surgically placed inside the portion of the inner ear that converts sound to neural signals (the cochlea). The implant receives signals from an external device worn behind the ear and stimulates electrodes in the cochlea; the electrodes stimulate the auditory nerve directly, bypassing the hair cells that implement the first stage of auditory neural processing in intact ears. Cochlear implants appear to improve hearing for adults who become deaf after having a spoken language. However, the jury is still out on the success of implants for prelingually deaf children who must *learn* spoken language through the device (Owens & Kessler, 1989; Svirsky, Robbins, Kirk, Pisoni, & Miyamoto, 2000).

In addition to encouraging deaf children to use whatever hearing they have, many oral programs also encourage children to use the visual cues that people produce when they speak. The problem, however, is that the information listeners get from reading visual cues off a speaker's lips is not sufficient to allow severely and profoundly deaf children to learn spoken language (Conrad, 1979; Farwell, 1976; Summerfield, 1983). Visual cues are generally ambiguous with respect to speech—the mapping from visual cues to words is one-to-many. In order to constrain the range of plausible lexical interpretations, other higher-order classes of information (e.g., the phonological, lexical, syntactic, semantic, and pragmatic regularities of a language) must come into play during speechreading. The most proficient speechreaders are those who can use their knowledge of the language to interpret an inadequate visual signal (Conrad, 1977). As a result, postlingually deafened individuals (people who had knowledge of a language before losing their hearing) are generally better speechreaders than individuals who have been deaf from birth (Summerfield, 1983). Since speechreading appears to require knowledge of a language to succeed, it is extremely difficult for a child to *learn* language solely through speechreading.

As a result, it is strikingly uncommon for deaf children with severe to profound hearing losses to achieve the kind of proficiency in spoken language that hearing children do. Even with instruction, deaf children's acquisition of speech is markedly delayed when compared to the acquisition of speech by hearing children of hearing parents (or when compared to the acquisition of sign by deaf children of deaf parents). By age 5 or 6, and despite intensive early training programs, the average profoundly deaf child has only a very reduced oral linguistic capacity (Conrad, 1979; Mayberry 1992; K. Meadow, 1968). However, speech is not the only route to language.

☐ Learning Sign Language

Deaf children born to deaf parents are very likely to be exposed to a natural sign language such as ASL from day 1. These children learn ASL as their first language with no need for additional instruction. Moreover, deaf children of deaf parents are socialized into Deaf culture (I follow common practice and use uppercase *Deaf* when referring to a cultural group, and a lowercase *deaf* when referring to hearing loss). For these children, Deaf is not the exception, Deaf is the norm (Padden & Humphries, 1988).

However, as mentioned above, 90% of deaf children in the United States are not born to deaf parents. They are born to hearing parents who are not likely to know a sign language. As a result, these deaf children will not be exposed to sign language at birth. Moreover, the hearing parents of these deaf children are likely to want their children to be part of their cultural world, not the Deaf world. Their first goal is to teach their children English.

Up until 1960, the only option open to hearing parents who wanted their children to learn English was to send them to an oral school. It was not until 1960 when Stokoe published the first linguistic analysis of ASL that educators began to realize that the manual modality could support language, and perhaps could be used to teach English. Although ASL was earning recognition as a "real" language, hearing parents had no interest in having their children learn a language they themselves did not know—they wanted their children to learn English, not ASL. As a result, educators invented a number of different sign systems (Signing Essential English, Seeing Essential English, Signing Exact English, Signed English; Lou, 1988) which, as a group, are referred to as "Manually Coded English." All of these systems borrow signs from ASL and syntactic structure from English—the goal is for children to learn the structure of English through the manual modality. In order to foster the development of speech, MCE is to be signed while simultaneously speaking English.

Although an excellent idea in principle, MCE systems are, in fact, difficult to process. Teachers of the deaf find it hard to sign and speak at the same time without distorting one of the two systems (Marmor & Petitto, 1979). Moreover, as mentioned in Chapter 5, deaf children frequently distort MCE systems as they learn them, often refashioning the systems so that they resemble natural sign languages like ASL. Some aspects of MCE are easy to learn, others are not (Schick & Moeller, 1992). One of the driving forces behind MCE systems is to teach deaf children how to read English. Unfortunately, however, MCE systems are no better at serving this function (and indeed may even be worse) than ASL (Chamberlain & Mayberry, 2000; Goldin-Meadow, & Mayberry, 2001).

The most current movement in deaf education holds that knowing one language (ASL) makes it easier to learn another (English). Under this model, the goal of the deaf school is to promote and, when necessary, teach ASL as deaf children's first language, and then teach English (either through print, sign, or sound) as their second language—in other words, to foster bilingual deaf education (Singleton, Supalla, Litchfield, & Schley, 1998).

It should now be clear why language-learning circumstances for deaf children vary so much from the typical. Spoken language is not accessible for children with severe to profound hearing losses without intensive instruction. Even with instruction and conventional hearing aids, only a few deaf children become oral successes. Sign language is available from day 1 only to those children born to deaf parents. The remaining 90% of deaf children, if they are to learn sign (ASL or, more likely, some form of MCE), will have to do so through an educational program; and that program can begin as soon as the child's hearing loss is discovered or it can be delayed until adolescence.

☐ The Deaf Children We Studied

We began our studies in 1972 when oral education for the deaf was still popular, although beginning to decline. The children we studied were in oral programs whose goal was to foster acquisition of English through heightened attention to sound and to the visual cues of speech. At the time of our observations, none of the children had made significant progress in learning spoken English—if they had, they would not have been included in the study. Our goal was not to test the merits of oral education, but to examine the language skills of children who had not yet benefited from the oral education to which they were exposed. Thus, we observed children who, at the time, were having difficulty with oral education. In addition, as recommended by the oral programs they attended, none of the children had been exposed to ASL or MCE.

We observed 10 deaf children of hearing parents, six from the Philadelphia area and four from the Chicago area. We recruited the children by obtaining names of deaf children from private speech therapists and from oral schools for the deaf in each area. Each child's parents were contacted and permission was obtained to observe and videotape the child over a period of time. We began videotaping the children as soon as we found them and, if possible, continued until age 5 or 6. We began observations on two children (Mildred and Kathy—the names of the children have been changed to protect their identities) when they were 1½, another five children (Abe, Marvin, David, Donald, and Dennis) during their 2nd year, two (Karen, Chris) at the beginning of their 3rd year, and the last child (Tracy) at the beginning of her 4th year. Table 1 lists the ten children, along with the number of sessions each child was observed and the child's age during that period.

To provide some sense of the data base we are working with, Table 1 also displays the number of gesture "utterances" each child produced per hour at the first session and at the last (I describe how we decided when a gesture utterance began and ended in Chapter 7). We typically observed a child from one to two hours, which means that we often had a large number of gesture utterances to code. On average, a third of a child's gesture utterances contained more than one gesture and conveyed a semantic proposition (sometimes several propositions, see Chapter 11; see the "Shovels" videoclip at www.psypress.com/goldinmeadow). The table also presents the longest gesture utterance that each child produced during the observation period.

The observation sessions described in Table 1 comprise the first wave of data that we coded and analyzed (see Feldman, Goldin-Meadow, & Gleitman, 1978; Goldin-Meadow, 1979; Goldin-Meadow & Mylander, 1984). However, we were able to continue observing a subset of the children—David until 5;2, Abe until 4;11, Marvin until 5;3, and Karen until 5;11. This second wave of data has been used for a variety of analyses, for example, to explore the children's morphological systems (Goldin-Meadow, Mylander, & Butcher, 1995) and their narratives (Phillips, Goldin-Meadow, & Miller, 2001) and to compare the American deaf children to Chinese deaf children (Goldin-Meadow, Gelman, & Mylander, 2003; Goldin-Meadow & Mylander, 1998; Zheng & Goldin-Meadow, 2002).

Hearing children learning to talk can vary a great deal in how much they talk—some talk all the time, others are relatively quiet. A child who is not a big talker is nevertheless developing a structured linguistic system, but the paucity of talk may make it harder to discover that system. So too with our deaf children—they varied a great deal in how much gesturing they did. One of the children, David, was particularly prolific—he was the only child to produce nearly 400 gesture utterances per hour (see Table 1). Moreover, he and his family really enjoyed our visits (as did we!). On occasion, we would stay at his home videotaping for three hours, and end up with a great deal of data. Because discovering a pattern is much easier when the data are

TABLE 1. Description of the Children

Child's Pseudonym	Number of Sessions Observed	Child's Age (years; months)		Number of Gesture Utterances Produced per Hour		Longest Gesture Utterance
		First Session	Last Session	First Session	Last Session	
Mildred	12	1;4	3;8	52.5	94.5	5
Kathy	9	1;5	2;8	40.0	93.0	6
Dennis	4	2;2	2;6	50.9	102.0	3
Abe	9	2;3	3;9	24.6	158.4	8
Donald	11	2;5	4;6	6.6	198.3	4
David	8	2;10	3;10	36.0	384.0	9
Marvin	6	2;11	4;2	91.8	187.5	8
Karen	6	3;1	4;2	67.5	133.1	6
Chris	3	3;2	3;6	92.2	120.9	4
Tracy	2	4;1	4;3	119.1	142.1	6

plentiful, we would often begin our analyses with David, find a pattern, and then confirm that pattern in the other children. At the moment, some of our analyses have been done only on David. These findings (which are described throughout the book) have therefore not yet been confirmed on the other children, although there is no particular reason to believe that David is unique.

The ten children we studied were relatively diverse—four were girls, and six were boys; two were African-American, and eight were European-American; six had at least one older sibling at the time of our observations, one had a younger sibling, and three had no siblings; two were from lower-class families, and eight were from middle-class families; two had only one parent (the mother) living in the home during all or part of the study, and eight had two parents living in the home, with mother as primary caretaker; fathers worked as plumbers, fire fighters, policemen, construction workers (see Goldin-Meadow, 1979; and Goldin-Meadow & Mylander, 1984, for additional details about the children). Despite these differences, the children shared the two characteristics necessary to be included in our study: None could rely on oral language for communication, and none was exposed to a conventional sign language system.

From a psychological perspective, all of the children were well integrated into family life. At this young age, much of a child's communication is about the here-and-now. As a result, the children had relatively little trouble making their desires known. They interacted with their siblings and parents as do all preschool children—sometimes with anger, sometimes with affection, sometimes with concern. As is the case in any group of individuals, temperaments varied widely—some of the children were cheerful and cooperative, some stubborn and defiant, others shy and cautious. All were loved and cared for by parents who were concerned about and involved in their children's lives.

Hearing Abilities and Oral Language Skills

All of the children in the study had received hearing evaluations at nearby medical centers. They were all judged congenitally deaf with no other physical or cognitive deficits. In one case, the cause of deafness was determined to be prenatal rubella; in the other nine cases, the cause of deafness was unknown. The medical reports indicated that the children had severe to profound hearing losses, that is, losses of 70 to 100 decibels. Nine of the children wore hearing aids. The aid improved each child's hearing, but not sufficiently to allow the natural acquisition of oral language. Dennis did not wear a hearing aid during the study but did acquire an aid later.

Nine of the children attended oral preschools where they were taught to vocalize and attend to sound. Dennis did not begin school until after we concluded our observations. Kathy, Chris, and Tracy all attended one oral preschool and David and Donald attended another in the Philadelphia area. Mildred, Karen, and Marvin attended the same preschool in the Chicago area, and Abe attended another. Thus, as a group, the children did not share the same school experiences. Moreover, the children saw each other only at school and didn't visit each others' homes.

We analyzed the children's vocalizations informally for the Philadelphia children (and more systematically for the Chicago children, see next paragraph). We observed that, during our taping sessions, Kathy and Chris neither read lips nor produced identifiable verbal words, although both produced sounds in what seemed like a haphazard fashion. Donald, David, and Tracy also verbalized haphazardly, but in addition they reliably produced verbal names in constrained situations for a very few objects; for example, "horse" and "bird." None of the Philadelphia children combined their spoken words into sentences.

We coded all of the vocalizations that the Chicago children produced during the first half hour of each visit (Goldin-Meadow & Mylander, 1984), and determined whether the vocalization was a recognizable word (meaningful vocalizations) or an unrecognizable sound spontaneously produced by the child or imitated in response to the caretaker (meaningless vocalizations). The children produced very few meaningful vocalizations—from 1% to 4% (representing 1 to 36 utterances) of all of each child's communications contained meaningful words. Moreover, almost half of all of the children's meaningful words were accompanied by gestures which conveyed the same meaning as the word. Finally, as in the Philadelphia group, all of each child's meaningful vocalizations were single words—they produced no spoken sentences whatsoever.

Thus, at the time of our observations, there was no evidence from the children's speech that they had learned English syntax. In addition, as we will see in Chapter 9, the sentence structure of the gestures created by the deaf children does *not* conform to the patterns of spoken English. For example, the deaf children produced gestures for patients (objects acted upon) before gestures for the actions themselves—they gestured "drum beat" rather than follow the "beat drum" order more commonly found in English. It is therefore extremely unlikely that the deaf children we studied had learned English and then patterned their gesture system after this spoken language model.

Manual Language Skills

As described above, none of the children in our study had been formally exposed to ASL or MCE. As preschoolers in oral schools for the deaf, the children spent very little time with the older deaf children in the schools who might have had some knowledge of a conventional sign system (the preschoolers only attended school a few hours a day and were not on the playground at the same time as the older children). Moreover, the children's families knew no deaf adults socially and interacted only with other hearing families, typically those with hearing children.

One of the primary reasons we were convinced that the children we studied had had no exposure to a conventional sign system was that they did not know even the most common lexical items of ASL or MCE. We asked a deaf native signer to review our videotapes of the play sessions. The signer found no evidence of any conventional signs. Moreover, when we informally presented common signs such as those for mother, father, boy, girl, and dog to some of the children, we found that they did not understand any of these signs. Thus, we were convinced that, at the time of our observations, the deaf children we were observing had not been exposed to conventional sign language.

With regard to the input issue in general, note that the goal of our research is to isolate properties of language that develop despite wide variations in learning conditions—what we have termed the "resilient" properties of language. The deaf children we study are clearly developing their communication systems under severely degraded input conditions—they have no input in conventional sign language and their hearing losses act as a massive filter on reception of speech, preventing spoken language data from reaching them in an undistorted form (cf. Swisher, 1989). Thus, even if the children in our study have acquired some words and signs, the properties of language that appear in their communications can still be said to have developed under atypical language-learning conditions. As a result, the children provide us with an opportunity to identify those properties of language so over-determined and buffered in humans that they will arise even under strikingly atypical acquisition conditions.

One other nagging question arises with respect to input. We were convinced that the deaf children we studied were not exposed to a conventional sign language. However, all of the children lived with hearing parents who wanted their children to learn to talk. The parents therefore talked to their children all of the time and, like all hearing speakers, gestured when they talked. Perhaps it was the hearing parents who generated the gesture systems that we describe in this book. In other words, the deaf children may have learned their gesture systems from the spontaneous gestures that their hearing parents produced while talking. This is a very real possibility, one that we have taken seriously in our studies. In Chapter 14, we will describe the gestures that the hearing parents produced when they talked to their deaf children, and we will analyze those gestures with the same tools that we use to analyze the children's gestures. We will find that the structure of the hearing parents' gestures is quite different from the structure of their children's gestures (perhaps not surprisingly given that the parents always produced their gestures while speaking, cf. Goldin-Meadow, 2003c; McNeill, 1992). Thus, the spontaneous gestural input that the deaf children received from their hearing parents cannot account for the gesture systems that the children create.

Our Procedures

The 10 deaf children were observed longitudinally, that is, over a period of time (see Table 1 for details). Each session was videotaped and lasted from one to two hours. Two experimenters were present at all sessions; one experimenter taped the interaction and the second interacted with the child. Usually the child's mother, and occasionally a sibling, was also present during some of the session and interacted with the child. In our Chicago sample, which was collected several years after the Philadelphia sample, we standardized our procedure and asked the mothers to interact with their children for at least one half hour of each session.

Our goal when playing with the children was to elicit communication. To this end, we brought a set of attractive and manipulatable toys, books, and puzzles to each session. The set of toys was carefully chosen to provide the children with choices (e.g., two puzzle pieces, a bare foot and a booted foot, that fit the same hole; the child could request one or the other by describing the picture on the piece); changes that the children might not expect (e.g., a mechanical toy that was missing the key to turn it on); and problems that the children might have to ask for help to solve (e.g., toys that were difficult to operate without assistance). The toy set is described in detail in Goldin-Meadow (1979).

The videotapes of the play sessions were transcribed according to a system of coding categories that took us years to work out. Because this system is the cornerstone of our analyses, we describe it in detail in the next chapter.

How Do We Begin?

Our goal was to see whether the deaf children's gestures were structured and, if so, what the nature of that structure was. We knew from earlier work that deaf children who are orally trained use gestures to communicate (Fant, 1972; Lenneberg, 1964; Mohay, 1982; Moores, 1974; Tervoort, 1961). These gestures even have a name—"home signs."

What no one knew was whether there was any rhyme or reason to the children's gestures. We set out to see whether children's home signs were structured in language-like ways. The first problem we had to solve was how to enter the system. Our strategy was to begin with preliminary decisions on how to categorize the gestures that the deaf children produce—for example, how to isolate gestures from the stream of motor behavior, how to segment those gestures, how to assign them meanings. We then "tested" these categories by applying them to the children's gestures to see if they made sense of the data.

Our preliminary coding categories were based on two sources. The first was the corpus of descriptions of spoken language, particularly child language, and the growing number of descriptions of conventional sign languages. The second source was our intuitions about the motoric forms and the semantic meanings of the gestures produced by the deaf children during our interactive play sessions.

Having established preliminary coding categories (which we describe below), we began to utilize those categories while transcribing videotapes. We tested the utility of our categories in two ways. First, we asked if the categories were reliable. We established reliability by comparing judgments between one experimenter and a second coder who was not at the original taping sessions and calculating how often the two coders' judgments agreed. The agreement scores for the coders were quite high (between 87% and 100%, depending on the coding category), confirming category reliability.

The second test of our category definitions was to ask if these particular categories work—that is, do they result in *coherent* descriptions of the deaf child's gesture system? The argument here is that if a description based on these particular coding categories is coherent, this fact is evidence for the usefulness of the categories themselves. Consider the following example. Suppose we tentatively apply the semantic categories "patient" (object acted on) and "act" to the deaf child's gestures. If we then discover a pattern based on those categories (e.g., a gesture-ordering rule following, say, a "patient-act" pattern), we have evidence that the particular categories "patient" and "act" are useful in descriptions of the deaf child's system. The existence of the pattern confirms the utility of the categories since the former is formulated in terms of the latter.

There is, of course, the very real possibility that these patterns and categories are products of our minds rather than the child's. There are several possible responses to this important concern. First, our study is no more vulnerable to this possibility than are studies investigating young hearing children who are learning spoken languages. Adult experimenters may be incapable of finding anything but language-like structures in a child's communication (for a discussion of this point, see Goldin-Meadow & Mylander, 1984, 18–26). Although this problem can never be completely avoided, the following assumption allows us to proceed: If a category turns out to "make sense of," or organize, the child's communications (e.g., by forming the basic unit of a predictable pattern), we are then justified in isolating that category as a unit of the system and in attributing that category to the child. Thus, the consistency of the results presented in Chapters 8 through 13 lends credence to our coding categories.

Two further methodological points are worth noting: (1) The coding categories described below were devised on the basis of the first wave of data from the Philadelphia children. However, these same categories, when applied to the second wave of Philadelphia data and the Chicago data (and even to our Taiwanese data, see Chapter 15), continue to yield coherent and systematic structures. (2) Our coding techniques do not *inevitably* unearth structure in spontaneous gestures. Later, in Chapter 14, we will see that the spontaneous gestures produced by the deaf children's hearing mothers do *not* form a linguistic system comparable to their children's, even though the mother's gestures were analyzed with the same coding categories.

☐ Identifying a Gesture

Our first task is to isolate communicative gestures from the stream of ongoing motor behavior. The problem here is to discriminate acts that communicate indirectly (e.g., pushing a plate away, which indicates that the eater has had enough) from those acts whose sole purpose is to communicate symbolically (e.g., a "stoplike" movement of the hands produced in order to suggest to the host that another helping is not necessary). We do not consider every nudge or facial expression produced by the deaf children to be a communicative gesture (no matter how much information is conveyed). Consequently, we are forced to develop a procedure that isolates only those acts used for deliberate communication.

Lacking a generally accepted behavioral index of deliberate or intentional communication (see MacKay, 1972, for discussion), we decided that a communicative gesture must meet both of the following criteria. First, the motion must be directed to another individual. This criterion is satisfied if the child attempts to establish eye contact with the communication partner (the criterion was strictly enforced unless there had been recent previous communication with eye contact such that the child could assume the continued attention of the partner).

Second, the gesture must not be a direct motor act on the partner or on some relevant object. As an example, if the child attempts to twist open a jar, the child is not considered to have made a gesture for "open," even if in some sense the child, by this act, is communicating to the experimenter that help is needed in opening the jar. But if the child makes a twisting motion in the air, with eyes first on the experimenter to establish contact, we consider the motion to be a communicative gesture. Once the gestures were isolated, we recorded gestures in terms of three dimensions commonly used to describe signs in ASL and other sign languages (Stokoe, 1960): shape of the hand, movement of the hand or body, and location of the hand with respect to places on the body or in space.

☐ Segmenting Strings of Gestures

We next decided on the units appropriate for describing combinations of gestures. Again, we borrowed a criterion often used in studies of ASL: Relaxation of the hand after a gesture or series of gestures was taken to signal the end of a string, that is, to demarcate a sentence boundary. For example, if a child pointed to a toy and then, without relaxing the hand, pointed to a table, the two pointing gestures were considered "within a string." The same two pointing gestures interrupted by a relaxation of the hand would be classified as two isolated gestures.

This criterion was validated by our subsequent analyses. We determined the boundaries of gesture strings on the basis of relaxation of the hand, and then examined the resulting strings to see if they had sentence-like qualities. We found that the deaf children's gesture strings, when isolated according to this criterion, resembled the early sentences of children learning conventional languages in three respects:

- The strings were used to express the same types of semantic relations as are typically expressed in early child language (Chapters 10 and 11).
- The strings were characterized by the same types of structural devices as are typically found in early child language (Chapters 10 and 11).
- The developmental onset of the strings used to express single propositions and multi-propositions fit well with the onset of simple and complex sentences in early child language (Chapter 12).

We therefore felt justified in continuing to use relaxation of the hand to determine boundaries and in calling the deaf children's gesture strings "sentences."

☐ Assigning Meaning to Gestures

The children produced three types of gestures. *Deictic* gestures typically were pointing gestures that maintained a constant kinesic form in all contexts. These deictics were used predominantly to single out objects, people, places, and the like in the surroundings. In contrast, *characterizing* or *iconic* gestures were stylized pantomimes whose forms varied with the intended meaning of each gesture (e.g., a fist pounded in the air as someone was hammering; two hands flapping in the presence of a pet bird). Finally, *marker* or *modulator* gestures were head or hand gestures (e.g., nods and headshakes, two-handed "flips" in which the palm rotates from down to up) that are conventionalized in American culture and that the children used to affirm, negate, and convey doubt.

We assigned lexical meanings to both deictic and iconic gestures. The problems we faced were comparable to those that arise in assigning lexical meanings to a hearing child's words. Consider an English-speaking child who utters "duck walk" as a toy Donald Duck waddles by. Adult listeners assume that since the child used two distinct phonological forms ("duck" and "walk"), the child intended to describe two distinct aspects of the event (the feathered object and the walking action). Moreover, we assume that the child's noun "duck" refers to the object, and that the verb "walk" refers to the action of the object; that is, that the child's lexical meanings for the words "duck" and "walk" coincide with adult meanings for these words. In general, we tend to assume that nouns refer to objects, people, places, and the like, and that verbs refer to actions, processes, and so forth. This decision, although difficult to justify (for discussion, see Braine, 1976; Dromi, 1987), is bolstered by data from the child's language system taken as a whole. To the extent that the child has mastered other aspects of the adult system that are based on the noun-verb distinction (e.g., verb agreement), the child can plausibly be said to have mastered the distinction in the instance of lexical meanings.

For the deaf children, we must also make relatively arbitrary assumptions at this stage of assigning lexical meanings, but we have no adult language model to guide us. As a result, we have chosen to use gesture *form* as a basis for assigning lexical meanings to the deaf children's gestures. We assume that deictic gestures (e.g., point at the duck) refer to objects, people, and places (duck). In addition, as a first cut, we assume that iconic gestures (e.g., walking motions produced by the hands; a round circle held in the air) refer to actions and attributes (walk; round). We make this assumption because, even if the child produces a walking gesture with the intent to identify an *object* (the duck), the child has done so by highlighting an *action* that the duck typically does. A hearing child who uses the word "duck" might have in mind the animal's walking actions, but we'd never know from the child's label. In contrast, when a deaf child uses a walking gesture to refer to the duck, we know from the form of the child's gestures precisely which attribute of the duck the child has in mind. Thus, in most of our analyses we assume that action gestures refer to actions, and that attribute gestures refer to attributes. However, there are times when action and attribute gestures appear to be playing a noun role, rather than a verb or adjective role. We look at these cases in Chapter 12.

We also use the form of the gesture and its context to classify action gestures as either transitive or intransitive. If the intended referent of a gesture involves action on an object (manipulating it, touching it, holding it, changing it, or moving it), we consider the gesture to be transitive—action on an object. If, however, the intended referent of the gesture involved an action in which a person or object moved on its own (either moving in place or moving to a new location), we consider the gesture to be intransitive—action which has no effect on an object. Often the form of the gesture is the deciding factor. For example, consider a situation in which a child pushes a toy truck and then watches the truck go forward on its own. A child learning English might describe this situation with the ambiguous word "move," meaning either "I move the truck" (transitive) or "the truck moves" (intransitive). The way the deaf child chooses to represent this event in gesture determines whether we call that gesture a transitive act or an intransitive act. If the child moves a hand in a short arc representing the pushing action done on the truck, the gesture is classified as the transitive act "push." If, however, the child moves a hand forward in a linear path representing the action of the truck, the gesture is classified as the intransitive act "go."

The task of gesture interpretation is, in general, made easier by the fact that we include as part of the context any responses the adults on the videotape made to the child's gestures and the child's reactions to those responses. On occasion, the adult responded in several different ways until a response was finally accepted by the child. This process of negotiation between the deaf children and the adults in their world is no different from the negotiations that take place between young hearing children and their communication partners, particularly when the subject of the conversation is a non-present object or event (cf. Sachs, 1983). Indeed, researchers routinely include the give-and-take between children and their interlocutors as part of the context when describing talk in young hearing children.

Gesture interpretation is also facilitated by the fact that we are familiar with the toys and the activities that typically occur during the taping sessions, and by the fact that the parents frequently share their intimate knowledge of the child's world with us during the taping sessions. Not only do we bring the same set of toys to each taping session, but this set is accessible to the coders when they transcribe the tapes, a procedure which allows the coders to verify, for example, that a particular toy does indeed have wheels or that the cowboy in a particular picture is in fact holding a gun. In addition, the parents are familiar with the child's own toys and activities outside the taping session and, if we are puzzled by a child's gestures, we ask the parents during the session what they think the child is looking for, commenting on, and so on. The parents' comments, as well as our own, are therefore on tape and are accessible even to coders who were not at the original taping session. Thus context, bolstered by the parents' and our own knowledge of the child's world, constrain the possible interpretations of the child's gestures and help to disambiguate the meanings of those gestures. Of course, at times the children move too far afield for their gestures to be interpretable even in context. These gestures, often no more than 5%, are considered "ambiguous."

How much or how little structure one discovers in children's *speech* is inevitably a function of the coding system one uses. So too for us. We feel confident of the coding system that we developed on the basis of the gestures produced by the deaf children in our Philadelphia sample because:

- Our coding decisions yield coherent patterns with prospective validity.
- These coherent patterns resemble the patterns of early child language, both spoken and signed.
- The same codes can be applied to the gestures produced by deaf children of hearing parents in Chicago and Taipei and yield similar coherent patterns.
- The codes yield a very different set of patterns when applied to the gestures that the deaf children's hearing parents produce while talking. In other words, the coding categories don't produce structure when applied to just any old set of gestures, only those that assume the full burden of communication (more on this in Chapter 17).

The remaining chapters in Part 2 of the book describe the patterns in the deaf children's gestures, and the non-patterns in the hearing parents' gestures, that give us this confidence.

Words

What do hearing children do when they have something to say and no words to say it with? When they want to say "no," they shake their heads. When they want mom to come closer, they beckon with their hands. When they want a cookie rather than milk, they point at the cookie. Some might even jab a fist toward their mouths while pretending to chew (see Acredolo & Goodwyn, 1988).

The deaf children in our study gesture like this too. But the gestures they produce are different from hearing children's—theirs are part of a system. The deaf children use their pointing gestures like hearing children use nouns and pronouns. They use their headshakes like hearing children use negative markers like "not" and "can't." And, unlike hearing children who produce only a few iconic gestures, the deaf children produce many, alone and in combination with other gestures. I begin by describing the deaf children's "lexicon"—the gestures that form the building blocks of the system.

☐ Pointing Gestures

Pointing gestures are not words. The pointing gesture directs a communication partner's gaze toward a particular person, place, or thing. The gesture explicitly specifies the location of its referent in a way that a word (even a pronoun like "this" or "that") never can. The pointing gesture does not, however, specify *what* the object is—it merely indicates *where* the object is. In contrast, words identify the objects to which they refer (e.g., "lion" classifies its referent into a particular set) but, unless accompanied by pointing gestures, they do not indicate where those objects are. Despite this fundamental difference, pointing gestures function for the deaf children like nouns and pronouns do for hearing children.

71

"Functioning like a word does for hearing children" is, in fact, a very important criterion that we use to decide when a category ought to be included in our coding system: When including a category produces a result that comports with what is known about language-learning in general, we include that category in our system. Note that we can then use the fact that the deaf children's gesture system resembles the linguistic systems developed by children under typical learning circumstances to make inferences about how all children learn language. We make use of this two-step process below—we use the fact that the deaf children's pointing gestures resemble hearing children's pronouns and nouns to rule out certain types of explanations for the patterns hearing children exhibit.

The deaf children's points work like hearing children's pronouns and nouns in three ways —in terms of the particular objects they refer to; in terms of the role they play in the child's linguistic system; and in terms of their ability to refer to objects that are not visible in the room. I elaborate on these three uses in the next paragraphs.

The Objects Points Refer To

When young hearing children begin to use nouns, they use them to refer to a relatively limited set of objects (Nelson, 1973). Why are their lexicons so limited? They could be limited simply because hearing children have to learn the names of each of the objects to which they refer, and learning names takes time and exposure to the label. However, the deaf children have no such constraint. If they wished to, they could use pointing gestures to refer to anything within view. But they don't. The deaf children use their pointing gestures to refer to precisely the same range of objects that young hearing children refer to with their words—and in precisely the same distribution (Feldman, Goldin-Meadow, & Gleitman, 1978:380). Like hearing children, the deaf children in our study refer most often to inanimate objects, followed by people and animals. Children in both groups also refer to body parts, food, clothing, vehicles, furniture, and places, but less frequently. Perhaps not surprisingly, it is what children want to communicate about that dictates the words they produce—having an "all-purpose" word like the pointing gesture does not encourage them to enlarge their noun vocabularies.

The Roles Points Assume in Gesture Sentences

The deaf children combine their pointing gestures with other points and with iconic gestures just as hearing children combine their nouns with other words. Although it may not be intuitively obvious that pointing gestures ought to be counted as the object-referring terms of a sentence, the proof of the pudding is in the eating. If pointing gestures *are* treated like nouns and pronouns, the deaf children's gesture combinations turn out to be structured in just the same ways as the early sentences hearing children produce (see Chapters 10 and 11). However, if pointing gestures are *excluded* from the system, the deaf children look as though they never refer to the most common objects in their environments and rarely use simple sentences, only complex ones—an unusual result, to say the least. On these grounds, we decided to include pointing gestures as part of the deaf children's linguistic system. As it turns out, this analytic step (although perhaps not intuitive) is not all that controversial—when researchers describe the communications of deaf children who are learning ASL from their deaf parents, they too include points as object-referring terms in the children's linguistic system (Hoffmeister, 1978; Kantor, 1982).

The Capacity Points Have to Refer to the Non-Present

At first glance, we might think that pointing gestures must limit the child to referring only to objects in the here-and-now. And, for the most part, that is precisely how the deaf children use their points—to refer to real-world objects in the immediate environment. For example, Karen points at a jar of bubbles, followed by a "blow" iconic gesture, to request her mother to blow bubbles. Importantly, however, the deaf children are *not* limited to these uses. They are able to take the here-and-now point and use it to refer to non-present objects. They do so in several ways.

First, the children can point at a real-world object that looks very much like the absent object to which they intend to refer. For example, Karen points at an *empty* jar of bubbles, followed by a "blow" gesture. From context, we know that Karen wants the bubbles blown. But then why does she point at an empty jar? Karen is using the empty jar as a stand-in for the full jar of bubbles that is not in view. As another example, David points at the pop-up toy at his side and does a "flick" gesture. It's clear from the context that this is a request and that the child wants a toy to be flicked so that it will pop up, but which toy? David can't be referring to the toy at his side simply because it is already in the popped-up position. He must be pointing at the toy near him as a stand-in for the pop-up toy that is behind the experimenter's back.

Another technique that the children use is to point at the habitual location of the person or object to which they intend to refer. For example, David points at the dining room chair at the head of the table and then produces a "sleep" gesture (Figure 1; see the "Dad-Sleep" videoclip at www.psypress.com/goldinmeadow). No one is sleeping in the chair, nor does anyone appear to be planning to nap in that location. What could the child mean? It turns out that the head dining-room chair is where the child's father typically sits, and his father is, at that moment, asleep in his bedroom down the hall. The child is telling us that his father (denoted by the chair) is sleeping.

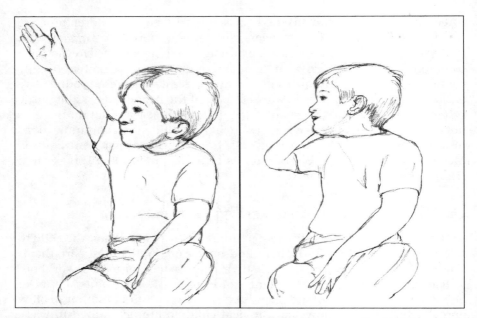

FIGURE 1. Pointing at the Present to Refer to the Non-Present. David points at the chair at the head of the dining room table in his home and then produces a "sleep" gesture to tell us that his father (who typically sits in that chair) is asleep in another room. He is pointing at one object to mean another and, in this way, manages to use a gesture that is grounded in the present to refer to someone who is not in the room at all.

Finally, the children can point at an arbitrary space that has been established as standing for the object to which they intend to refer. For example, David is telling us about a sledding incident. He "hangs" an imaginary sled over a spot in front of him above eye level, then points at that spot and finally "hammers" in the spot. The point at essentially nothing only makes sense because the spot has been established as the place where the hanging-nail for the sled sits.

We examined pointing gestures in detail in one of the deaf children in our study (David; see Butcher, Mylander, & Goldin-Meadow, 1991), and found that, when he was first observed at age 2;10, David was already using points to indicate objects in the room. In later sessions, he began to use points to indicate objects that were not present. He did so by indicating the habitual location of the non-present object at age 3;3, and by indicating an object that was perceptually similar to the non-present object at age 3;5. David did not use points to indicate arbitrary locations set up as place-holders for non-present objects until age 3;11. Hoffmeister (1978) finds a similar developmental trajectory from points at real-world objects, to "semi-real-world" objects, to arbitrary loci in deaf children learning ASL from their deaf parents.

Interestingly, hearing children use pointing gestures at comparable ages, but they do not use those points to refer to absent objects (Butcher et al., 1991). They do, of course, use nouns and pronouns to refer to absent objects, and do so about as often as David uses his pointing gestures for this purpose. The urge to communicate about non-present objects is strong even in very young children. If ready-made words are not available to talk about the non–here-and-now, children will expand the role of the pointing gesture so that it can do the job.

☐ Iconic Gestures

Iconic gestures also differ from words. The form of an iconic gesture captures an aspect of its referent. The form of a word does not. There is nothing about the word "walk" that brings to mind the act of putting one foot in front of another to move forward. Making the fingers of an upside-down-V hand wiggle as the hand moves forward—an iconic gesture—can, however, evoke the act of walking, even in individuals who have never seen such a gesture before. Thus, unlike pointing gestures—but like words—iconic gestures specify the identity of their referents. However, unlike words, iconic gestures specify the identity of their referents through iconicity. Interestingly, as we noted in Chapter 4, although iconicity is present in many of the signs of ASL, deaf children learning ASL do not seem to notice. Most of their early signs are either not iconic (Bonvillian et al., 1983) or, if iconic from an adult's point of view, not recognized as iconic by the child (Schlesinger, 1978).

The deaf children in our study are forced by their social situation to create gestures that are transparent. If they didn't, no one would be able to take any meaning from their gestures. Remember that our hearing parents are interested in having their children learn to talk, not learn to gesture—although they respond to their children's gestures, they are typically not aware of the role those gestures play in the give-and-take they have with their children.

Despite the strong pressure to create transparent gestures, the deaf children do at times use gestures that do not map as accurately onto the situations they represent as they could have. For example, David holds two fists together side-by-side and then breaks the fists apart to indicate that an object had been broken (Figure 2A; see the "Break" videoclip at www.psypress.com/goldinmeadow). David uses the "break-apart" gesture even though the toy that is now broken was not severed in half but is merely missing a small part. Thus, the "break" gesture is not always finely tuned to the actual circumstances surrounding the broken toy.

As another example, all of the deaf children use the "give" gesture—a flat hand, palm-up, extended to request the transfer of an object (Figure 2B; see the "Give" videoclip at www.psypress.com/goldinmeadow). When hearing

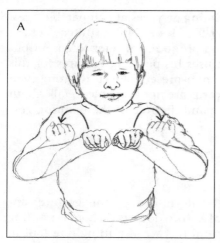
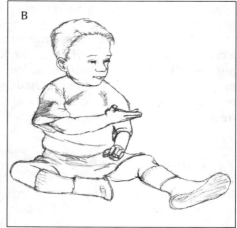

FIGURE 2. Examples of Conventional Emblems Whose Meanings Are Not as Transparent as They Seem. In panel A, David is shown producing a "break" gesture. Although this gesture looks like it should be used only to describe snapping long thin objects into two pieces with the hands, all of the children used the gesture to refer to objects of a variety of sizes and shapes, many of which had not been broken by the hands. In panel B, Marvin is shown producing a "give" gesture. This gesture looks like it should mean "put something small in my hand," but all of the children used it to request the transfer of an object, big or small, to a place that was not necessarily the child's hand. Thus, many of the gestures that the deaf children used were not as transparent in meaning as a quick glance would suggest.

children use this gesture (and most do), they use it to mean "put something in my hand." But the deaf children use this gesture to request the transfer of objects, not only to themselves, but also to other people and locations. Moreover, the gesture is used for objects that will fit in the hand but also for those that won't. The gesture thus has an extended meaning for the deaf children, one that begins to eat away at the transparency between gesture form and meaning.

The examples of semi-transparent iconic gestures that I have given thus far may well have been borrowed from the gestures that hearing speakers produce. But the iconic gestures that the children create on their own are also not always as transparent as they could be. For example, David pats his head with a flat palm to represent a crown, despite the fact that crowns do not sit flat on the head. In addition, the deaf children often break their self-created iconic gestures into component parts in ways that are reminiscent of deaf children breaking the signs of ASL into parts (Supalla, 1982; see also Chapter 4)—and breaking a gesture into parts results in a series of gestures that look *less* like the event they represent than the gesture as a whole would have. For example, to describe snow falling, David makes a flutter gesture, wiggling his fingers with his hand held in place over his head. He then moves his palm straight down, his fingers no longer wiggling, to indicate the direction in which the snow falls (Figure 3; see the "Flutter-Fall" videoclip at www.psypress.com/goldinmeadow). A more accurate depiction of snow falling would have combined the wiggling motion and directional path into a single gesture since the fluttering and falling, in fact, take place at the same time. By decomposing their lexical items, a tendency found in all children whether or not they are exposed to a conventional language, the deaf children are actually making their gestures *less* veridical (but more language-like).

The majority of the deaf children's gestures are, however, quite transparent and closely linked to their referents. For example, Donald holds a fist near his mouth and makes chewing movements to comment on eating a birthday cake. Tracy moves her hand forward in the air to describe the path a pig takes in a picture book. David forms a round shape with his hand to describe a Christmas tree ornament. We explore just how closely linked these forms are to the meanings they represent in Chapter 9.

Do the children's iconic gestures form a stable lexicon? If the children have a stable store of lexical items, we might expect to find relatively little

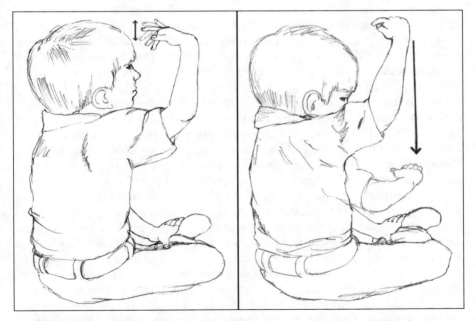

FIGURE 3. Decomposing an Action Gesture Into Parts. David is gesturing about snow falling. In the first gesture, he wiggles his fingers in place above his head, illustrating how snowflakes flutter. In the second gesture, he holds his fingers still and moves his hand straight down, thus indicating the path that snowflakes follow when they fall. David has broken up the action of snow falling into its component parts—*fluttering* and *falling*—and, in so doing, has made his gestural representation less veridical than it would have been had he combined the two motions into a single form.

variability in the set of forms they use to convey a particular meaning. However, it's very possible that the deaf children might not have a stable lexicon to call upon, but instead create each gesture anew every time they use it. If so, we might expect some consistency in the forms the gestures take (the gestures are iconic and iconicity constrains the set of forms that can be used to convey a meaning), but there should also be a great deal of variability around the iconic prototype—variability that crops up simply because each situation is a little different, and the gesture created specifically for that situation might be expected to reflect that difference.

We have thus far explored this question in only one child (David). We examined the iconic gestures that David created over a two-year period, and found remarkable stability in his lexicon (Goldin-Meadow, Butcher, Mylander, & Dodge, 1994). David produced 190 different types of gestures during this period, 81 of which were used only once and thus couldn't vary in form. The remaining 109 accounted for 706 gesture tokens. Only 10% of these 706 gestures varied from prototype. For example, David produced his "break" gesture by moving two fists apart in a short arc. Only once in 15 times did David vary from this prototype, moving his two fists apart in a *long* arc rather than a short one. In fact, in two-thirds of the 109 gesture types that he produced more than once, David *always* produced the same form, never varying from prototype even once. Thus, David had a stable store of iconic gestures. Moreover, his gestures adhered to standards of form, albeit standards that were idiosyncratic to him rather than shared by a community of language users.

Finally, it is important to point out that the deaf children produce a wide variety of iconic gestures. They all produce gestures akin to bleached verbs in conventional languages, forms that convey movement but without specifying the manner or path of that movement (for example give, transfer, move). But they also produce gestures that convey the path of motion (put in, put on, put together, go around, go away, go up) and gestures that convey the manner of motion (scamper, wiggle, dance, swim, crawl, fly, climb, drive, hop, pull, twist, paddle, scoop, strum, bounce, wash, jump, spray, nibble, push, float, dive, cradle). The children even produce gestures that capture both path and manner (hop + forward, in which the hand moves up and down while at the same time moving forward; see Zheng & Goldin-Meadow, 2002, and Goldin-Meadow, 1979, for listings of action gestures created by the deaf children). Given how transparently action can be portrayed in the manual modality, it is not surprising that the deaf children develop and use so many action gestures. But the children also produce gestures that capture the properties of objects, concrete properties like size (little, long) or shape (round-and-long, tree-shaped) and also more abstract properties (ugly, afraid). In general, the lexicons that the deaf children create are very similar to the lexicons that children develop at the early stages of learning a conventional language.

☐ Modulating Gestures

The deaf children produce a third type of lexical item that they use to modulate the meanings of their gesture sentences. All of these gestures are "borrowed" from gestures that hearing individuals use when they speak. The most common three are nods, side-to-side headshakes, and one- or two-handed flips (the hand begins with the palm facing down and then rotates so that the palm is facing up; the gesture is often, but always, accompanied by a shrug). All of the children we studied use these gestures, alone and in combination with other gestures. As an example, here's how David communicated "Lisa is not going to eat lunch but I am" (pointing gestures are displayed in lowercase, iconic characterizing gestures in uppercase, modulating gestures in brackets):

Lisa + [headshake] + CHEW—David + [nod]—EAT—David

David first points at Lisa, one of our assistants, while shaking his head back and forth, and produces a "chew" gesture. He thus makes it clear that Lisa will not be eating. Without pausing or dropping his hands, he points at himself and produces an "eat" gesture while nodding, thus affirming his own role as eater (see the "Headshakes & Nods" videoclip at www.psypress.com/goldinmeadow). Both the headshake and the nod are integrated into the sentence, the headshake negating the first proposition (Lisa is not eating lunch) and the nod affirming the second (I am eating lunch).

The third gesture, "flip," is used to convey doubt, often to comment on an unexpected event. For example, a block tower falls and Abe "flips" as though to say "What happened?" Flips are also used to query the whereabouts of an object, which may or may not be present in the room. For example, Karen pats the top of her head and produces a "flip" while looking for a missing crown. The children's hearing parents, like all speakers of English, also use the "flip" gesture, but they use it only to express doubt and uncertainty and not to comment on nonvisible objects (Morford & Goldin-Meadow, 1997). For example, a mother produces the "flip" gesture while asking her child how many books are in a pile. Moreover, the hearing parents typically produce the "flip" gesture in isolation, that is, not in combination with other gestures, whereas their deaf children often combine the "flip" with other gestures.

The children also appropriate a fourth gesture from hearing speakers. This gesture, which we gloss as "wait," is formed by holding up the index finger (Figure 4A; see the "Wait" videoclip at www.psypress.com/goldinmeadow). It is frequently used in the United States to request a brief delay or time-out. In addition to using the gesture for this conventional meaning, the deaf children also use it to signal the immediate future (Morford & Goldin-Meadow, 1997). For example, Marvin gestures "wait" and then points at the

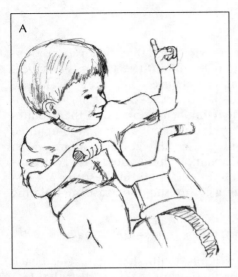
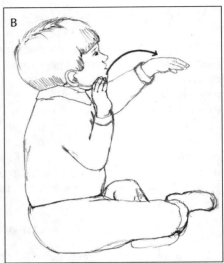

FIGURE 4. The Gestures, Borrowed and Invented, That the Deaf Children Use as Modulators. In panel A, Marvin is shown using a gesture that he has appropriated from hearing speakers around him—the "wait" gesture typically used in the United States to request a brief delay or time-out. Marvin is using the gesture to inform his mother that he is about to go to the bag to get a new toy and, in so doing, extends the gesture's meaning to include signaling the immediate future. In panel B, David is shown using a gesture that he created to refer to non-present events—the "away" gesture which David uses to indicate that what he is gesturing about is displaced in time and space (akin to the phrase "once upon a time" used to introduce stories).

toy bag to indicate that he is going to retrieve a new toy from the bag. It is clear from the context that Marvin is using the gesture, not to get his mother's attention, but to signal his next actions. Again, the children's hearing parents use this gesture but don't use it in the same way as their children. The parents use the gesture only for its conventional meaning—to get the child to stop and pay attention—and not to signal immediate future. For example, a parent produces the "wait" gesture in combination with a point to a dog. She wants the child to look at the dog and is using her gesture, not to talk about future action, but to get her child to attend to her.

Finally, two children also generated novel modulating gestures which they use to flag a communication as being about a non-present event. For example, Marvin is looking at flashcards with his mother. When he sees a picture of a poodle, he shows it to his mother with a look of excitement and recognition. His mother responds, "That's right. We used to have a gray poodle, hunh?" Marvin then points over his shoulder behind himself, points to the picture, and finally points to the floor in front of himself (to indicate where the poodle once was). Marvin uses the point over his shoulder to refer to the remote past. A second child, David, produces his novel gesture to refer to both remote future and remote past events—for example, needing to repair a toy (future) and having visited Santa (past). The gesture is made by holding the hand vertically near the chest, palm out, and making an arcing motion away from the body (Figure 4B; see the "Away" and "Away Embedded" videoclips at www.psypress.com/goldinmeadow). David's parents gloss this gesture as "away," as though it refers to spatially remote occurrences. In fact, the events David describes with this gesture are all both spatially and temporally distanced—they all take the form of simple narratives displaced in time and space (Phillips, Goldin-Meadow, & Miller, 2001).

Thus, aside from the two novel gestures, modulating gestures are conventional in form. They also assume conventional meanings. However, some of the modulating gestures take on additional meanings—meanings that turn the gestures into markers for the non-present. Interestingly, these derived meanings appear to be constrained by the semantic starting points given them by the culture-at-large—all of the children end up with the *same* derived meanings for their modulating gestures despite the fact that none of the hearing parents use their own gestures for those meanings.

☐ Summary: Gestures That Function as Words in a Linguistic System

The types of gestures that the deaf children use are no different from the types of gestures used by hearing children. However, the deaf children's gestures form a *linguistic system* in a way that hearing children's gestures do not (the gestures that hearing children produce form a system with the words they accompany, see Goldin-Meadow, 1999b; 2003c). The deaf children produce almost as many iconic gestures as pointing gestures and fewer modulating gestures. Hearing children produce many pointing and modulating gestures and far fewer iconic gestures. The deaf children use pointing gestures to refer to present and non-present objects, places, and people, despite the fact that pointing gestures seem to do nothing more than direct attention to things in the immediate surround. They also use iconic gestures that specify the identity of their referents and that form a stable lexicon, despite the fact that each gesture could easily be reinvented with each use. Finally, the deaf children borrow modulating gestures from the gestures that hearing speakers produce, but they alter those gestures to serve as linguistic markers for past and future. In the next chapters, we will continue to see how these gestures are used by the deaf children as the building blocks of a linguistic system.

9 CHAPTER

The Parts of Words

Human languages are distinct from all other animal communication systems in having a set of elements (words) that combine systematically to form potentially novel larger units (sentences). What further distinguishes human language is the fact that this combinatorial feature is found at several different levels. For example, in all human languages, the words that combine to form sentences are themselves composed of parts (morphemes). Although there is great variability in how much within-word structure a given language has, it is nevertheless difficult to find a language that has *no* structure at the word level (be it the result of inflectional processes or stem-formation processes, including derivational morphology, compounding, or incorporation; cf. Anderson, 1985). Indeed, in her review of the Perkins (1980) sample of 50 languages chosen to represent the languages of the world, Bybee (1985) found that all languages have at least some morphologically complex words. Do the gesture systems invented by the deaf children we studied?

There were hints that the children's iconic gestures might be composed of parts. On one occasion, we were being deliberately obtuse with David who had produced the following (perfectly understandable) gesture to ask us to put a penny down flat (we had put the penny on its edge so that it stood vertically in the slot)—David formed his index finger and thumb into a circle and moved the circle downward in a short arc as though placing it flat. Disgusted with our apparent inability (or unwillingness) to understand his gesture, David then broke his gesture into two parts—he produced the circle shape, holding it in the air; he then changed his handshape to a flat palm and moved his palm downward in a short arc (see the "Round-Put Down" videoclip at www.psypress.com/goldinmeadow). The gesture had decomposed into its handshape (circle) and motion (short arc) parts right before our eyes. It is very likely that David altered his original gesture because it didn't achieve the results he wanted. However, the fact that he used a "breaking-gestures-into-parts" strategy when frustrated suggests that, at the least, his gestures do have parts.

Although suggestive, anecdotes of this sort do not convincingly make the case for a *system* of handshape and motion components underlying the deaf children's gestures. To argue for such a system, we need to review all of the iconic gestures that a child produces and show that:

- the child uses a limited set of discrete handshape and motion forms, that is, the forms are *categorical* rather than continuous;
- the child consistently associates each handshape or motion form with a particular meaning (or set of meanings) throughout the corpus, that is, each form is *meaningful*;
- the child produces most of the handshapes with more than one motion, and most of the motions with more than one handshape, that is, each handshape and motion is an independent and meaningful morpheme that could combine with other morphemes in the system to create larger meaningful units—the system is *combinatorial*.

There are many small, yet important, steps that we need to take in order to uncover a morphological system in a deaf child's gestures. We have taken these steps and done the necessary analyses on four of the deaf children. Rather than take you through every step of our discovery procedures, I present only the results of our analyses in the next several sections—that is, the morphological systems that our procedures unearthed. However, each step of our discovery procedure is described in exquisite detail in Goldin-Meadow, Mylander, and Butcher (1995).

☐ A Limited Number of Forms

The deaf children produce two different types of iconic gestures. In the first type, the parts of the gesture don't conform to the object and/or action it represents; "break" and "give" which do not change their form as a function of the object described are good examples (see Chapter 8). This first type of gesture is akin to "frozen" signs in ASL, signs whose stems contain only one morpheme and thus are unanalyzable (cf. Kegl, 1985), and tend to be gestures that the deaf children borrow from hearing speakers (the gestural emblems that vary from culture to culture, Ekman & Friesen, 1969).

In the second type of gesture the deaf children produce, the parts of the gesture do vary with particular circumstances of the situation. For example, the child produces a different "put down" gesture when describing putting down a cup versus a large box. These gestures comprise approximately three-quarters of each child's iconic gestures and our analyses focus on them. We ask just how closely the form of a gesture matches the situation it represents.

Notice that the manual modality offers children the opportunity to represent the actions that they do on objects with a great deal of accuracy. To gesture beating a drum, all the child need do is replay the motions that he or she produces when actually beating the drum. If the deaf children were to exploit this analog way of mapping actions, they would end up producing in their gestures all of the handshapes and motions that they typically use when manipulating objects. They would consequently have a very large set of handshape and motion forms in their gestural repertoires. However, languages—even sign languages—do not have unlimited forms at their disposal. Rather, they have a constrained set of forms that provides the basis for discrete categories.

It turns out that the deaf children in our studies also have a limited set of handshape and a limited set of motion forms in their gestures—which means that the deaf children do *not* take advantage of the potential for analog representation that the manual modality offers. On the positive side, however, this circumscribed set of forms means that the children have at their disposal the elements necessary to construct a categorical system—which is precisely what they do, as we see in the next section.

☐ Each Form Has a Consistent Meaning

The children use their handshapes in two distinct ways: (1) to represent a HAND as it manipulates an object, and (2) to represent the OBJECT itself. The HAND handshapes are akin to handle classifiers in ASL, and the OBJECT handshapes are akin to size-and-shape classifiers (cf. McDonald, 1982; Schick, 1987). As an example of a HAND handshape, to describe a knife, David produces a *Fist* handshape (with a back-and-forth movement), mirroring a person's hand manipulating a knife. In contrast, to again describe the knife in a separate sentence, David produces a *Palm* handshape held perpendicular to the table (with the same back-and-forth movement), mirroring the flat shape of the knife itself (Figures 5A and B; see the "To&Fro + Fist" and the "To&Fro + Palm" videoclips at www.psypress.com/goldinmeadow).

The children use each of their handshape forms, as well as their motion forms, to convey a particular meaning (or set of meanings) throughout the corpus. We discovered the pairings between form and meaning by constructing grids with forms down the left-hand column and meanings across the top. We constructed three grids for each child, one for HAND handshapes, one for OBJECT handshapes, and one for motions. I use David's HAND handshapes as an illustration. Table 2 presents David's 8 HAND forms categorized according to the width of the object described by that form. Thus, the table shows the number of times a particular form—for example, *OTouch*—is used to refer to objects that are 0–1 inches in diameter, 1–2 inches in diameter, and so on. There is, in fact, a consistent relation between forms

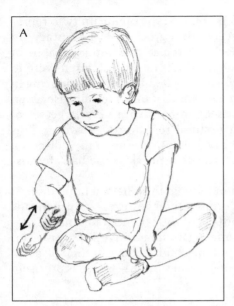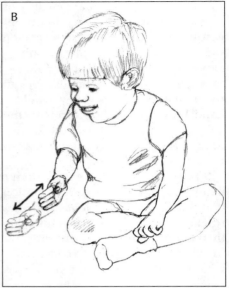

FIGURE 5. The Same Motion Can Occur with Different Handshapes. In panel A, David has his hand in a fist shape and is moving the fist back and forth as though cutting with a knife. In panel B, he holds his hand in a straight palm and again moves it back and forth, this time representing the knife as it moves when it cuts. Thus, David uses two different handshapes (*Fist, Palm*) with the same *To-and-Fro* motion.

and meanings—the numbers that are boxed in the table represent the form-meaning pairings that meet our criterion for consistent use (see Goldin-Meadow, Mylander, & Butcher, 1995, for a description of this criterion and how it was applied to each category). For example, David uses his *O* handshapes to refer to objects that are 0–2 inches wide. In contrast, he uses his *CMedium* handshape to refer to objects that are 2–3 inches wide and his *CLarge* handshape to refer to objects that are 2–5 inches wide. We constructed comparable grids for David's OBJECT handshapes and for his motions, and used those grids to discover the consistent form-meaning pairings for these categories as well (see Goldin-Meadow et al., 1995, for a more complete description).

Table 3 displays the results of these analyses. It lists David's consistent form-meaning pairings for HAND (two left columns) and OBJECT (two middle columns) handshapes and for motions (two right columns). The forms are listed in the left-hand column for each category and the meaning consistently paired with that form is listed to its right. Each form-meaning pair is a morpheme in David's system. Note that David can use the same handshape as either a HAND or an OBJECT morpheme. For example, he uses the *Fist* handshape to represent handling objects less than 2 inches wide and greater

TABLE 2. David's HAND Forms Displayed in Relation to the Object Each Form Represents[a]

| Hand Forms | Object Width (in inches) | | | | | Many Small Surfaces |
	0 – 1	1 – 2	2 – 3	3 – 5	> 5	
Point	3					
Thumb	1					
Fist [b]	43	30	5			
OTouch	66	9	1			
OSmall	3	3				
CMedium		2	4	1		
CLarge			7	4		
Palm	1	4		10	11	3

a. The numbers enclosed in boxes represent the form-meaning pairings that meet our criterion for consistent use; that is, the form-meaning pairings considered to be HAND morphemes.
b. The *Fist* handshape was distinguished from the *OTouch* and *OSmall* in David's gestures by length: David used the *Fist* for objects > 3 inches in length but used the *O* forms for objects of any length.

than 3 inches long (a balloon string, where the handshape mirrors the handgrip around the object, i.e., HAND). But he also uses the *Fist* handshape to represent bulky objects (a hammer head, where the handshape represents the object itself, i.e., OBJECT). Note also that different aspects of form are relevant to HAND and OBJECT morphemes. For example, David uses the "distance between thumb and finger" form parameter (the difference between an *O*, a *CMedium*, and a *CLarge* form) distinctively for HAND handshapes. However, he uses the "shape of the palm" form parameter (the difference between an *OCurved*, an *OAngled*, and a *CCurved* form) distinctively for OBJECT handshapes (see Goldin-Meadow et al., 1995, for a detailed description of the procedures we used to discover these differences). Importantly, the set of morphemes displayed in Table 3 accounts for almost all of the gestures David produced over a two-year period: 91% (N = 232) of his handshapes used as a HAND, 93% (N = 135) of his handshapes used as an OBJECT; and 90% (N = 439) of his motions conform to the system displayed in Table 3.

David's morphemes are not always accurate representations of the way a hand manipulates a particular object in the real world. For example, David uses the same form, the *Fist*, to describe manipulating a balloon string, a newspaper, a flag pole, a string of tree lights, the brim of a hat, and an umbrella handle—objects that would be handled quite differently in the real world. These objects need not be manipulated with the hand in a fist and, even if a fist were used to manipulate them, the tightness of the fist

TABLE 3. David's Handshape and Motion Morphemes[a]

HAND Forms	HAND Meanings	OBJECT Forms	OBJECT Meanings	Motion Forms	Motion Meanings
Point	Handle a surface < 1" wide e.g., gun trigger	Point	Straight skinny object e.g., straw	Linear Path	Change location by moving in a path with or without an endpoint e.g., glide-forward
Fist	Handle an object < 2" wide, > 3" long e.g., balloon string	Fist	Bulky object e.g., hammer head	Long Arc	Change location by moving in a path with an endpoint e.g., scoop-to-mouth
O	Handle an object < 2" wide e.g., Band-Aid	OCurved	Surface of a round object e.g., ball	Medium or Short Arc	Reposition to reorient e.g., fall-together
CMedium	Handle an object 2" to 3" wide e.g., horn	OAngled	Surface of an angled object e.g., Santa's hat	Arc To-and-Fro	Reposition by moving back and forth e.g., flap
CLarge	Handle an object 2" to 5" wide e.g., cup	CCurved	Surface of a curved object e.g., cowboy's legs	Circle	Reposition by moving in a circle e.g., sew-in-circle
Palm	Handle a 3" × >5" surface e.g., drawer Handle many small surfaces e.g., piano keys	Palm Broad	Individuated points or lines e.g., snowflakes, teeth of comb	Revolve	Rotate around an axis e.g., twist
		Palm Straight	Vehicle e.g., airplane	Open & Close	Open-close or expand-contract e.g., squeeze
		Palm Straight or Curved	Straight wide object e.g., butterfly wings	No Motion	Hold or exist in place e.g., wand-hold
		Palm Straight or Angled	Animate object e.g., Santa Claus		

a. The table displays the HAND handshape forms, the OBJECT handshape forms, and the Motion forms that David used over a two-year period. The column next to each form displays the meaning that was consistently associated with this form in David's gestures. These form-meaning pairings constitute David's handshape and motion morphemes.

would vary across the set of objects. Nevertheless, David uses the same *Fist* form, and without any variation in the tightness of the handshape, when gesturing about these objects. Thus, David does not distinguish objects of varying widths within the *Fist* category. However, he does use his handshapes to distinguish handling objects with narrow widths *as a set* from handling objects with larger widths (> 2 inches, e.g., a cup, a horn) which he conveys with his *C* hands. David thus relies on discrete categories, rather than analog representations of "real-world" objects.

We stress again that David is not alone in developing a morphological system. Each of the four deaf children analyzed thus for uses consistent form-meaning pairings—morphemes—for handshapes and motions (Goldin-Meadow et al., 1995). Interestingly, however, there are subtle differences across the children's systems. For example, Table 4 displays how the children use handshape forms that vary in the distance between the thumb and fingers: *OTouch* = fingers touch thumb; *OSmall* = fingers less than 1 inch from thumb; *CMedium* = fingers 1 inch to 3 inches from thumb; *CLarge* = fingers greater than 3 inches from thumb. The children use the forms for meanings that resemble one another at a general level but differ in detail. For example, the *OTouch* form is used by all four children for narrow objects. However, the precise boundary for a narrow object differs across the children: for David, Marvin, and Karen,[1] the boundary for this handshape is 2 inches, for Abe it's 1 inch.

In addition, the relation particular morphemes hold to other morphemes differs across the children—in other words, the systems themselves differ. For example, in Marvin's and Abe's gestures, *OSmall* is a category unto itself and is distinct in meaning from the other forms the child uses. In contrast, in David's gestures, *OSmall* is not distinguished from *OTouch*—both are used for objects less than 2 inches in width and thus form a single category. In Karen's gestures, *OSmall* is also not unique, but it is aligned with *CMedium* (rather than *OTouch*)—both are used for objects 1 to 2 inches in width and thus form a single category for Karen. Similarly for motions, all four children use the *Medium Arc* and the *Short Arc* forms to mean reposition to reorient. However, David also uses both forms to mean reposition to affect an object, whereas Marvin uses only the *Short Arc* form for this meaning, Abe uses only the *Medium Arc* form, and Karen uses a different form entirely (the *Linear Path*).

The similarities across the deaf children's systems are not surprising given that the children's gestures must be relatively transparent to be understood by their hearing parents. The differences across the systems are also not unexpected since we would anticipate some randomness in where children set boundaries for their categories. The fact that there are differences in the

---

[1]In some publications, the pseudonyms for Karen and Kathy were inadvertently switched. Thus, in Goldin-Meadow et al. (1995) and in Morford & Goldin-Meadow (1997), the child observed was actually Karen, not Kathy.

TABLE 4. Examples of Different Handshape Form-Meaning Pairings in Four Children

Forms	David's Meanings	Marvin's Meanings	Abe's Meanings	Karen's Meanings
OTouch	Handle an object < 2" wide	Handle an object < 2" wide	Handle an object < 1" wide	Handle an object < 2" wide
	e.g., Band-Aid	e.g., steering wheel	e.g., tiny knob	e.g., penny
OSmall		Handle an object < 2" wide, < 2" long	Handle an object 1" to 2" wide	Handle an object 1" to 2" wide
		e.g., jar lid	e.g., banana	e.g., jar lid
CMedium	Handle an object 2" to 3" wide	Handle an object 2" to 3" wide	Handle an object 1" to 2" wide, 1" to 5" long	
	e.g., cup	e.g., box	e.g., toy soldier	
CLarge	Handle an object 2" to 5" wide	Handle an object 2" to > 5" wide	Handle an object 2" to 3" wide	Handle an object 2" to 3" wide
	e.g., horn	e.g., bowling ball	e.g., horn	e.g., puzzle envelope

ways the children define a particular morpheme suggests that there are choices to be made (although all of the choices are still transparent with respect to their referents). Moreover, the choices that a given child makes cannot be determined without knowing that child's individual system. In other words, we cannot predict the precise boundaries of a child's morphemes without knowing that child's individual system. It is in this sense that the deaf children's gesture systems can be said to be *arbitrary*.

In addition to suggesting that they are able to introduce arbitrariness into their gesture systems, the differences across the deaf children's systems suggest that the children have different *standards of well-formedness* within their individual systems. The children's gestures are not only adequate representations of objects and movements in the world, but they also conform to an internally consistent system and, in this sense, each system has standards of form.

We became convinced that the children's systems adhere to standards of form after we gave David an experimental test of his morphological system. We tested David when he was age 9;5, several years after our naturalistic observations ended (Singleton, Morford, & Goldin-Meadow, 1993). Not wanting to exclude David's hearing sister from our interactions, we gave her the test along with her brother and asked her to generate gestures without talking. The interesting point is that David found his sister's gestures to be inadequate and spontaneously corrected the handshapes she produced that did not conform to his gestural system. Although it is not necessary for a language-user to correct another's "mispronunciation" in order to suggest that the user adheres to standards of form (such corrections imply a certain level of consciousness which a user need not have), corrections of another's performance do offer firm evidence of a standard. David appears to have a well-developed and articulated sense of what counts as an acceptable form for a given meaning, and he is not shy about informing others of his standards.

☐ Form-Meaning Pairings Combine Freely With Each Other

Up to this point, we have shown that each of the four children's gestures can be described in terms of a set of handshape morphemes (i.e., handshape form-meaning pairings) and a set of motion morphemes (i.e., motion form-meaning pairings). Although isolable as separable units from the experimenter's point of view, it is still possible that handshape and motion form a single, unanalyzed whole from the child's point of view. Since gestures are composed of hands moving in space, it is not possible to find handshapes that are actually separated from their motions. Nevertheless, if we find that a handshape is not uniquely associated with one motion but rather is combined with several different motions in different gestures, we then have evidence that the handshape morpheme may be an independent unit in the child's gesture system. Similarly, if a motion is combined with different handshapes in different gestures, we have evidence for the separability of that motion morpheme.

The children used from 12 to 17 different handshape morphemes. On average, 84% of these handshape morphemes were used with at least two different motion morphemes. Conversely, the children used from 8 to 11 different motion morphemes. On average, 94% of these motion morphemes were used with at least two different handshape morphemes. Thus, most of each child's handshape morphemes could be found in combination with more than one motion morpheme, and vice versa. A good example of two different handshapes combined with the same motion appears in Figures 5A and B (see the "To&Fro + Fist" and the "To&Fro + Palm" videoclips at www.psypress.com/goldinmeadow)—David uses the *Fist* handshape in combination with the *To-and-Fro* motion to mean "move a narrow, long object back and forth" (move a knife; Figure 5A), and a *Palm* handshape with this same motion to mean "move a straight, wide object back and forth" (a knife moves; Figure 5B). Figures 6A and B (see the "Fist + Linear Path" and the "Fist + Circle" videoclips at www.psypress.com/goldinmeadow) present an

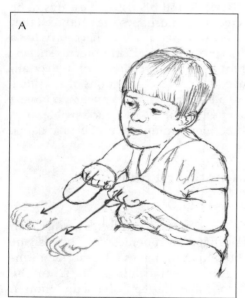

FIGURE 6. The Same Handshape Can Occur with Different Motions. In panel A, David holds two fists together and moves them along a straight path as though pushing a lawnmower. In panel B, he holds the same fist handshape in the air and moves it in a circle as though waving a balloon. Thus, David uses two different motions (*Linear Path, Circle*) with the same *Fist* handshape.

example of the same handshape used with two different motions—David uses the *Fist* handshape in combination with a *Linear Path* motion to mean "change the location of a narrow, long object by moving it along a path" (push the handle of a lawnmower forward, Figure 6A), and the same handshape with a *Circle* motion to mean "move a narrow, long object in a circle" (wave a balloon string, Figure 6B). The handshape morphemes in each child's gestures thus formed a matrix or *paradigm of contrasts* with the motion morphemes in the corpus of gestures.

☐ The Parts Grow Out of Wholes

We saw in Chapter 1 that, at the very earliest stages of development, children acquiring conventional languages initially learn words as rote wholes (MacWhinney, 1978). They then realize—relatively quickly in some languages such as K'iche' Maya (Pye, 1992), Turkish (Aksu-Koc & Slobin, 1985), West Greenlandic (Fortescue & Olsen, 1992), and more slowly in other languages such as English (Bowerman, 1982b) and ASL (Newport, 1984)—that those wholes are composed of meaningful parts and begin to use those parts as productive morphemes. Since the deaf children in our study are not learning their gestures from adult models, we might expect them to show a different developmental pattern—that is, to use their sub-gesture hand and motion components productively even at the earliest stages of development. If so, we would then conclude that children begin by learning words as wholes rather than as combinations of parts *only* when they learn their words from a conventional language model.

On the other hand, it is possible that, even without a conventional language model, the child's first representation of an event is not in terms of parts, but rather in terms of the event as a whole. If so, the deaf child's first lexical items would not be composed of component parts but would instead be unanalyzed wholes which map (as wholes) onto an event. For example, the gesture *OTouch + Revolve*, if used in the context of twisting a small key and for no other objects or actions, may early in development function as an unanalyzed label for key-twisting. Later, perhaps when the child has accumulated a sufficient number of gestures in the lexicon, the child begins to consider his or her gestures in relation to one another and organizes the gestures around any regularities that happen to appear in the lexicon (i.e., the child treats his or her own gestures as a "problem space" that needs systematization; cf. Karmiloff-Smith, 1979). For example, over time the child adds to his or her repertoire an *OTouch + Short Arc* combination used exclusively for hat-putting-on, and a *CLarge + Revolve* combination used exclusively for jar-twisting. At some point, the child pulls back and considers the relation between these three gestures: *OTouch + Revolve*, *OTouch + Short Arc*, and *CLarge + Revolve*. The child notices that the *OTouch* handshape recurs across the gestures, as does the *Revolve* motion. These recurring forms are, for the first time, separated out from the wholes and treated as component parts. The transition is from a state in which the child considers a gesture only in relation to the situation conveyed—that is, a gesture-*world* relation—to a state in which the child begins to consider gestures in relation to other gestures in the system—a gesture-*gesture* relation.

If the deaf children were to follow this developmental path, we would expect that a particular handshape-motion combination, when still an undecomposed whole, might be used exclusively for a single object-action pairing. Later, when the parts of the gesture have been isolated, that same combination would be used for a variety of related objects and a variety of related actions. For example, David first uses a *Fist + Arc To-and-Fro* combination only in relation to drumstick-beating. In later sessions, he uses the *Fist + Arc To-and-Fro* combination not only for "drumstick-beat" but also for "toothbrush-brush" or "handlebars-jiggle." That is, the *Fist* handshape in this and in other gestures is now used in relation to a variety of related objects (drumsticks, toothbrushes, handlebars—all of which are narrow and long), and the *Arc To-and-Fro* motion in this and in other gestures is used in relation to a variety of related actions (beating, brushing, jiggling—all of which involve repositioning by moving back and forth). This is precisely the pattern we find in three of the four children—David, Karen, and Marvin (Goldin-Meadow et al., 1995). The fourth child, Abe, was already using a large number of handshape-motion combinations for a variety of object and actions during his first observation session. We may not have caught Abe early enough to observe the first steps he took in fashioning a morphological system—or Abe may have begun his gesture system, not with representations of events as wholes, but with representations of parts of events.

What I am suggesting is that the deaf children induce their morphological systems from the earliest gestures they themselves create. Indeed, the first holistic gestures that the children used seemed to set the stage for the system each child eventually generated. For example, in Session 1, David used the *OTouch + No Motion* combination to describe holding a bubble wand, a narrow *long* object. In addition, he also used the *OTouch + Circle* combination to describe twisting a small key, a narrow *short* object. If these examples are representative of the gestures David used at the time, he would infer that the *OTouch* handshape is used for objects that have relatively narrow diameters but that can be either long (like the wand) or short (like the key). Thus, on the basis of *his own* gestures, David would infer a form-meaning pairing in which the *OTouch* form is associated with the meaning "handle an object < 2 inches in width and any length" (see Table 3).

In contrast, the first time David produced the *Fist* handshape, he used it in Session 2 combined with *No Motion* to describe holding a bubble wand; that is, the *Fist + No Motion* combination was used for the same event as the *OTouch*

+ *No Motion* combination. However, the *Fist* was *not* used to describe any other objects during the early sessions: It was used only for narrow, long objects and not for narrow, short objects. On the basis of these gestures, David would infer that the *Fist* handshape is used for objects that have narrow diameters and *long* lengths. In fact, when he began to consistently use gestures in relation to a variety of objects and actions in Session 4, David used the *Fist* (combined with the *Arc To-and-Fro* and the *Short Arc* motions) to describe a set of objects, all having narrow diameters (< 2 inches) and long lengths (> 3 inches), for example, the handle of a hammer, the handlebars of a bike, a newspaper, and the brim of a hat—precisely the range of objects eventually seen for this form in his HAND morphemes (see Table 3).

The earliest gestures that Karen and Marvin created also set the stage for the categories they eventually settled on in their gesture systems (Goldin-Meadow et al., 1995, 241–242)—and thus set the stage for the similarities and differences seen across the children's systems (see Table 4). Before each child began to consistently use a handshape-motion combination in relation to a variety of objects and actions, the child had already used that handshape in different gestures in relation to precisely the range of objects that would eventually fall within a given morpheme type in that child's system. Thus, when the child was ready to survey his or her gestures and analyze them to extract handshape and motion components, the outlines of the system were already present. Just as children provided with a conventional language model induce rules and categories from the input they receive, the deaf children in this study induce the structure of their categories from their input—the difference is that the deaf children are forced by their circumstances to provide, and reflect upon, their own gestures as input.

☐ Summary: A Simple Morphology

The deaf children produce gestures that are themselves composed of parts. The children could have faithfully reproduced the actions that they perform in the world in their gestures. They could have, for example, created gestures that capture the difference between holding a balloon string and holding an umbrella. But they don't. Instead, they produce gestures composed of a limited set of handshape forms, each standing for a class of objects, and a limited set of motion forms, each standing for a class of actions. These handshape and motion components combine freely to create gestures, and the meanings of these gestures are predictable from the meanings of their component parts. For example, *OTouch* combined with *Revolve* means "rotate an object < 2 inches wide around an axis," a meaning that can be transparently derived from the meanings of its two component parts (*OTouch* = handle an object < 2 inches wide; *Revolve* = rotate around an axis). The gestures that the deaf children create thus form a simple morphology akin to the morphologies found in all conventional sign languages.

Our first step was to show that the deaf children's gestures have morphological structure. We then used this fact to make inferences about the developmental course that all children follow when developing a morphological system. Children learning conventional languages go through an initial stage in which they learn words as wholes or amalgams, only later breaking those wholes into the component parts that characterize the language they are learning. This "start-with-the-whole" strategy could reflect the fact that children are learning an established system handed down to them by their communities. However, the fact that the deaf children in our studies also go through an initial stage in which their gestures are unanalyzed amalgams suggests that this strategy is more basic. It is a strategy that all children bring to language-learning whether or not they are exposed to a conventional language.

After their initial holistic period, children begin to derive a morphological system using whatever input they have. If learning a conventional language, they survey the words they've learned and extract regularities across those words. If constructing their own gesture system, they survey the gestures they've created and extract whatever regularities exist in those gestures. Thus, the morphological systems that children construct reflect regularities in input, even in deaf children who must provide their own input. The important point to note, however, is that the drive to analyze and systematize one's lexicon is robust in young children, robust enough that it does not have to be catalyzed by a conventional language.

Combining Words Into Simple Sentences

Unlike other animals who typically produce their signals as single units not combined with other signals (cf. Seyfarth & Cheney, 1997), humans produce words in combination with other words. The deaf children in our study are no exception—the children frequently combine their gestures with one another, and use those combinations to convey different meanings. For example, a deaf child combines a point at a toy grape with an "eat" gesture to comment on the fact that grapes can be eaten, and at another time combines the "eat" gesture with a point at the experimenter to invite her to lunch with the family. Moreover, and equally important, the deaf children's gesture combinations function like the sentences of early child language in a number of respects. To be specific, the gesture combinations:

- convey the same types of meanings that children learning conventional languages convey in their early sentences;
- are characterized by predicate frames comparable to those underlying the sentences of early child language; and
- are characterized by surface regularities that mark who does what to whom and that are comparable to marking devices found in early child language.

On this basis, the deaf children's gesture combinations warrant the label "sentence." I describe each of these features of the deaf children's sentences in the next sections.

☐ The Meanings Simple Sentences Convey

As described in Chapter 7, we use motoric criteria to determine the boundaries of the deaf children's gesture sentences: relaxation of the hand signals the end of a sentence. We set single gestures aside for this analysis and look only at sentences containing more than one gesture. We then determine how many propositions are conveyed by the gestures. For example, Marvin points at a train and produces a "circle" gesture (recall that pointing gestures are displayed in lowercase, iconic characterizing gestures in uppercase):

> train—CIRCLE

The battery-powered train is circling around the track and Marvin uses his gestures to comment on this event. His gestures constitute a simple sentence containing a single proposition: "train circles."

In contrast, Abe produces a longer string of gestures before dropping his hands:

> Susan—WAVE—Susan—CLOSE

I had earlier waved at Abe before closing the door and Abe is commenting on my past actions. He produced a complex sentence containing two propositions: "Susan waves" (proposition 1) and "Susan closes door" (proposition 2). In this chapter, I focus exclusively on the children's simple, one-proposition gesture sentences, leaving their complex multi-proposition sentences for Chapter 11.

The deaf children convey both action and attribute relations in their gesture sentences and, like English-learning children (Bloom, Lightbown, & Hood, 1975), produce action sentences more frequently than attribute sentences (Goldin-Meadow & Mylander, 1984). They gesture about actions that involve transferring objects to a new location or person. Marvin produces the following gesture sentence before he himself moves a puzzle piece to the puzzle board:

> TRANSFER—puzzle board

The children also gesture about actions on objects but ones that don't involve changing the location of the object. Karen produces the following gesture sentence when she wants me to open a jar of bubbles for her:

> bubble jar—TWIST

In addition, the children gesture about actions that don't involve any objects at all. They describe actions in which an actor moves to a new location. For example, Marvin produces the following sentence to ask his mother to come to his side:

> COME—mother

And they describe actions in which an actor moves but doesn't change location. For example, David produces the following gesture sentence to describe a picture of a bear who is dancing in place:

> bear—DANCE

As far as attributes are concerned, the children describe an object's size, shape, posture, and so forth in their gesture sentences. Karen uses the following gesture sentence to comment on the unusual size of a miniature ketchup bottle:

> ketchup bottle—LITTLE

The children use strings of pointing gestures to comment on the relation between objects. Abe uses the following gesture sentences to indicate the similarity between two objects, a toy elephant's back and his own back in the first example, and a picture of a potato chip and the chip itself in the second:

> elephant's back—Abe's back
> picture of a potato chip—potato chip

Finally, the children use pointing gestures to comment on an object's typical location, as in the first example below in which Mildred points out that Band-Aids go on fingers. They also use pointing gestures to comment on an object's owner, as in the second example in which Abe points at a picture that belongs to him (it's not a picture of him) and then at his own chest.

> Band-Aid—finger
> picture—Abe

These types of events and properties are just the ones that children communicate about whether they are learning a spoken language (Bowerman, 1973a; Brown, 1973) or a signed language (Hoffmeister, 1978; Kantor, 1982; Newport & Ashbrook, 1977; Schlesinger & Meadow, 1972). Indeed, they seem to be topics that are on the minds of young children even if those children are not exposed to a conventional language.

☐ Underlying Predicate Frames Organize the Sentence

Sentences are organized around verbs. The verb conveys the action which determines the thematic roles or arguments (θ-roles, Chomsky, 1982) that underlie the sentence. For example, if the verb is "give" in English or "donner" in French, the framework underlying the sentence contains three arguments—the giver (actor), the given (patient), and the givee (recipient). In contrast, if the verb is "eat" or "manger," the framework underlying the sentence contains two arguments—the eater (actor) and the eaten (patient). Do frameworks of this sort underlie the deaf children's gesture sentences?

All of the deaf children produce sentences about transferring objects and, at one time or another, they produce gestures for each of the three arguments that we would expect to underlie such a predicate. They never produce all three arguments in a single sentence but, across all of their sentences, they produce a selection of two-gesture combinations that, taken together, displays all three of the arguments. For example, David produces the following two-gesture sentences to describe different events, all of which are about a person transferring an object to another person. In the first three, he is asking his sister to give him a cookie. In the fourth, he is asking his sister to give a toy duck to me so that I will wind it to make it go.

> cookie—GIVE (patient—act)
> sister—David (actor—recipient)
> GIVE—David (act—recipient)
> duck—Susan (patient—recipient)

By overtly expressing the actor, patient, and recipient in this predicate context, David and the other children exhibit knowledge that these three arguments are associated with the transfer-object predicate.

The children also produce sentences about acting on objects without changing their location and, again, produce gestures for each of the two arguments that we would expect to underlie such a predicate. For example, Karen produces the following two-gesture sentences to describe different events, all of which are about a person acting on an object. In the first two, she is asking someone (me in the first example, Marolyn in the second) to twist open a bubble jar. In the third, she is saying that she herself will twist the object.

> bubbles—TWIST (patient—act)
> Marolyn—bubbles (actor—patient)
> TWIST—Karen (act—actor)

By overtly expressing the actor and patient in this predicate context, the children exhibit knowledge that these two arguments are associated with the act-on-object predicate.

As described in the previous section, the children also produce sentences about actions that do not involve objects. For example, Abe produces the following gesture sentences to describe different events in which an object or person moves on its own to a new location (or, in our terms, recipient). In the first, Abe is saying that he will go outside. In the second, he is saying that the penny will go to the slot on the toy bank after he pulls a trigger which propels the penny forward. In the third, which actually contains three gestures, he is asking his friend to go to the candle on a nearby birthday cake.

> outside—Abe (recipient—actor)
> GO—slot (act—recipient)
> candle—friend—GO (recipient—actor—act)

By overtly expressing the actor and recipient in this predicate context, the children exhibit knowledge that these two arguments are associated with the move-to-location predicate.

Finally, Tracy produces the following two-gesture sentence to describe a picture of an octopus wriggling in place:

octopus—WRIGGLE (actor—act)

By overtly expressing the actor with these predicates, the children exhibit knowledge that this argument is associated with the perform-in-place predicate.

Most of the children's sentences that convey a single proposition contain only two gestures (like hearing children learning a language such as Inuktitut who continue to produce short sentences as they develop simply because their language permits a great deal of deletion). As a result, the deaf children rarely produce all of the arguments that belong to a predicate in a single sentence. What then makes us think that the entire predicate frame underlies a sentence? Is there evidence, for example, that the recipient and actor arguments underlie the sentence "cookie give" even though the patient "cookie" and the act "give" are the only elements that appear in the surface structure of the sentence? Yes. The evidence comes from how likely the child is to produce gestures for various arguments—what we've called "production probability."

Production probability is the likelihood that an argument will be gestured when it can be. The children cannot produce gestures for all of the arguments that belong to a two- or three-argument predicate in their two-gesture sentences—they are not yet capable of producing sentences that long. Counting the predicate, there are three candidate units for the two slots in a sentence with a two-argument predicate frame (actor, patient, act; or actor, recipient, act), and four candidate units for the two slots in a sentence with a three-argument predicate frame (actor, patient, recipient, act). The children must therefore leave some arguments out of their gesture sentences. They could leave elements out haphazardly—but they don't. They are quite systematic in how often they omit and produce gestures for various arguments in different predicate frames. This is just the pattern we would expect if the predicate frame is the organizing force behind a sentence.

Take the actor as an example. If we are correct in attributing predicate frames to the deaf children's gesture sentences, a *giver* (i.e., the actor in a "give" predicate) should be gestured *less* often than an *eater* (the actor in an "eat" predicate) simply because there is more competition for slots in a three-argument "give" predicate (four units in the underlying predicate frame) than in a two-argument "eat" predicate (three units in the underlying predicate frame). The *giver* has to compete with the *act,* the *given,* and the *givee.* The *eater* has to compete only with the *act* and the *eaten.* This is precisely the pattern we find. Figure 7 presents production probability for actors in two-gesture sentences that have predicate frames of differing sizes. Each of the ten children is *less* likely to produce an actor in a sentence with a four-unit underlying predicate frame (e.g., the *giver*, white bars) than an actor in a sentence with a three-unit underlying predicate frame (e.g., the *eater*, hatched bars).

Following the same logic, an *eater* should be gestured *less* often than a *dancer* (the actor in a "dance" predicate) because there is more competition for slots in a two-argument "eat" predicate (three units in the underlying predicate frame) than in a two-argument "dance" predicate (two units in the underlying predicate frame). The *eater* has to compete with the *act* and the *eaten*, but the *dancer* has no competition at all since the predicate frame has only two slots, one for the *act* and one for the *dancer*. We see this pattern in Figure 7 as well. The children are *less* likely to produce an actor in a sentence with a three-unit underlying predicate frame (e.g., the *eater*, hatched bars) than an actor in a sentence with a two-unit underlying predicate frame (e.g., the *dancer*, black bars). Actor production probability is not 100% for sentences with two underlying units for Marvin and Karen simply because these children occasionally produced gestures for non-essential elements rather than for the actor (e.g., the "place" where the action is taking place, a non-essential but allowable element in any action sentence). Dennis produced no sentences with two-units in the underlying predicate frame.

In general, what we see in Figure 7 is that production probability *decreases* systematically as the number of units in the underlying predicate frame *increases* from two to three to four, and it does so for each of the ten children. Importantly, we see the same pattern for patients: The children are *less* likely to produce a gesture for a *given* apple than for an *eaten* apple simply because there is more competition for slots in a three-argument "give" predicate (four units in the underlying predicate frame) than in a two-argument "eat" predicate (three units in the underlying predicate frame; Goldin-Meadow, 1985).

It is worth making one final point—it is the underlying predicate frame that dictates actor production probability in the deaf children's gesture sentences, not how easy it is to guess from context who the actor of a sentence is. We convinced ourselves of this by examining production probability separately for first-person actors (i.e., the child him or herself), second-person actors (the communication partner), and third-person actors. If predictability in context is the key, first- and second-person actors should be omitted regardless of underlying predicate frame because their identity can be easily guessed in context (both persons are on the scene); and third-person actors should be gestured quite often regardless of underlying predicate frame because they are less easily guessed from context. We found, however, that the production probability patterns seen in Figure 7 hold for first-person, second-person, and third-person actors when each is analyzed separately (Goldin-Meadow, 1985, 237). The predicate frame underlying a sentence is indeed an essential factor in determining how often an actor will be gestured in that sentence.

This is an important result. It suggests that children come to the language-learning situation with actions already organized into just the types of

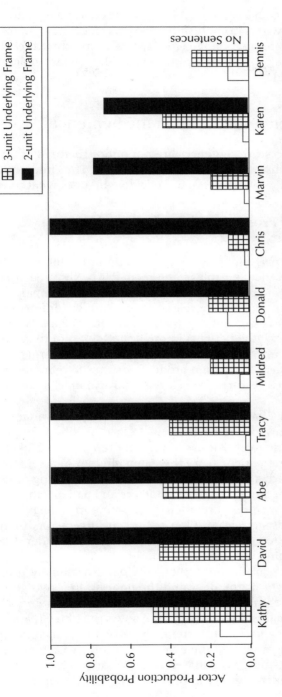

FIGURE 7. The Production of Gestures for Semantic Elements in a Sentence Depends on the Predicate Frame Underlying That Sentence. The figure displays the likelihood that a deaf child will produce a gesture for an actor in a two-gesture sentence as a function of the predicate frame underlying that sentence. Children are more likely to produce actors in sentences with a two-unit than a three-unit underlying frame, and in sentences with three-unit than a four-unit underlying frame, simply because there is less "competition" for the two slots in surface structure when the underlying frame contains fewer units and thus offers fewer candidates for those slots.

frameworks that languages exploit. As a result, there is no need for children to learn these frameworks from the input they receive. They can instead use the frameworks *they* bring to language-learning to interpret their input—a step that simplifies, although certainly doesn't solve, the language-learning problem for the child.

☐ Marking Semantic Roles in the Sentence

The deaf children's gesture sentences are not only structured at underlying levels, but they are also structured at surface levels. The children use three different devices, all of which serve to indicate who does what to whom.

Marking Roles by Producing Them at a Particular Rate in a Sentence: Syntax

As described in the preceding section, production probability is the likelihood that a particular thematic role or argument will be gestured in a sentence of a given length. Unlike the above analysis where we compared the production probability of a given role (e.g., the actor) across different predicate frames, in this analysis we compare the production probability of different roles (e.g., the actor vs. the patient) in predicate frames of the same size. If the children haphazardly produce gestures for the thematic roles associated with a given predicate, they should produce gestures for patients equally as often as they produce gestures for actors in, for example, sentences about eating.

We find, however, that here again the children are *not* random in their production of gestures for thematic roles—in fact, likelihood of production distinguishes thematic roles. All ten of the children are more likely to produce a gesture for the patient (e.g., the eaten cheese) in a sentence about eating than to produce a gesture for the actor (e.g., the eating mouse). Figure 8 presents production probability for actors and patients in two-gesture transitive sentences with two-argument predicate frames (e.g., "eat"). Production probability is significantly lower for transitive actors than for patients for each of the ten children (Goldin-Meadow & Mylander, 1984). Two points are worth noting.

First, the children's production probability patterns convey probabilistic information about who is the doer and the done-to in a two-gesture sentence. If, for example, a deaf child produces the gesture sentence "boy hit," we would guess from this utterance that the boy is the hittee (patient) in the scene rather than the hitter (actor) simply because the deaf children tend to produce gestures for patients at the expense of transitive actors.

Second, note that the deaf children's particular production probability pattern tends to result in two-gesture sentences that preserve the unity of

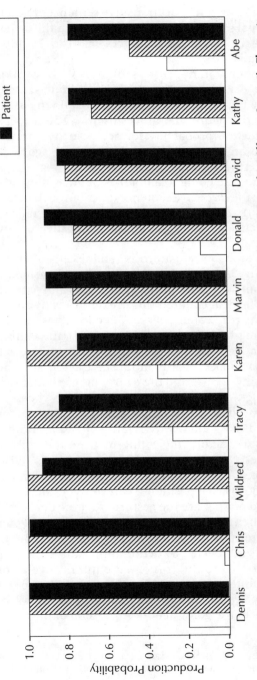

FIGURE 8. The Deaf Children Follow an Ergative Pattern When They Omit and Produce Gestures for Different Semantic Elements. The figure displays the likelihood that a deaf child will produce a gesture for a transitive actor, a patient, or an intransitive actor in a two-gesture sentence. All of the children except Abe produced gestures for intransitive actors as often as for patients, and more often than they produced gestures for transitive actors. They thus displayed a structural arrangement reminiscent of the patterns found in ergative languages.

the predicate—that is, patient + act transitive sentences (akin to OV [Object-Verb] in conventional systems) are more frequent in the deaf children's gestures than actor + act transitive sentences (akin to SV [Subject-Verb] in conventional systems).

Actors appear not only in transitive sentences with two-argument predicate frames (*mouse*, eat, cheese) but also in *intransitive* sentences with two-argument predicate frames (*mouse*, go, hole). How do the deaf children treat intransitive actors, the figure that moves itself to a new location? Figure 8 also presents production probability for actors in two-gesture intransitive sentences with two-argument predicate frames (e.g., "go"). Nine of the ten children produce gestures for the intransitive actor (e.g., the *mouse* in a sentence describing a mouse going to a hole) as often as they produce gestures for the patient (e.g., the *cheese* in a sentence describing a mouse eating cheese), and far more often than they produce gestures for the transitive actor (e.g., the *mouse* in a sentence describing a mouse eating cheese)—Abe is the only exception.

This production probability pattern is reminiscent of case-marking patterns found in ergative languages (cf., Dixon, 1979; Silverstein, 1976). Gesture production is high and equal for intransitive actors and patients, and low for transitive actors.[1] The deaf children thus treat intransitive actors (the going-mouse) and patients (the eaten-cheese) alike in terms of production probability, distinguishing both from transitive actors (the eating-mouse). The hallmark of an ergative pattern is the way the intransitive actor is marked. In accusative languages like English, intransitive actors are marked like transitive actors (the going-mouse and the eating-mouse both precede the verb), and both are distinguished from patients (the eaten-cheese) which follow the verb. In contrast, in ergative languages, intransitive actors (the going-mouse) are marked like patients (the eaten-cheese), and both are distinguished from transitive actors (the eating-mouse). If English were ergative, we would say "goes *mouse*" (rather than "mouse goes"). The intransitive actor would be placed *after* the verb, aligning it with the patient which typically occupies the postverbal position ("eats *cheese*"). But, of course, English is not ergative—and neither are the gestures that the deaf children's hearing parents produce when they talk to their children (see Chapter 14).

The ergative pattern in the deaf children's gestures could reflect a tendency to see objects as affected by action rather than as effectors of action. In the sentence "you go to the corner," the intransitive actor "you" has a double meaning. On the one hand, "you" refers to the goer, the actor, the effector of the going action. On the other hand, "you" refers to the gone, the patient, the affectee of the going action. At the end of the action, "you" both

---

[1]In conventional ergative systems, it is the transitive actor that is marked. However, in the deaf children's gesture systems the transitive actor tends to be omitted and, in this sense, could be considered unmarked.

"have gone" and "are gone," and the decision to emphasize one aspect of the actor's condition over the other is arbitrary. By treating intransitive actors like patients, the deaf children are highlighting the affectee properties of the intranstive actor over the effector properties.

It is important to note that the deaf children really are marking thematic role, and not just producing gestures for the most salient or most informative element in the context. One very sensible (albeit wrong) possibility is that the deaf children produce gestures for intransitive actors and patients more often than for transitive actors because intransitive actors and patients tend to be new to the discourse more often than transitive actors (cf. DuBois, 1987). In other words, the production probability patterns seen in Figure 8 could be an outgrowth of a semantic element's status as "new" or "old" in the discourse. If the novelty of a semantic element is responsible for how often that element is gestured, we would expect production probability to be high for all "new" elements (regardless of role) and low for all "old" elements (again, regardless of role). We find no evidence for this hypothesis (Schulman, Mylander, & Goldin-Meadow, 2001; see also Goldin-Meadow & Mylander, 1984, 49). Rather, we find an ergative production probablity pattern for "new" elements when analyzed on their own, as well as for "old" elements when analyzed on their own. Figure 9 presents averaged data from four of the deaf children—Karen, Marvin, David, and Abe. The children produce gestures for transitive actors less often than they produce them for

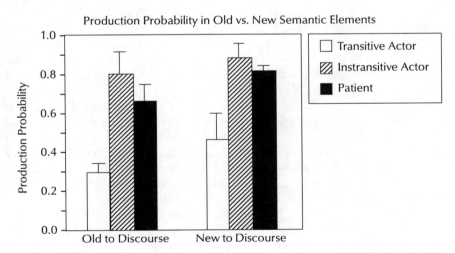

FIGURE 9. The Deaf Children Follow an Ergative Pattern Whether They Are Gesturing About New or Old Semantic Elements. The figure displays the likelihood that four deaf children will produce gestures for transitive actors, intransitive actors, or patients when those elements are old (left) or new (right) to the discourse. The ergative pattern is evident in both graphs, suggesting that ergative structure at the sentence level is independent of the newness of the elements in discourse. Error bars indicate standard errors.

intransitive actors or patients, whether those elements are new (right bars) or old (left bars). This is as it should be if thematic role, rather than novelty, determines how often an element is gestured.

Marking Roles by Placing Them in a Particular Position in a Sentence: Syntax

In addition to reliably producing gestures for some thematic roles at the expense of others, the children are also consistent in where they position the gestures they do produce in their two-gesture sentences. The children order gestures for patients, acts, and recipients in a consistent way in their two-gesture sentences. Many, but not all, of the children produce sentences conforming to the following three ordering patterns (Goldin-Meadow & Feldman, 1977; Goldin-Meadow & Mylander, 1984, 35–6): (1) gestures for *patients* (e.g., cheese) precede gestures for *acts* (e.g., eat); (2) gestures for *patients* (e.g., hat) precede gestures for *recipients* (e.g., cowboy's head), and (3) gestures for *acts* (e.g., move-to) precede gestures for *recipients* (e.g., table).

Importantly, these ordering patterns are not reducible to the discourse status of the semantic elements—if we re-analyze the sentences in terms of whether an element is "new" or "old" to the discourse, we find that most of the children's gesture sentences are "old-old" or "new-new," and that the "old-new" sentences are approximately as frequent as "new-old" sentences. In other words, "new" elements do not consistently occupy the initial position in the deaf children's gestures sentences, nor do "old" elements (Goldin-Meadow & Mylander, 1984, 51).

Nine of the 10 children produce gestures for patients before gestures for acts (Abe is the exception; see Figure 10, top). Moreover, 7 of the 10 also produce gestures for intransitive actors before gestures for acts (Mildred and Chris are the exceptions; Dennis produced no relevant sentences at all; see Figure 10, bottom, Goldin-Meadow, 2003b). Thus, many of the children treat intransitive actors like patients with respect to gesture order as well as production probability.

David is the only child who produces a sufficient number of sentences with transitive actors to allow us to discern an ordering pattern for this thematic role. David not only treats patients and intransitive actors alike with respect to gesture order, but he orders them differently from transitive actors—he produces gestures for patients and intransitive actors *before* gestures for acts, but gestures for transitive actors *after* gestures for acts (Goldin-Meadow & Mylander, 1984, 39). For example, David produces the following gesture sentence to tell me to eat the snack that his mother had just brought into the room (Figure 11; see the "Snack-Eat-Susan" videoclip at www.psypress.com/goldinmeadow):

snack—EAT—Susan (patient—act—actor)

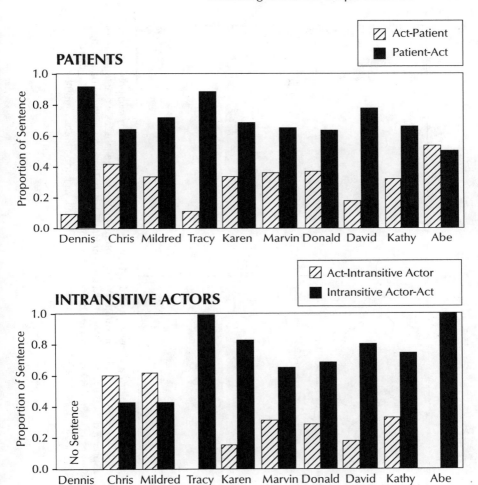

FIGURE 10. The Deaf Children Follow Consistent Gesture Orders When They Produce Patients and Intransitive Actors in Sentences with Acts. The figure displays the proportion of sentences in act-patient vs. patient-act orders (top graph) and act-intransitive actor vs. intransitive actor-act orders (bottom graph) that each child produced. The children tended to produce both patients and intransitive actors before acts. Exceptions were Abe (patients) and Chris and Mildred (intransitive actors); Dennis produced no relevant sentences with intransitive actors.

Note that in this sentence the patient (snack) precedes the act (eat) and the actor (Susan) follows it. In contrast, when David asks me to move to a particular spot—that is, when I play the role of intransitive actor rather than transitive actor—he produces the following gesture sentence:

Susan—MOVE OVER (actor—act)

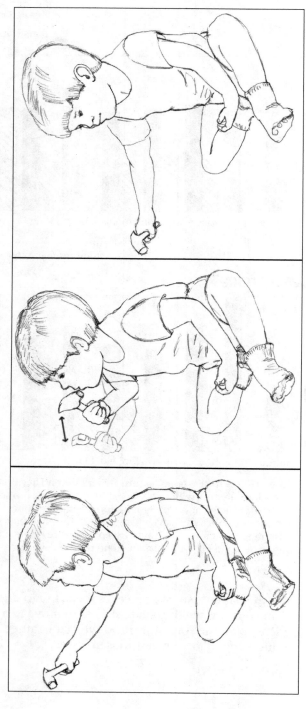

FIGURE 11. The Gestures in the Deaf Children's Sentences Follow a Consistent Order. David is holding a toy and uses it to point at a tray of snacks that his mother is carrying = *snack* (the tray is not shown in the drawing). Without dropping the toy, he jabs it several times at his mouth = *eat*. Finally, he points with the toy at me sprawled on the floor in front of him (not shown) = *Susan*. This is an ordering pattern that David frequently follows in his gestures—the patient [snacks, in this case] occurs before the action [eat] which occurs before the transitive actor [Susan]. The fact that he does not drop the toy before gesturing is reminiscent of children who talk with food in their mouths.

110

In this sentence, the intransitive actor (Susan) precedes the act (move over). David thus treats patients and intransitive actors alike (both precede the act) and distinct from transitive actors (which follow the act). He thus displays an ergative pattern not only with respect to production probability, but also with respect to gesture order.

Marking Roles by Inflecting the Verb in a Sentence: Inflectional Morphology

In addition to indicating who does what to whom via gesture order and production probability, the children use displacement of their gestures in space to achieve this same function. This technique is reminiscent of inflectional systems in ASL in which signs are displaced so that they "agree" with their noun arguments. For example, the sign "give" is moved from the signer to the addressee to mean "I give to you," but from the addressee to the signer to mean "You give to me" (Fischer & Gough, 1978; Padden, 1983).

The deaf children in our study often produce gestures in neutral space. For example, in Figure 12A, Donald is shown producing a "twist" gesture at chest level in neutral space. However, at times, the children orient their gestures toward particular objects in the room. For example, Figure 12B shows Karen producing a "twist" gesture with her hand extended toward the jar (note that she is not actually twisting the jar, else we would not

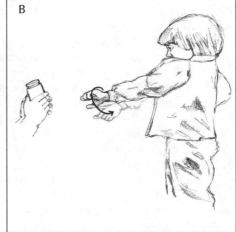

FIGURE 12. The Placement of the Deaf Children's Gestures Matters. The deaf children can produce the same gesture in different locations. In panel A, Donald produces a "twist" gesture in front of his body at chest level. In panel B, Karen produces the same "twist" gesture extended toward, but not on, the bubble jar. The second gesture, but not the first, incorporates the object of the twisting action into its form and, in this way, marks the patient of the action.

consider the act a gesture). We call these displacements "inflections," adopting terminology used in the sign language literature. These inflections are obligatory in three-argument predicates (they're used close to 100% of the time), optional in two-argument predicates, and very rare in one-argument predicates (Goldin-Meadow et al., 1994).

Importantly, the children do not displace their gestures toward just any objects—they displace them toward objects playing particular thematic roles. In transitive sentences, gestures are oriented toward objects playing patient roles. For example, David produces his "transfer" gesture near the puzzle piece, thereby marking the piece as the patient of the predicate. In addition, in intransitive sentences involving change of location, gestures are oriented toward objects playing recipient roles. For example, David moves his "go" gesture toward the open end of a car-trailer to indicate that cars go into the trailer, thereby marking the trailer as the recipient of the predicate. In contrast, the children rarely displace gestures toward actors of either transitive or intransitive predicates.

The deaf children's inflectional system resembles ASL in that the gestures needn't be displaced toward the actual topic of conversation (cf. Hoffmeister, 1978). The children can produce their gestures near objects that are not the actual objects they're gesturing about but are similar to those objects. For example, David produces a "twist" gesture near an empty jar of bubbles, a seemingly nonsensical request—why twist open an already open jar? However, we can tell from the preceding and subsequent events that David wants the full jar of bubbles which is in the kitchen twisted open (Butcher et al., 1991). The placement of his gesture helps to tell us which type of object ought to be acted upon.

However, the deaf children's inflectional patterns differ from ASL in *which* thematic roles are marked: three-argument transitive predicates (e.g., "give") agree with *patients* in the deaf children's gesture systems, but with *recipients* in ASL (Meier, 2002). For example, if a deaf child in our study were to ask that a jar be given to his mother, the child would displace the "give" gesture toward the jar (the patient). In contrast, an ASL signer would displace the sign for "give" toward the mother (the recipient). This difference makes it clear that the choice of which object to mark is indeed a choice. The patient-marking that the children in our studies display is consistent with the focus on the patient found in their other marking techniques (producing gestures for patients with high probability and in first position of a two-gesture sentence), and thus contributes to the coherence of the system.

The children's marking techniques work together in one other way—a predicate is *less* likely to be marked with a patient inflection if there is already a pointing gesture for the patient in the sentence than if it there is not (this is true for two-argument transitive predicates where inflectional marking is optional, but not for three-argument transitive predicates where inflectional marking is obligatory and occurs no matter what happens to pointing gestures; Goldin-Meadow et al., 1994). Thus, in the relevant sentences, there is a trade-off between inflections and pointing gestures—as in ASL (Lillo-Martin, 1986), the deaf child can omit a morphological inflection for a thematic role if that role is already indicated by a pointing gesture.

☐ Summary: A Simple Syntax

To summarize, the deaf children not only combine their gestures into strings but those strings act like sentences in the following ways.

They convey the meanings that young children learning conventional languages typically convey with their sentences. Thus, at the earliest stages of language-learning, the content of young children's communications is determined more by what's on their minds than by the particular linguistic models their language provides for them.

They are structured at underlying levels just like the early sentences of children learning conventional languages. Thus, children come to the language-learning situation with actions organized into frameworks—predicate frames. Those frameworks serve as the organizing structure for children's earliest sentences, whether those sentences are learned from conventional language models or invented *de novo*.

They are structured at surface levels, containing many of the devices to mark "who does what to whom" that are found in the early sentences of children learning conventional languages. The children indicate objects that play different thematic roles by preferentially producing pointing gestures for those objects and putting the gestures in particular positions (e.g., pointing at the drum as opposed to the drummer, and producing that gesture before the "beat" gesture), or by inflecting predicate gestures for the objects (e.g., displacing the "beat" gesture toward the drum). The production and ordering techniques are syntactic in that they deal with the relation between gestures; the displacement technique is morphologic in that it deals with variations within a single gesture. The techniques form a coherent system in that they are all used primarily to mark patients, and they complement one another in that a morphologic marking can trade off with a syntactic marking. The sentences therefore adhere to a syntax, albeit a simple one.

Thus, whether or not children are exposed to a model for language, they communicate certain ideas and structure those communications at underlying and surface levels. And they do so using devices found in natural languages across the globe. If not handed a language, children will invent a system that looks very much like language.

CHAPTER

Making Complex Sentences out of Simple Ones: Recursion

Recursion allows language users to express more than one proposition within a single sentence. Recursive rules are those that can be applied repeatedly. They transform simple sentences into complex sentences, give language its generative capacity, and thus are an essential component of all natural languages (Hauser, Chomsky, & Fitch, 2002). With recursive devices, speakers and signers can produce an infinite number of sentences, all conforming to the grammar of their language. The question is whether the deaf children's gesture systems contain recursion.

☐ The Meanings Complex Sentences Convey

As described earlier, the boundaries of a gesture sentence are determined by tension and relaxation of the hands: If a child produces two or more gestures without breaking the flow of movement and without relaxing hand or arm, we consider those gestures to be part of one sentence. If the gestures in that sentence convey two or more propositions (even if those propositions are conveyed incompletely), that sentence is considered complex. Using these criteria, we find that all 10 of the deaf children produce complex sentences. Complex sentences account for 7% to 31% (mean = 17.4%) of the gesture sentences the children produce during the early years (our first wave of data collection, Goldin-Meadow & Mylander, 1984; see Chapter 6), and 32% to 45% (mean = 36.7%) of the sentences they produce during the later years (our second wave of data collection, Goldin-Meadow & Mylander, 1998). Although sometimes the numbers of complex sentences are small, the important point is that each child produces at least some multi-proposition gesture sentences and the number increases with age. For example, David produced 177 complex gesture sentences, Abe 55, Marvin 26, and Karen 20 during two observation sessions each between the ages of 3;8 and 4;11 These multi-proposition gesture sentences often contain more than two gestures; indeed, some contain eight or more gestures.

Most often, the children conjoin two action propositions. An example is shown in Figure 13. Marvin produces the following gesture sentence to tell his mother that he had just blown a bubble (proposition 1) and then the bubble went forward in the air (proposition 2).

BLOW—GO FORWARD

As another example, David produces the following sentence to request his mother to twist open the jar (proposition 1) and blow a bubble (proposition 2) so that he can clap it (proposition 3).

CLAP—David—TWIST—BLOW—Mother

The children also conjoin two attribute propositions, as well as action and attribute propositions. For example, Marvin produces the following sentence to comment on the fact that watches go on wrists (proposition 1) and are round (proposition 2).

wrist—watch—ROUND

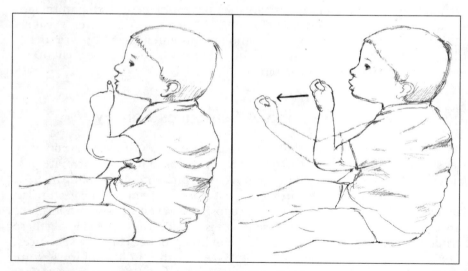

FIGURE 13. The Deaf Children Can Convey More Than One Proposition in a Gesture Sentence. Marvin holds his index finger at his mouth as though blowing on a bubble wand. Without breaking his flow of movement, he then forms his hand into an "O" shape which he moves away from his mouth, thus representing the bubble as it is blown forward. Marvin has concatenated two propositions into a single gesture sentence: *I blow bubbles* and *bubbles go forward*.

As another example of a complex sentence containing an attribute proposition, David produces the following sentence to comment on the fact that a lobster is ugly (attribute proposition) and dives (action proposition).

lobster—UGLY—DIVE—lobster

None of the children created explicit gestures for the links between the propositions within a sentence, that is, none created conjunctions. However, it is quite easy to infer such links from context (Goldin-Meadow & Mylander, 1984, 39–42). And when we do infer these links, we find that the deaf children's inferred conjunctions are precisely the same as those explicitly produced by children learning conventional languages (Bloom, Lahey, Hood, Lifter, & Fiess, 1980; Brown, 1973; Clark, 1973; El'konin, 1973; Menyuk, 1971; Miller, 1973; Smith, 1970).

Marvin's watch sentence and David's lobster sentence are good examples of propositions conjoined by "and." "Then" sentences contain propositions that are temporally (and perhaps even causally) related to each other. Marvin's bubble sentence is an example, as is the following example from David. David is asking Heidi (my fellow experimenter) to take out the glasses (proposition 1) *and then* he will don them (proposition 2).

TAKE OUT—glasses—DON

"But" sentences typically contain either a side-to-side headshake or a two-handed flip (see discussion of modulators in Chapter 8). As an example, David produces the following sentence while we are playing a game rolling toys to each other's legs. He is telling me that he thinks the pear will roll toward his leg (proposition 1) *but* the banana will not (proposition 2).

pear—banana + [headshake]—ROLL

Finally, "which" sentences are those in which an element in one proposition is restricted or qualified by the second proposition. For example, David produces the following sentence to ask Heidi to give him the penny (proposition 1) *which* is round (proposition 2).

ROUND—penny—David

Note that even if the "round" gesture is considered to be an adjective modifying penny, it still functions to convey a second piece of information about the penny and, in this sense, counts as a second proposition.

☐ Combining Underlying Predicate Frames

A complex sentence is the conjunction of two propositions. The frame underlying such a sentence ought to reflect this conjunction—it ought to be the sum of the predicate frames for the two propositions. For example, a sentence about a soldier beating a drum (proposition 1) and a cowboy sipping a straw (proposition 2) ought to have an underlying frame of six units—two predicates (beat, sip), two actors (soldier, cowboy), and two patients (drum, straw). If the deaf children's complex sentences are structured at an underlying level as their simple sentences are, we ought to see precisely the same pattern in their complex sentences as we saw in their simple sentences—that is, we should see a systematic decrease in, say, actor production probability as the number of units in the conjoined predicate frames increases. And the reasoning is the same—we should see this decrease in actor production probability because the actor has more competition for the limited number of slots in the sentence when it's part of a large underlying frame than when it's part of a smaller underlying frame.

This is precisely the pattern we find. Figure 14 presents David's production probability for actors in two-, three-, and four-gesture sentences that have six units underlying them (white bars), five units (gray bars), four units (hatched bars), and three units (black bars). Production probability, of course, increases as the number of gestures in the sentence increases from two to three to four. But what's important is that, for gesture sentences of a given length, production probability for actors decreases systematically as the number of units in the underlying propositions increases from three to four to five to six. We find systematic decreases not only for actors (as shown in Figure 14), but also for patients (Goldin-Meadow, 1982, 66). David produced enough complex sentences to do the analyses on his sentences alone. The other children did not, but when we combine all of the data for the other children, they too show the pattern seen in Figure 14 for actors and for patients (Goldin-Meadow, 1982, 66).

Sometimes when two propositions are conjoined, one element is redundant or "shared" across the propositions. For example, in the English sentence "Elaine cut apples and Mike ate apples," *apples* is shared across the two propositions (the second *apples* could be replaced by *them* and the pronoun would then mark in surface structure the fact that the element is shared). The deaf children's complex sentences also exhibit this type of redundancy, and at approximately the same rate as children learning language from conventional models (Goldin-Meadow, 1987, 117). The deaf children's sentences, at times, have one, two, and even three shared elements in underlying structure. For example, David produces the following sentence to comment on the fact that the horse climbs the house (proposition 1) and the horse sleeps (proposition 2).

CLIMB—SLEEP—horse

There are three units underlying the first proposition (actor, act, object—*horse, climb, house*) and two in the second (actor, act—*horse, sleep*), but one of those units is redundant (*horse* appears in both propositions).

The question is whether the shared element—the horse—should appear once or twice in the underlying predicate frame of the conjoined proposi-

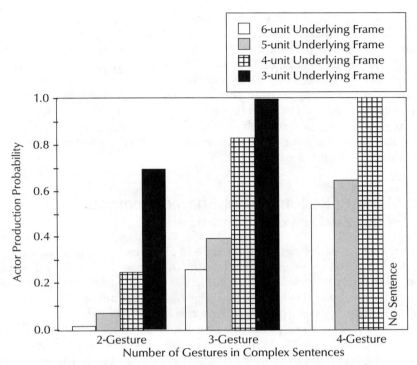

FIGURE 14. The Production of Gestures for Semantic Elements in Complex Sentences Depends on the Conjoined Predicate Frames Underlying That Sentence. The figure displays the likelihood that David will produce a gesture for an actor in two-, three-, and four-gesture complex sentences as a function of the conjoined predicate frames underlying that sentence. Like the production probability patterns seen in the simple sentences displayed in Figure 7, actors are more likely to be produced in sentences with smaller underlying frames, presumably because there is less "competition" for the limited number of slots in surface structure in these sentences. Not surprisingly, production probability goes up overall as the number of gestures in the sentences increases—but the pattern in relation to the underlying frame remains the same.

tions. If *horse* is allowed to appear twice—[(*horse* climbs house) & (*horse* sleeps)]—the sentence will have an underlying frame of five units. If *horse* is allowed to appear only once—*horse* [(climbs house) & (sleeps)]—the sentence will have an underlying frame of four units. In fact, it turns out that production probability decreases systematically with increases in underlying predicate frame *only if* shared elements appear once in the underlying frame (Goldin-Meadow, 1982).[1]

_____

[1] This finding has implications for which types of units can be conjoined in underlying predicate frames. "Horse climbs house" and "horse sleeps" are two full sentences. If we conjoin them at the underlying level, "horse" will appear twice—[(*horse* climbs house) & (*horse* sleeps)], which results in an underlying frame of five units. But some theorists suggest that units smaller

I am not arguing that the deaf children fail to attribute two roles to the climbing and sleeping horse at some, perhaps semantic or propositional, level. There is no reason to think they don't. However, the children's production probability patterns make it clear that we need a level between this semantic-propositional level and the surface level of the sentence—a level in which dual-role elements appear only once. We call this level underlying structure (see Goldin-Meadow, 1982, for discussion). This underlying level is a necessary feature of our descriptions of the deaf children's gesture systems because it is an essential component in our account of the surface properties of the children's sentences.

☐ Marking Redundant or Shared Elements in the Surface of a Sentence

Shared and unshared elements are treated alike in the underlying frame of the deaf children's complex sentences in the sense that they both appear only once. But these elements might be distinguished in the surface structure of complex sentences. In other words, the children might have some way of marking shared (or redundant) versus unshared elements.

The deaf children use production probability to mark thematic roles in their simple sentences. Might they use production probability to mark shared versus unshared roles in complex sentences? I am, in effect, suggesting that the probability of producing a gesture for a particular semantic element when it is involved in *both* propositions of a complex sentence (the shared element) might differ systematically from the probability of producing that same semantic element when it is involved in only *one* proposition of a complex sentence (the unshared element).

We conducted this analysis on David's sentences because only he had a sufficient number of shared and unshared elements to serve as a database. We found that David does indeed distinguish shared from unshared elements (Goldin-Meadow, 1987). Holding the number of gestures in surface structure constant, as well as the number of units in the underlying predicate frame, a patient that is shared across propositions is *less* likely to be gestured than a patient that appears in only one proposition (see Figure 15). The same pattern

than sentences can be conjoined at underlying levels, for example, verb phrase units like "climbs house" and "sleeps" (see Dik, 1968; Dougherty, 1970, 1971; Gleitman, 1965; and Lakoff & Peters, 1969, for discussion). If we allow verb phrases to be conjoined in the underlying predicate frame, "horse" will appear only once—*horse* [(climbs house) & (sleeps)], which results in an underlying frame of four units. We find that there is a systematic pattern in the data (a systematic decrease in production probability as the number of elements in the underlying predicate frame increases) only if we allow units smaller than the sentence to be conjoined in the underlying frame, that is, only if phrasal conjunction, as well as sentence conjunction, is allowed at underlying levels.

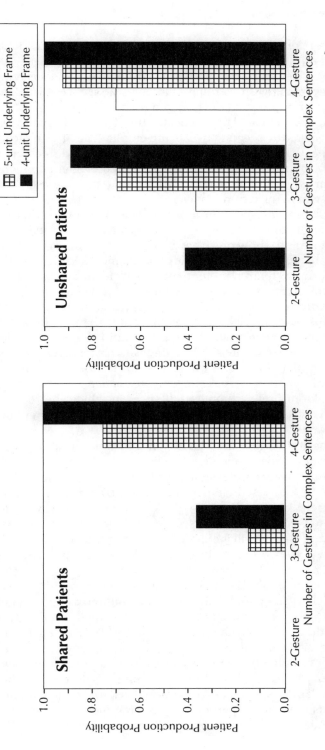

FIGURE 15. Shared Elements Are Less Likely to be Produced Than Unshared Elements. The figure displays how likely David is to produce a gesture for a shared (left graph) versus unshared (right graph) patient in two-, three-, and four-gesture complex sentences as a function of the conjoined predicate frames underlying that sentence. Shared patients are those that play a role in both propositions of a complex sentence; unshared patients play a role in only one. For both shared and unshared patients, production probability increases as the size of the frame underlying the sentence decreases from six to five to four units and, of course, it increases as the number of gestures in the sentence increases from two to three to four. Note, however, that, at every comparison point, shared patients are *less* likely to be produced than unshared patients. David thus reduces redundancy in his complex sentences.

121

holds for actors—actors that are shared across propositions are *less* likely to be gestured than actors that appear in only one proposition.

Gesturing shared elements less often than unshared elements is reminiscent of the strategy that English-learning children use to reduce redundancy— eliminating the second appearance of a shared element, for example, "I came and θ stayed." The speaker could have repeated the "I" ("I came and I stayed") but doing so feels like the second "I" is being emphasized. The typical pattern is to *not* repeat the redundant element. In fact, David's gesture sentences frequently involve complete ellipsis of shared elements, much like reduction in Japanese or Sinhalese (e.g., θ came and θ stayed; Lust, personal communication) where the redundant element is not mentioned at all. Thus, the basic principle of using some form of *reduction* to deal with shared elements is characteristic of child language, be it learned or invented.

However, David fails to show one bias that children learning conventional languages display in dealing with underlying redundancy. Recall from Chapter 3 that English-learning children prefer to produce and imitate complex sentences in which the element that can be reduced (i.e., the null element) is to the *right* of the expressed element (e.g., "*frogs* jump and θ catch flies," where θ follows and thus is to the right of "frogs"), rather than to the left (e.g., "frogs θ and kangaroos *jump*," where θ precedes and thus is to the left of "jump"). What this means, in effect, is that English-learners prefer sentences with shared actors (*frogs* jump and catch flies) rather than sentences with shared actions and/or patients (frogs and kangaroos *jump*). In contrast, Japanese-learning children prefer complex sentences in which the reduced or null element is to the *left* of the expressed element. David shows neither bias (Goldin-Meadow, 1987).

Lust (1981) has argued that the biases found in English- and Japanese-learners reflect the principal branching direction of the language each group is learning. English-learners prefer sentences in which the reduced element is to the *right* of the expressed element because they are learning a *right*-branching language. Japanese-learners prefer sentences in which the reduced element is to the *left* of the expressed element because they are learning a *left*-branching language. David is exposed to no language model and shows no bias whatsoever. David's data thus provide indirect support for Lust's hypothesis (1981).

At a larger level, this analysis of David's complex sentences illustrates another way in which the invented gestures of deaf children can bear on problems of language-learning. To the extent that the deaf children *fail* to develop regularities found in child languages learned from conventional language models, we have evidence (albeit tentative) for the importance of a language model in developing those regularities. In other words, the *absence* of a language property in the deaf children's gestural repertoire (e.g., a bias in underlying redundancy and its reduction traced back to principal branching direction) suggests that the property is fragile—a property whose development requires guidance from a conventional language model.

☐ Summary of Recursion

In sum, each of the 10 deaf children we have observed has developed a gesture system with the important property of recursion. Their gesture systems are generative. The children conjoin action and attribute propositions within a single sentence, as do children learning conventional languages, and the relations between those propositions (e.g., temporal, causal, contrastive, restrictive) are precisely the ones found in early child language.

Moreover, the complex gesture sentences the deaf children produce, like their simple sentences, are characterized by underlying predicate frames. These predicate frames combine systematically to create organizing structures that determine surface properties of sentences. The underlying frame is not just the conjunction of two predicate frames—it must take into account whether a semantic element plays a role in both frames. As such, it is a level of structure *between* semantic-propositional structure and surface structure, a level that we need to posit in order to account for regularities in the deaf children's complex gesture sentences.

Finally, the children's complex sentences have elements that are shared across propositions, and those shared elements are treated differently from unshared elements in surface structure—shared elements are gestured less often than unshared elements. This strategy is reminiscent of the strategy that children learning conventional languages use to reduce redundancy. However, the deaf child shows none of the biases for the *direction* of redundancy reduction found in children learning language from conventional models. Recursion is resilient, but other aspects of language that bear on how recursion is expressed (e.g., principal branching direction) may be fragile and crucially dependent on linguistic input.

These findings are important because they underscore how much like natural language the deaf children's gesture systems really are. Recursion is an essential property of all languages as it gives language its capacity to generate an infinite number of sentences. And the deaf children incorporate recursion into their systems. They also develop systematic ways of dealing with the redundancy that is introduced by recursion—they reduce it, as do all natural languages. However, they fail to display a bias in how redundancy is reduced, thus strongly suggesting that linguistic input (exposure to a language with a principal branching direction) is needed for a child to exhibit this bias. Here again, we have followed our two-step process. We first establish an equivalence between the deaf children's systems and the linguistic systems developed by children learning conventional languages. We then make inferences about how language is learned in general from the fact that the deaf children display certain properties of language in their gesture systems but fail to display others.

Building a System

I have, with minor exceptions, been describing the deaf children's gesture system as a steady state. But over the course of our observations, we did see some changes in the children's gestures. Some of the children were quite young when we first observed them (around a year and a half) and thus had a long way to go. Others were relatively advanced during our first observation sessions. Thus, a combination of longitudinal and cross-sectional observations contribute to what we know about the children's developmental trajectory. The most obvious developmental finding is that the children's utterances grow in size and scope.

☐ An Utterance Grows in Size and Scope

When we first observed Kathy and Abe, they were gesturing. However, they produced no more than one gesture at a time. Some of their gestures were pointing gestures and some were iconic gestures, but at no time during these early sessions did the children combine two gestures into a single sentence. Kathy and Abe were thus in a "one-gesture" period, akin to the one-word stage found in children learning conventional languages (e.g., Bloom, 1973). We can use the fact that these deaf children are limited to producing a single gesture at a time to make inferences about what makes all children go through a period in which they are limited to a single unit.

Why might a hearing child be limited to producing one word at a time? One possibility is that young children find it hard to remember two different words at one time. Another is that it is motorically difficult for young children to produce two different words as a single unit. But these explanations won't work for gesture. It seems easy enough to combine one pointing gesture with another pointing gesture—the child does not have to produce or hold two lexical forms in mind and thus there is little strain on either motor function or memory. The one-unit constraint found in all young communicators may therefore stem from deeper causes, ones tied to neither the modality nor the arbitrariness of the language.

The fact that the deaf children experience a one-gesture period comparable to the one-word period of children learning conventional languages suggests that the deaf children are following a *language* trajectory—their early gestures have the same constraints as early words. Moreover, their later steps are also in synchrony with children learning conventional languages.

Before describing the remaining stages that the deaf children go through, I need to say a word about the criterion we are using for "begins to produce." We give a child credit for a construction when that child first produces an instance of the construction, even if it is only one instance. Typically, the children do not produce only a single instance of a new construction and, more importantly, they almost always continue to produce instances of the construction in subsequent observation sessions. In other words, the construction really has entered the child's repertoire.

Kathy and Abe first began producing two-gesture sentences at ages 1;6 and 2;5, respectively—around the same time as English-learning children first produce two-word sentences (Brown, 1973), and only slightly later than ASL-learning children first produce two-sign sentences (Bonvillian et al., 1983). These early two-gesture sentences, for the most part, convey only one proposition, and do so using structures found in early child language learned from conventional models (see Chapter 10).

Four of the deaf children began producing more than one proposition within the bounds of a single sentence—complex sentences—during our observation sessions (the other six produced complex sentences when first observed). Mildred and Kathy first produced complex sentences at 2;2, Abe began at 2;5, and Donald began sometime between 3;1 and 3;11 (we did not observe Donald during this time period; when we resumed observations, he was already producing complex sentences). Children learning spoken (Brown, 1973) and signed (Hoffmeister, 1978) languages first produce sentences conveying more than one proposition around these same ages.

Thus, the deaf children's sentences grow in the same way as sentences do when children are exposed to conventional language models. The children first experience a one-word period during which they are limited to one gesture at a time. They then combine those gestures into two-word sentences characterized by simple structural properties. Finally, they produce longer sentences which convey two or more propositions. The deaf children's gesture sentences never get as consistently long as the sentences English-learners produce—they are closer in length to sentences produced by children whose language permits a great deal of ellipsis (e.g., Japanese or Sinhalese). Yet they do grow in patterned ways.

☐ The Utterance Grows Not Only in Size but Also in Organization: Nouns, Verbs, and Adjectives

Not only do the deaf children's gestures grow in length, but they also grow in coherence—they take on the properties of a *system*. One excellent way to explore the system underlying a language is to look at how nouns and verbs are treated within that language. Although we often think of nouns as names for objects and verbs as names for actions, in fact, nouns and verbs are defined by the roles they play in the structure of the language.

Do the deaf children have grammatical categories akin to nouns, verbs, and adjectives? We addressed this question by examining the gestures produced by David, our most prolific gesturer, over a two-year time period, from ages 2;10 to 4;10 (Goldin-Meadow et al., 1994). Our challenge was to figure out how to break into David's system of grammatical categories without knowing the properties of that system (or even whether the system existed).

Identifying Nouns, Verbs, and Adjectives in David's Gestures

No natural language wholly fails to distinguish noun and verb. Indeed, the noun-verb distinction is one of the 10 properties of language that Hockett (1977, 181) includes in his list of grammatical universals and it is a distinction that Sapir (1921, 119) considers essential to the "life of language." In fact, the noun-verb distinction is one of the few that has traditionally been accepted as a linguistic universal (e.g., Robins, 1952; Sapir, 1921) and whose status as a universal continues to be uncontested (e.g., Givon, 1979; Hawkins, 1988; Hopper & Thompson, 1984, 1988; Schachter, 1985; Thompson, 1988). Not surprisingly given its universal status, the noun-verb distinction is also found in conventional sign languages (Supalla & Newport, 1978).

However, languages vary in the way nouns and verbs manifest themselves—the syntactic positions they occupy, and the morphological inflections they assume. What is common across languages is the functional roles nouns and verbs play in discourse, and the semantic characteristics that have evolved as a function of these discourse roles (Hopper & Thompson, 1984, 1988; Sapir, 1921). Sapir (1921) grounds the universality of the noun-verb distinction in the basic fact that language consists of a series of propositions. On intuitive grounds, there must be something to talk about and something to be said (or to predicate) of this subject once it is brought into focus. According to Sapir, this particular distinction is of such fundamental importance that languages emphasize it by creating a formal barrier between the two terms of the proposition—the subject of discourse, that is, the noun, and the predicate of the discourse, the verb.

We follow Sapir (1921) in considering a noun to be the focus or subject of the discourse (i.e., the something that is talked about), and verbs and adjectives to be the predicates of the discourse (i.e., what is said of this something). Thus, if David uses an iconic gesture to focus attention on an object, it is coded as a noun. But if he uses the gesture to say something about that object (i.e., to predicate something of the object), it is coded as either a verb or an adjective, depending upon whether the gesture depicts an action or an attribute.

For example, if David uses the "flap" gesture (two palms, each held at a shoulder, arced to and fro as though flapping wings) to comment on a picture of a bird riding a bicycle with its wings on the handlebars (i.e., to focus attention on the bird rather than to comment on wing-flapping), the gesture is considered a *noun*. In contrast, if the "flap" gesture is used to describe a toy penguin that is flapping its wings, the gesture is considered a *verb* (although we do recognize that David could be commenting on the presence of the bird itself). As a second example, if David uses the "high" gesture (a flat palm held horizontally in the air) to comment on the fact that a cardboard chimney typically stands in the corner at Christmas time (i.e., to focus attention on the chimney rather than to comment on the chimney's height), the gesture is considered a *noun*. In contrast, if the "high" gesture is used to describe the temporary height of the tower before urging his mother to hit it with a hammer and topple it, the gesture is considered an *adjective*. Not surprisingly, material entities (cf. Bloom, 1990) turn out to be the most common subjects of the discourse—the nouns—and relations (actions and attributes) turn out to be the most common predicates—the verbs and adjectives.

There were, of course, occasions when it was particularly difficult to decide whether a gesture was a noun, verb, or adjective (just as it is often hard to decide whether a hearing child's word is a noun, verb, or adjective). In order not to force our intuitions into categorical decisions when none seemed just right, we classified such gestures as "unclear"—12% of the 915 gestures David produced could not unequivocally be assigned a grammatical category and thus were placed in this unclear category. Moreover, reliability for making our coding decisions was quite good. Reliability was established by having a second observer independently code a randomly selected portion of the videotapes. Interrater agreement between the two coders was 94% for determining whether a gesture was a noun, verb, adjective, or unclear. As in all of our analyses, the proof of the pudding is in the eating—the fact that the form distinctions described in the next sections pattern consistently with our noun, verb, and adjective decisions (made on the basis of discourse function) provides evidence for the categories themselves.

We found that David distinguishes nouns from verbs throughout the two-year period. Thus, like all natural languages, David's gestures have a noun-verb distinction. Interestingly, however, the way in which David maintains the distinction between nouns and verbs changes over time, becoming more and more linguistically sophisticated with age. I describe the three stages David traverses in the next section.

From Separate Forms, to Separate Lexicons, to Separate Grammatical Markings and Positions

Initially, David uses pointing gestures to fill noun roles and iconic gestures to fill verb and adjective roles. Thus, at the earliest stage, David distinguishes nouns from verbs and adjectives through a gross distinction in gesture form: The point, a stationary and directed index finger, signals nominal functions; iconic gesture forms signal predicate functions.

Sometime after age 2;10, David starts to use his iconic gestures as nouns, while continuing to use them as verbs and adjectives. The question is whether he finds some other way to distinguish between nouns, verbs, and adjectives now that gesture form no longer serves the purpose. English-learners, at the earliest stages, maintain inter-category boundaries by having distinct lexicons for nouns, verbs, and adjectives. And they do so despite the fact that the English language does *not* have distinct lexicons. In other words, there are words in English that cross noun-verb boundaries, but young learners don't seem to notice. For example, "comb" can be both a noun and a verb. Although young English-learners do use words like "comb" at the earliest stages of language-learning, they use these words in only one role (Macnamara, 1982). A child might use "comb" to describe what she does to her doll's hair, but then would *not* also use "comb" to refer to the instrument involved in this activity. It is not until later in development that the child begins to use the same word in two different roles.

David shows this same constraint. He restricts his use of a particular iconic gesture to a single role. For example, David uses his "laugh" gesture as a noun (to refer to Santa Claus) and never as a verb. He violates these boundaries for the first time at age 3;3, when he uses the same gesture as a noun and a verb. Thus, like young children learning conventional languages, David does *not* violate inter-category boundaries at the earliest stages of development. His first inclination is to respect these boundaries as do all young communicators. When gesture form (i.e., pointing versus iconic forms) no longer serves to distinguish nouns from verbs and adjectives in David's gesture system, he maintains the distinction lexically, that is, by using separate lexical items as nouns, verbs, and adjectives.

Eventually, however, English-learning children do learn words that cross the noun-verb boundary, that is, words like "comb." But when they do, they treat the noun uses of the word differently from the verb uses: (1) Noun uses appear in different positions within a sentence than do verb uses; that is, they are marked differently with respect to syntax (e.g., "I *comb* my hair" vs. "The *comb* is lovely"). (2) Noun uses are marked with different inflections than are verb uses; that is, they are marked differently with respect to morphology (e.g, "I *combed* my hair" vs. "The *combs* are lovely").

David begins to use the same iconic gesture as both noun and verb at age 3;3. And, like children learning conventional languages, when he does, he uses morphological and syntactic techniques to distinguish the different uses (see Figure 16). Nouns are more likely to be abbreviated and less likely to be inflected (morphological distinctions) than verbs in David's system. In addition, nouns are more likely to precede pointing gestures and verbs are more likely to follow them (a syntactic distinction) in David's system. For example, if using a twist gesture as a noun to mean "jar," David produces the gesture with only one rotation rather than several (with abbreviation), produces it in neutral space (without inflection), and produces it *before* a pointing gesture at the jar (pre-point). In contrast, if using the gesture as a verb to mean "twist," he produces the gesture with several rotations (without abbreviation), produces it near the jar (with inflection), and produces it *after* the pointing gesture at the jar (post-point).

Interestingly, adjectives are a mixed category in David's system, as they are in many languages (Thompson, 1988; Dixon, 1994). In David's gestures,

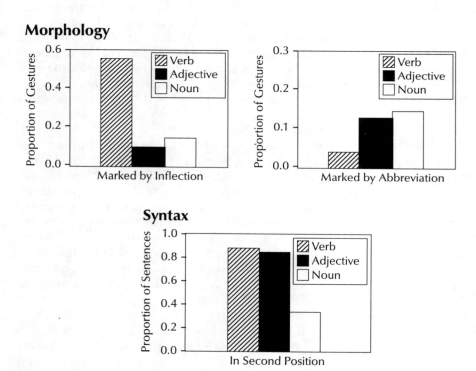

FIGURE 16. The Deaf Child Can Distinguish Nouns from Verbs from Adjectives. The figure displays the proportion of verb, adjective, and noun gestures that David inflected (top left graph), abbreviated (top right graph), or placed in the second position of a two-gesture sentence (bottom graph). Nouns were abbreviated and rarely placed in second position; verbs were inflected and frequently placed in second position. Adjectives resembled nouns in terms of morphology (abbreviated rather than inflected) but verbs in terms of syntax (placed in second rather than first position).

adjectives resemble nouns in terms of morphological markings, but verbs in terms of syntactic position. For example, when David uses the adjective "broken," he produces only one breaking-apart motion rather than several, or the motion with only one hand rather than two (with abbreviation), and produces the gesture in neutral space (without inflection)—that is, he treats it like a noun. However, when positioning it in a sentence, David produces "broken" *after* a pointing gesture at the broken object (post-point)—that is, he treats it like a verb. David thus maintains a distinction between nouns, verbs, and adjectives, but now he does so *grammatically* rather than lexically.

Are the Nouns and Verbs Grammatical Categories or Names for Objects and Actions?

We began our search for a noun-verb distinction in David's gesture system with an intuitive guess as to which of his iconic gestures are nouns and which are verbs. Using these noun and verb categories, we found both morphological (i.e., variations within the gesture itself) and syntactic (i.e., variations across a string of gestures) patterns that distinguish between nouns and verbs in David's system. We take these formal patterns to be evidence for the noun and verb categories we code in David's gestures since (as described in Chapter 7) the former (the patterns) are formulated in terms of the latter (the categories). The question then arises—what are these categories that we call *nouns* and *verbs* in David's gestures? Are they truly grammatical categories that are part of a linguistic system, or are they semantic categories naming objects and actions? After all, as is the case in all natural languages and particularly child language (Brown, 1958), most of David's nouns turned out to refer to objects, and most of his verbs turned out to refer to actions.

To pursue this question, we recoded a subset of David's gestures in terms of whether they referred to objects and actions (as opposed to nouns and verbs). We used contextual criteria developed by Huttenlocher and Smiley (1987, 1989) to determine when a lexical item refers to an object versus an action, and we then determined whether David's noun-verb categories could be reduced to object-action categories. We found that they could *not*, particularly after age 3;3. Before age 3;3, coding David's gestures in terms of nouns and verbs resulted in precisely the same distributions as coding them in terms of objects and actions. However, after age 3;3, the two sets of categories were distinguishable and, where the two sets of codes diverged, the morphological and syntactic devices displayed in Figure 16 patterned according to the noun-verb codes rather than object-action codes (Goldin-Meadow, 2003a; Goldin-Meadow et al., 1994, 300–1). In other words, prior to age 3;3, David's categories could have been grammatical (noun-verb) or semantic (object-action), but after 3;3, there was good evidence that they were grammatical.

Do these findings guarantee that the categories we have isolated are truly the grammatical categories of noun and verb rather than the semantic categories of object and action? In fact, the data suggest only that the noun and verb codes we have used to describe David's gestures are not reducible to one particular set of contextual codes (albeit one that has been used in the literature exploring early nouns and verbs in hearing children; cf. Huttenlocher & Smiley, 1987, 1989). Given the bootstrap nature of our coding procedure, this is as good as it gets. We can never prove beyond a doubt that the categories we isolate are the grammatical categories of noun and verb. Nevertheless, the fact that these categories pattern as do nouns and verbs in natural language suggests that the categories are grammatical and part of a linguistic system. I highlight three of the ways in which David's nouns and verbs resemble natural languages in the following paragraphs.

First, there is coherence between the morphological and syntactic devices in David's system. The morphological devices work together to distinguish the grammatical categories noun and verb: inflections mark verbs, abbreviations mark nouns. Importantly, virtually *no* gestures are produced with both markings (Goldin-Meadow et al,, 1994, 290). Moreover, nouns and verbs occupy different positions in gesture sentences, verbs occurring after the pointing gesture and nouns occurring before the pointing gesture.

Second, the particular way in which the morphological and syntactic devices are used to distinguish adjectives from nouns and verbs is reminiscent of patterns found in natural languages. In particular, adjectives in David's system behave like nouns morphologically (they are abbreviated rather than inflected) but like verbs syntactically (they occur after the pointing gesture), as do adjectives in some natural languages (cf. Thompson, 1988; Dixon, 1994).

Finally, in the few instances in David's system where verbs are combined within a single sentence with iconic gestures used as nouns (as opposed to pointing gestures), the gestures adhere to the syntactic rules of the system. For example, David produces the following gesture sentence to ask me to give him a grape:

  GRAPE—GIVE

In this sentence, the iconic gesture "eat" is used as a noun referring to the grape. David has therefore placed his noun iconic gesture playing a patient role ("grape") before his verb iconic gesture ("eat"), just as he routinely places pointing gestures playing a patient role before verb iconic gestures:

  grape—GIVE

In other words, when noun iconic gestures are produced in sentences with verbs, they take over the slot typically filled by pronoun pointing gestures. Thus, the grammatical categories noun and verb are elements within David's syntactic system and, as such, are governed by the rules of that system, just as nouns and verbs are governed by the rules of syntax in natural language.

☐ Reorganization Across the System

To recap David's trajectory—after abandoning a distinction between nouns, verbs, and adjectives based purely on gesture form, David uses separate sets of lexical items as nouns, verbs, and adjectives. Thus, he persistently respects inter-category boundaries in his early lexicon, as do children learning conventional languages, be they spoken (Huttenlocher & Smiley, 1987) or signed (Petitto, 1992). At 3;3, David changes once again. He now uses some of his lexical items for more than one function, most commonly using the same gestural form as a noun and a verb. However, he continues to maintain a distinction between categories by abbreviating nouns but not verbs (akin to derivational morphology), by producing verbs but not nouns in marked locations (akin to inflectional morphology), and by producing verbs and nouns in distinct positions in gesture sentences (akin to syntax). Thus, at 3;3, David begins to use grammatical devices to maintain inter-category boundaries.

There are other changes that coincide with what appears to be the onset of a grammatical system in David's gestures. Prior to age 3;3, David produces all of his iconic gestures in contexts consistent with their grammatical function (Goldin-Meadow et al., 1994, 301). During the first three observation sessions, he produces verbs *only* in contexts in which the relevant action and object are both present, and nouns *only* in contexts in which the action and object are both absent—prototypical contexts for identifying actions and objects (cf. Huttenlocher & Smiley, 1987; 1989). Thus, just as children learning English initially distinguish between nouns and verbs on the basis of a semantic rather than a grammatical distinction (Macnamara, 1982), David may be basing his first categories on a semantic (object-action) rather than a grammatical (noun-verb) distinction. However, at age 3;3, David starts using noun and verb gestures in intermediate contexts where the action is absent and the object is present—precisely the moment when he introduces grammatical devices to keep noun and verb categories distinct. Thus, David begins to use gestures in what amounts to ambiguous action and object contexts at just the moment that he secures his grammatical system for distinguishing nouns from verbs.

At this same point in development, David's gestures can, for the first time, be characterized as having two levels of structure—structure across gestures within a sentence (akin to syntactic structure), and structure within each gesture (akin to morphological structure). Before this age, there is evidence for structure across gestures in the deaf child's gesture system (Chapters 10 and 11), but no evidence that David has broken his gestures into component parts. At age 3;3, however, David begins to systematize his lexicon, changing it from a collection of gestures, each treated as a whole, into a system in which the component parts of each gesture contrast in a meaningful way with the component parts of the other gestures in the lexicon (Chapter

9; Goldin-Meadow & Mylander, 1990; Goldin-Meadow et al., 1995). Handshape and motion components combine to form word-stems. These stems are then fed to the next level of the system—they are abbreviated when used as nouns or inflected when used as verbs, and placed into distinctive positions in sentences. Thus, we see sets of units corresponding to the different levels found in conventional languages (word-stem morphology, derivational and inflectional morphology, syntax) which come together at the same moment in development and constitute the building blocks of David's gesture system.

The transformation of David's lexicon from an unorganized collection of gestures into a system of contrasting morphemes that work within a grammatical system co-occurs with yet one other change. At age 3;3, David begins to refer, either via pointing gestures (Chapter 8) or the placement of iconic gestures (Chapter 10), to objects that are not in the here-and-now. Recall that at this age, David begins to point at (or displace his iconic gestures toward) objects in the room to refer to objects that are *not* in the room (Butcher et al., 1991). Thus, David begins to systematize his lexicon in the context of a grammatical system at the same time as he begins to use his gestures in an increasingly symbolic fashion.

To summarize, we see the onset of four different types of changes in David's gesture system taking place at precisely the same point in development:

- David begins to use gestures in ambiguous contexts; no longer are all of his gestures that refer to objects found in noun contexts, nor are all of his gestures that refer to actions found in verb contexts.
- David begins to use grammatical devices (inflectional morphology, syntactic ordering) to mark nouns, verbs, and adjectives.
- David begins to form lexical stems out of smaller gestural components (derivational morphology).
- David begins to use pointing gestures and the placement of his iconic gestures to refer to objects that are not in the here-and-now.

The relationship among these changes is not clear. Some seem clearly linked—the first two, for example. David's initial categories may be semantic. At that point, he can't even be said to have nouns and verbs in his system, just names for objects and actions. But at some point, David starts to use forms that look like nouns in contexts that are not prototypical object contexts, and forms that look like verbs in contexts that are not prototypical action contexts. It is at this moment that David can be said to have grammatical categories, and it is at this moment that David introduces devices (inflections, order) to mark those categories and thus resolve whatever uncertainty is introduced by using nouns and verbs in ambiguous contexts. The first two changes thus both seem to result from the introduction of grammatical categories into the system.

The second and the third changes both result from the decomposition of gestures into their component parts—morphemic units that serve a syntactic function (marking grammatical categories), and morphemic units that serve a word-building function (creating lexical stems).

Finally, the fourth change reflects a continuing pull away from the here-and-now, a pressure that could contribute to the formation of a linguistic system guided by its own rules. In fact, all four changes may reflect the child's ever-growing inclination to treat the language he is developing as a system unto itself—a problem space of its own (cf. Karmiloff-Smith, 1992).

Thus, the changes seen in David's gesture system at age 3;3 could result from a single developmental process. The impetus for a massive reorganization of this sort might be the child's maturational state—that is, the fact that he has reached a certain age. Or perhaps the impetus comes from the state of the gesture system itself—that is, the fact that the system has become sufficiently cumbersome to require reorganization. We hope to do developmental analyses of the gesture systems of the remaining deaf children in our study to pull apart these possibilities. If changes of this sort occur in all of the children at precisely the same moment, we will have good evidence that the reorganization reflects a single process—a maturational process if the reorganization occurs at the same age across all of the children, or a data-driven process if the reorganization occurs at the same point in the development of the children's gesture systems. If, however, the changes occur at different moments in different children, or don't occur at all, we will be able to search for factors in the child's world or gesture system that might account for the individually paced changes.

Whatever the outcome of such analyses, it is clear that the reorganization that occurs in David's gestures results in a *system* that looks very much like natural language. Once again, we can make inferences about language-learning in general from these findings. We know that the development of this system does *not* depend on guidance from a conventional language model. The process may, however, be data-driven in the sense that each developmental step depends on input from the previous step—input that the child himself has generated.

CHAPTER

Beyond the Here-and-Now:
The Functions Gesture Serves

The deaf children use their gestures in the same way that hearing children use their words—to make requests and to make comments, not only about the here-and-now, but also about objects and events that are not in the room. In addition to these rather obvious uses for language, the children use their gestures for some of language's more subtle uses—to make generic statements, to tells stories, to talk to themselves, and even to comment on their own and others' gestures.

☐ Making Requests and Comments in the Here-and-Now

Like children learning conventional languages, the deaf children request objects and actions from others but they do so with gesture. Donald produces the following gesture sentence to ask Robyn, one of my assistants, to blow up a balloon.

>balloon—Robyn

Or Kathy produces the following sentence to ask Heidi to move a puzzle piece to the board.

>MOVE—puzzle board

As a final example, Dennis produces the following sentence to ask his mother to hammer a nail.

>nail—HAMMER

Moreover, and again like children learning conventional languages, the deaf children comment on the actions and attributes of objects and people in the room. For example, Chris produces the following gesture sentence to comment on the fact that a toy soldier is, at that very moment, marching.

MARCH—soldier

Or Donald produces the following sentence to comment on the fact that a balloon in a picture is floating off in space.

balloon—GO UP

Finally, Tracy produces the following sentence to comment that the trunk of an elephant in a picture book is quite long.

trunk—LONG

☐ Commenting on the Non-Present

Among language's most important functions is making reference to objects and events that are not perceptible to either the speaker or the listener— displaced reference (cf. Hockett, 1960). Displacement allows us to describe a lost hat, to complain about a friend's slight, and to ask advice on college applications. If we were to communicate only about what is immediately in front of us, it is not at all clear that we'd need as complex and productive a system as language is.

Can our deaf children communicate about non-present objects and events? We addressed this question by looking for instances of displaced reference on the videotapes of four deaf children (Abe, David, Marvin, and Karen) between the ages of 2;3 and 5;1, and as a comparison group, 18 English-learning hearing children between the ages of 1;4 and 3;5 (Morford & Goldin-Meadow, 1997). We found that all four of the deaf children and all 18 of the hearing children communicated about non-present topics, and produced more and more of these communications over time. However, we also found that the deaf children did not begin to communicate about non-present topics until age 2;7, while the hearing children were already communicating about the non-present when we first observed them at 1;4 (see Figure 17).

Despite their delay in the onset of displaced reference, the deaf children's developmental trajectory, once begun, was precisely the same as the hearing children's. The children first referred to non-present objects, actions, attributes, and locations (dark portions of the bars in Figure 17), next to proximal events (that is, events that had just recently taken place; striped portions), and finally to distal or non-actual events (events in the more distant past or even events that had never actually happened; white portions). This pattern is evident at the group level in Figure 17, but it holds as well for each of the four deaf children observed longitudinally. Karen first referred

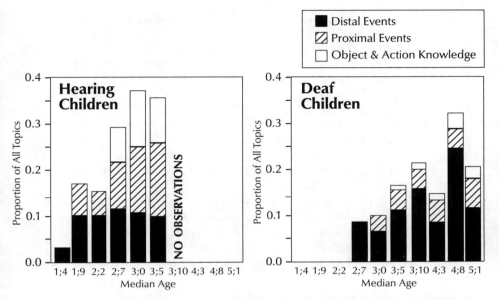

FIGURE 17. Deaf Children Follow the Same Developmental Steps as Hearing Children in Communicating about the Non-Present but They Start Later. The figure displays the proportion of topics that are about the non-present in a group of English-learning hearing children and gesture-creating deaf children. Note that the hearing children begin producing communications about the non-present approximately a year before the deaf children. However, once begun, the children's developmental pattern is the same: The children first convey non-present information about present objects and actions; they then convey proximal events not present in the immediate context; finally they convey distal events in the past, future, or hypothetical.

to non-present objects, actions, attributes, or locations at age 3;4, to proximal events at 3;6, and to distal and non-actual events at 4;0. Comparable onset ages were 2;5, 2;10, and 3;7 for Abe, and 2;11, 3;1, and 3;9 for Marvin. David referred both to non-present objects, actions, attributes, or locations and to proximal events in his first session at 2;10, but did not begin to refer to distal or non-actual events until 3;3.

In their earliest references to the non-present, the children describe what they know about an object or action and go beyond what's visible in doing so (dark bars in Figure 17). Marvin produces the following gesture sentence to comment on the action that is characteristically done on footballs and rubber balls but that is *not* taking place at the time.

football—rubber ball—KICK

A hearing child says, "This is for looking with," when her mother hands her a toy mirror covered with nonreflective foil, thus referring to an action that is typically done with mirrors but cannot be done with this mirror.

Next, both groups of children refer to events that take place prior to or after the communicative act but that still occur during the observation session, that is, they refer to proximal events (striped bars). After blowing a large bubble, Abe produces the following gesture sentence to indicate what happened to the bubble.

    bubble—EXPAND

As a comparable example in speech, a hearing child says, "See, I flipped over," immediately after doing a flip on the couch. This second type of displaced reference differs from the first in that the child describes an entire, specific event rather than a piece of an event. However, the event described is still very much tied to the present context.

In the final type of displaced communication the children develop, they refer to an event in the past, an event in the future, a potential event, or a fantasy event (white bars). As an example, David produces the following string of gesture sentences to indicate that, in preparation for setting up the cardboard chimney for Christmas, the family is going to move a chair downstairs.

    chair—MOVE AWAY
    chair—downstairs
    CHIMNEY—MOVE AWAY—MOVE HERE

The "move away" gesture is produced in the direction of the chair (that is, it's inflected for its patient), and the "move here" gesture is produced in the direction of the cardboard chimney (it too is inflected for its patient). As an example in speech, a hearing child talks of the future when asked how old she is: "And after three, I'm going to be four." Distal and non-actual events provide particularly striking evidence of the deaf children's ability to think and communicate about the non-present, and each of the four deaf children we have examined has examples of such references. However, these references are relatively rare in comparison to the first two categories of displaced reference, and relatively rare in comparison to hearing children's use of this category.

Thus, despite the absence of a shared linguistic code, the deaf children succeed in evoking the non-present in their communications. The deaf children refer to the non-present less frequently and at later ages than the hearing children. However, both groups follow an identical developmental path, adding increasingly abstract categories of displaced reference to their repertoires in the same sequence.

☐ Making Generic Statements

Generic statements ("birds fly") refer to an entire category of objects (all birds, not just the bird in my livingroom) and highlight qualities of that category that are essential, enduring, and timeless (flying, as opposed to having a broken wing; Lyons, 1977). Generic statements are thus made about categories that are coherent, stable entities, often called *kinds* (cf. Gopnik & Meltzoff, 1997). The way in which languages express generics varies considerably (Krifka et al., 1995), but all languages provide some means for making generic statements.

Do the deaf children use their gestures to make generic statements? Individual objects (the bird in my livingroom) are there for the naming, but a class of objects (all birds) does not present itself as such and must be constructed. It might therefore be difficult, perhaps impossible, for a deaf child who is not exposed to conventional language not only to construct classes of objects but also to use gesture to make statements about those classes. We addressed this question by looking for generics in the gestures of four deaf children—Abe, David, Marvin, and Karen—when they were between 3;8 and 4;11 (Goldin-Meadow, Gelman, & Mylander, 2003).

If it turns out that the deaf children do make generic statements (as it will), we can then ask whether they use those generics in the same way as children exposed to conventional language. There are no formal restrictions on which domains can support generic statements—it is possible to make generic claims about animals, artifacts, plants, food, and so on. However, Gelman and Tardif (1998) found that both Chinese and American adults produced many more generics for animals than for artifacts. Gelman and Tardif (1998, 227) suggest that this bias reflects the fact that the adults' animal concepts are structured differently from their concepts in other domains—animal concepts are conceptualized as deep (retaining identity over transformations; Keil, 1989, and having many similarities in common that promote rich inferences, Gelman, 1988). This conceptual difference is then reflected in the adults' propensity to form category-broad, generic statements. Hearing children receive models for this animacy bias in the generics they hear. If they display the bias, it could reflect either their own conceptual organization or the influence of the linguistic model that their parents provide. However, if the deaf children display the animacy bias in their gestures, it must reflect the children's own conceptual organization developed without benefit of a language model.

We began our search for generics in the deaf children's gestures by examining all of their references to objects. Recall that the deaf children have two ways of referring to objects: (1) deictic gestures, such as pointing at the bird, and (2) iconic gestures, such as flapping two hands in the air, a "fly" gesture used as a noun to refer to a bird (see Chapter 12). When a deaf child uses a gesture like "fly" to refer to a bird, that child is, in effect, saying "that's a bird." However, the "fly" gesture goes beyond the label "bird" in that it identifies the particular property of the bird the child is focusing on. The gesture consequently reveals what the child means by "bird." Thus, all of the deaf child's iconic gestures used as nouns are, in this sense, categoricals. The question is whether any of them can be considered generic.

We relied on contextual cues, both from the discourse and from our knowledge of the available objects and pictures, to identify generics in the deaf children's gestures. We coded a gesture as a *generic* if it represented a prototypical property found in all members of the class to which the object belonged, and if it appeared to refer, not to that particular object, but to a class of objects. To this end, we required that the properties reflected in the child's gesture *not* be present in the particular object that elicited the gesture. For example, if the child produced a "fly" gesture to comment on a bird that was clearly not flying, that gesture was a candidate for a generic. More convincing still, there were times when the property highlighted in the child's comment on an object was true of the class to which that object belonged, but not true of the particular object itself, for instance, "fly" was used to identify a bird that could not fly (a picture of a bird that had its wings grasped firmly on the handlebars of the bicycle it was riding). These were the most convincing cases simply because they illustrate a crucial aspect of generic knowledge—that it is not rendered invalid by the existence of what appears to be a counterexample (Prasada, 2000). In addition, we noted the domain of each generic, classifying it as either animal (including people and animal parts), artifact, or other.

We found that three of the four deaf children made generic statements. The children produced generics in 1.4% of their references to objects (including both points and iconic gestures used as nouns). Although low, these rates are similar to those found in American and Chinese hearing adults (Gelman & Tardif, 1998)—0.79% and 0.19% of utterances, respectively, in naturally occurring activities in the home, and 3.6% and 1.4%, respectively, in book-reading contexts that are more like our spontaneous play sessions.

As an example of a generic, David produced a "fly" gesture meaning "bird" in response to a picture of an empty nest to indicate that birds live there. He was making the generic statement "nests are where birds live." As another example, David pointed at a picture of an unmoving pinwheel, pointed at a picture of an unconnected wheel, and then produced a "go around" gesture. The child was making the generic statement "wheels go around." As a final example, Abe produced an "eat" gesture in response to a picture of a squirrel in a tree. There were nuts nearby but, importantly, there was no eating taking place in the picture. The child was making the generic statement "squirrels eat nuts."

In addition, the deaf children used a greater percentage of their generics for animals than for artifacts: 61% versus 13%. Importantly, this animacy bias was *not* found in the gestures the children used to refer to objects but not to categorize those objects (e.g., a point at a cat or a table): 35% versus 47%. Thus, the animacy bias is specific to generics—it doesn't reflect a general tendency to gesture more about animals than artifacts.

To summarize, the deaf children produce generics in their gestures despite the fact that they are not exposed to conventional language. A language model is clearly not essential for a child to come up with the idea of making generic statements. In addition, the deaf children produce more generics for animals than for artifacts—the same animacy bias seen in both American and Chinese hearing adults. Gelman and Tardif (1998) suggest that this bias reflects a common conceptual basis for generic use in English and Mandarin. Our data take the argument one step farther and suggest that this conceptual basis does not underlie conventional languages alone but also guides self-created communication systems. The conceptual organization that leads communicators to form generic statements about animals more often than artifacts thus appears to be present in child minds, even those developed without benefit of a language model.

☐ Telling Stories

Narrative is one of the most powerful tools that human beings possess for organizing and interpreting experience. Not only is narrative found universally across cultures (Miller & Moore, 1989), but no other species is endowed with this capacity. Moreover, narrative emerges remarkably early in human development. Children from many sociocultural backgrounds, both within and beyond the United States, begin to recount their past experiences during the second and third years of life

Do the deaf children use their gestures to tell stories? We examined the videotapes of four deaf children (Abe, David, Karen, and Marvin) between the ages of 2;3 to 5;11 looking for examples of narratives (Phillips, Goldin-Meadow, & Miller, 1999, 2001). Narratives, by definition, describe events that are displaced from the here-and-now (Bruner, 1986; Labov & Waletzky, 1967; Polanyi, 1985). To identify narratives in our deaf children's gestures, we used the criterion that Sperry (Sperry & Sperry, 1996; Miller & Sperry, 1988) uses to isolate the earliest narratives in hearing children's talk: A narrative contains at least two topic-centered utterances, one of which refers to displaced action. For example, a preschool hearing child produced the following string of sentences which meet the criterion for a narrative: "A duck went out on Halloween. When the duck dressed up like a bear, he scared people. Then went trick-or-treating" (Hudson & Shapiro, 1991). The narratives young children produce are not likely to win any literary prizes but they do count as stories, albeit simple ones.

As in all of our analyses, we determine the boundaries between gestured utterances using motoric criteria. If a child drops his or her hands or pauses between gestured strings, this signals the end of a gesture "utterance." The child has to produce two such utterances, each centered on the same non-present event, in order to produce a narrative. Using this criterion, we find that all four of the deaf children examined produce simple narratives. They tell stories about events they or others have experienced in the past, events they hope will occur in the future, and events that are flights of imagination. For example, Marvin produced the following narrative at age 5;3 in response to a picture of a car. His mother confirmed the tale by telling it later in her own words.

Utterance 1: BREAK—[away = narrative marker]—dad—CAR GOES ONTO TRUCK (flat right hand glides onto back of flat left hand)

Utterance 2: CRASH—[away = narrative marker]

Gloss: Dad's car broke and went onto a tow truck. It crashed.

Note that, in addition to producing gestures to describe the event itself, Marvin produces what we've called a narrative marker. Marvin recognizes that he is not talking about an event that is taking place in the here-and-now. Rather, he is describing a real event that happened in another time and place. Marvin indicates this stance with an "away" gesture—a palm or point hand extended or arced away from the body (see Chapter 8 and Morford & Goldin-Meadow, 1997). David also uses this gesture, and both children produce it exclusively in narratives. The "away" gesture marks a piece of gestural discourse as a narrative in the same way that "once upon a time" is often used to signal a story in spoken discourse.

Like children learning conventional languages (Burger & Miller, 1999), some of the deaf children told many stories, others told few. Despite this variability, the children display very similar structural patterns in their narratives. All of the children include in their stories *setting information* (implicit references to the details of the situation in which the story takes place), *voluntary actions* (the major goal-directed action of the protagonist that weaves the story together), and *complications* (actions by other people, animals, or things "out there" in the world which interfere with the protagonist's action). Three (David, Abe, and Karen) go further and produce narratives containing *temporal order* (the order in which the events are laid out in the story mirror the order in which those events actually occurred) as well. Only David produces narratives containing an explicit *orientation* (an explicit, summarizing statement encapsulating information concerning setting and action at the beginning of a narrative before the details of the story are divulged). For example, David produced the following narrative at age 5;2 illustrating all five features. David was playing with an assortment of toys on the floor in the living room and came upon a toy rabbit, which triggered a memory of an incident involving the family's pet rabbit (see the "Rabbit Story" videoclip at www.psypress.com/goldinmeadow).

> **Utterance 1:** toy rabbit
>
> **Utterance 2:** backyard (where the pet rabbit is in a cage)
>
> **Utterance 3:** backyard—OPEN—HOP—CHOMP—backyard—toy rabbit—backyard
>
> **Gloss:** We have a rabbit like this one out there. Someone opened the cage and the rabbit hopped out and chomped on something in the backyard.

This narrative is more fully formed than the story about the broken car. David establishes from the beginning where the story takes place and that it is about his pet rabbit by providing a simple *orientation* ("We have a rabbit like this out there"). David then moves through the tale describing how someone opened the cage (presumably to play with the rabbit), which constitutes the *voluntary action* of the protagonist. The rabbit provides a *complication* through its actions, which were independent of the protagonist's wishes or goals. Finally, David recounts the events in the order in which they actually occurred, thus displaying *temporal ordering*. The order and content of this story were corroborated by David's mother, who later told it in her own words adding such details as who let the rabbit out of its cage and what the rabbit ate.

David was the only child who produced enough narratives for us to examine a developmental trajectory. He acquired his narrative skill by adding one feature at a time in a manner completely consistent with the way hearing children develop their narratives (McCabe & Peterson, 1991; Hudson & Shapiro, 1991). David's earliest narratives contained *setting information* but no other features. He systematically added features over developmental time, first incorporating *voluntary actions* into his narratives, then *complications, temporal order*, and eventually *orientation*.

In addition to these structural and developmental similarities, we also find similarities in content. The deaf children's narratives focus on the same types of events as those told by hearing children (Burger & Miller, 1999; Miller & Sperry, 1988)—emotional gain in their positive narratives (e.g., enjoying an activity, being praised for completing a difficult task) and physical harm in their negative narratives (e.g., falling down, getting a shot). Moreover, the deaf children show a bias toward narrating events with a positive valence, consistent with patterns found in studies of some European-American children (middle-class children; Burger & Miller, 1999) but not others (working-class children; Miller & Sperry, 1988). The different biases found in the children studied by Miller and her colleagues undoubtedly reflect the kinds of stories these children hear. The deaf children's biases cannot, of course, reflect the *verbal* information in stories that the adults in their lives tell (although they could reflect patterns in whatever nonverbal behaviors accompany those stories, cf. Ochs & Capps, 1996). Their biases thus provide insight into the kinds of events children experience and witness, and how those events are keyed in their cultures through nonverbal means.

The narratives told by the hearing children studied by Miller and her colleagues (Miller, 1996; Miller, Wiley, Fung, & Liang, 1997) are co-narrated collaborations between caregiver and child—some turns are contributed by the caregiver, others by the child. In contrast, the deaf children's narratives are entirely self-generated. However, the hearing parents of our deaf children were committed to teaching their children spoken language and treating them like normally hearing children. Thus, it is possible that the parents engineered co-narrations with their children, despite the children's inability to hear. These co-narrations, particularly if they included mother's gestures that their children could understand, might then have served as models for the children's self-generated narrations.

We reviewed our tapes to determine whether the deaf children engaged in co-narrations with their hearing mothers, and found only three co-narrations, two from David and one from Marvin. In two of these co-narrations, the mothers produced no gestures along with their speech. It is thus unclear how much (if any) of the narrative the child actually understood. The co-narration that contained gesture was produced by David and his mother when he was age 4;10. David was playing on the floor in the living room with me, and his mother was sitting in a nearby easy chair. The mother noticed a Santa Claus doll in the pile of toys and began the following narrative.

1. *Mom*	"David . . . Hey . . . Dave . . . David, does Santa Claus . . . look at me" [+ tap on David's head for attention] "come down the chimney? Does he come down the chimney?"
2. *David*	(standing) GO DOWN—JUMP DOWN (with body) = *go down, jump down*
3. *Mom*	"Oh! And he lands you-know-where!"
4. *David*	Santa doll—GO DOWN (with doll)—[nod] = *yes, Santa goes down*
5. *Mom*	"And he gets all dirty?"
6. *David*	own backside = *Santa's backside*
7. *Susan*	"That's Santa Claus. Does he bring presents?"

8.	*Mom*	"And then he brushes himself off? [+ BRUSH ARM ges-ture] "Hey! Because he gets all dirty from the chimney, from coming down the chimney?"
9.	*David*	[headshake]—[away]—[headshake] + BRUSH ARM—down—own backside = *No (narrative marker), Santa doesn't brush arm, he brushes his backside when he comes down*
10.	*Mom*	"Oh! He doesn't get dirty? Oh . . . "
11.	*Susan*	"Just on the seat!"
12.	*Mom*	"Oh! Yeah, on his backside, back here . . . "
13.	*David*	own backside = *Santa's backside*
14.	*David*	Santa doll—GO UP—GO DOWN = *Santa goes up, then goes down*
15.	*Mom*	"And he brings you all of the toys . . . he brings toys . . . ? For David?" [+ GIVE gesture toward David]

Mother works very hard to structure a narrative around David's utter-ances and does so through speech in the first seven turns. Structurally, this interchange looks much like a narration constructed by two people who have access to a shared conventional language. But the lack of a shared system does create challenges to developing the story. Mother introduces the topic of the story in speech during turn 1. David, however, understands the topic through the presence of a toy Santa Claus, which serves as the focal referent for him. In turns 2 through 4, Mother and David repeat the same information without any elaboration (they both note that Santa lands on his backside when he comes down the chimney). Narrative development does not really begin until turn 8 when Mother *gestures* along with her spo-ken contributions; she queries, "And he brushes himself off?" while at the same time brushing her right arm. In the next turn, David corrects Mother by shaking his head while at the same time brushing his arm, followed by an emphatic point at his own backside. In essence, David is saying, "No, Mom! Santa doesn't brush off his arm, he brushes off his backside!" This comment builds on his initial statement in turn 2 that Santa lands on his backside when he comes down the chimney. It is not until turn 8 that David under-stands that Santa's getting dirty has been introduced into the story. Once David understands this contribution, he is able to build on it and, indeed, correct his mother—if Santa lands on his backside, he obviously dirties his backside, not his arm. Interestingly, it is at this point that David produces an "away" gesture which marks the discourse as a narrative.

In sum, the hearing mothers of these deaf children, like all hearing mothers, create narratives around their children's communications. However, they produce these co-narrations with their deaf children far less frequently than hearing mothers talking to hearing children do (0.06 co-narrations per hour for our deaf children versus 2.4 for American hearing children; Phillips et al., 2001). Moreover, the mothers rarely produce their own contributions in gesture, and therefore do not ensure the child's access to those contributions. Thus, the mothers do not provide their deaf children with explicit models for narrative structure—although their support as listeners is likely to be important in encouraging the deaf children to narrate at all. Telling stories appears to be a robust activity in humans, an activity that not only cuts across diverse sociocultural traditions, but also flourishes even when an explicit model for narration is not provided.

☐ Talking to Oneself

In addition to using their gestures to communicate with others, the children also use their gestures for a number of the other functions that language serves. These functions are not particularly frequent even in the communications of young children learning conventional languages. As a result, we have only anecdotal examples of the functions, and all of our examples come from David, the child on whom we have the most data. Nevertheless, it is impressive that a child can extend his homemade gesture system to cover these rather sophisticated linguistic functions.

We occasionally saw David using his gestures when he thought no one was paying attention, as though "talking" to himself. Once when David was trying to copy a configuration of blocks off of a model, he made an "arced" gesture in the air to indicate the block that he needed next to complete the design. When I offered him a block that fit this description, David ignored me, making it clear that his gesture was not intended for me but was for his use only. As another example, David and his sister were sitting side-by-side playing with clay and not with each other. David needed a plastic knife to cut the clay. He got up, looked around, and without making eye contact with any of the people in the room, produced a "where" flip and then a point at his chest, as though asking himself where the object that belonged to him was (see the "Talking to Self" videoclip at www.psypress.com/goldinmeadow).

It is extremely unlikely that a child would invent a language in order to talk to him or herself. Genie who was left alone with no one to talk to for the first 13 years of her life did not, for example, invent a language to share thoughts with herself (Curtiss, 1977). However, it is striking that, once having invented a language to communicate with others, children are able to use that system to communicate with themselves.

☐ Talking About Talk

Another important use of language is its metalinguistic function—using language to talk about language. Language is unique in providing a system that can be used to refer to itself. It requires a certain level of competence for a child to say, "the dog smells." It requires an entirely different and more sophisticated level for that child to say, "I said 'the dog smells'." The child must be aware of her own talk and be able to report on that talk.

David did, on occasion, use gesture to refer to his own gestures. For example, to request a Donald Duck toy that Heidi held behind her back, David pursed his lips, thus referring to the Donald Duck toy. He then pointed at his own pursed lips and pointed toward the Donald Duck toy. When Heidi offered him a Mickey Mouse toy instead, David shook his head, pursed his lips and pointed at his own pursed lips once again (Goldin-Meadow, 1993). The point at his own lips is roughly comparable to the words "I said," as in "I said 'Donald Duck'." It therefore represents a communicative act in which gesture is used to refer to a particular act of gesturing and, in this sense, is reminiscent of young hearing children's quoted speech (cf. Miller & Hoogstra, 1989).

David also used gesture to comment on the gestures of others. For example, at one point we asked David and his hearing sister to respond, in turn, to videotaped scenes of objects moving in space. David was using his gesture system to describe the scenes, and his sister was inventing gestures on the spot (Singleton et al., 1993). As described in Chapter 9, David considered his sister's response to be inappropriate on a number of the items, and he used his own gestures to correct her gestures. The sister extended her index finger and thumb as though holding a small object to describe a tree in a particular segment. Reacting to his sister's choice of handshape, David teased her by reproducing the handshape, pretending to gesture with it, and finally completely ridiculing the handshape by using it to poke himself in the eyes. His sister then shrugged and said, "okay, so what should I do?"—a reaction which both acknowledged the fact that there was a system of which David was the keeper, and admitted her ignorance of this system. David then indicated that a point handshape (which is an appropriate handshape for straight thin objects in his system, see Table 3 in Chapter 9, and therefore an appropriate handshape for a tree) would be a correct way to respond to this item. Thus, David not only produced gestures that adhered to the standards of his system, but he used his gestures to impose those standards on the gestures of others.

These examples are remarkable in that they indicate the distance David has achieved from his gesture system. It is one thing for a child to gesture in order to achieve a goal or make a comment, that is, to use gesture for a specific communicative act. It is quite another for the child to recognize that he is gesturing and to call attention to his gestures as communicative acts. David was able to treat other peoples' gestures as objects to be reflected on and, at times, corrected. Moreover, he was able to distance himself from his own gestures and treat them as objects to be reflected on and referred to. He therefore exhibited in his self-styled gesture system the very beginnings of the reflexive capacity that is found in all languages and that underlies much of the power of language (cf. Lucy, 1993).

☐ Summary: The Uses to Which Gesture Is Put

The deaf children could have used gesture only for the basics—to get people to give them objects and perform actions. Indeed, when chimpanzees are taught sign language, the only purpose to which they seem to put those signs is to request objects and activities (Greenfield & Savage-Rumbaugh, 1991). But the deaf children do much more with their gestures. They use them to comment not only on the here-and-now but also on the distant past, the future, and the hypothetical. They use them to make generic statements so that they can converse about classes of objects. They use them to tell stories, to talk to themselves, and to talk about their own and others' gestures. In other words, they use them for the functions to which all natural languages are put.

Thus, the deaf children not only structure their gestures according to the patterns of natural languages, but they also use their gestures to serve the functions of natural languages. It is interesting that language structure and language function go hand-in-hand in the deaf children's gesture systems. However, the relationship between the two is far from clear. For example, the functions to which the deaf children put their gestures could provide the impetus for building a language-like structure. Conversely, the structures that the deaf children develop in their gestures could provide the means by which more sophisticated language-like functions can be fulfilled. More than likely, language structure and language function complement one another, with small developments in one domain furthering additional developments in the other. One conclusion is quite clear from our data, however: A conventional language model is *not* necessary for children to use their communications for the basic and not-so-basic functions of language. These functions are resilient properties of language.

How Might Hearing Parents Foster Gesture Creation in Their Deaf Children?

The deaf children we study are not exposed to a conventional sign language and thus cannot be fashioning their gestures after such a system. They are, however, exposed to the gestures that their parents use when they speak—and these gestures could serve as a model for the deaf children's system. Moreover, the deaf children's gestures evoke reactions from their parents—and these parental responses might also help shape the deaf children's system.

We have considered these possibilities but have not found support for them. I begin by exploring whether the patterns seen in the deaf children's gestures are particularly comprehensible to hearing adults, *any* hearing adults. It turns out that they are not. I then ask whether the hearing parents of *these particular* deaf children respond differently to gestures that conform to their children's patterns than to gestures that do not conform to those patterns. Again, we find that they do not. Finally, I ask whether the deaf children's hearing parents create gestures that could serve as a model for the gesture systems that the deaf children create. And again, we find that they do not. The children themselves seem to be responsible for the structure in their gesture systems.

☐ Do Parents Shape Their Children's Gestures by Responding Differentially to Those Gestures?

The deaf children's hearing parents are committed to teaching their children how to talk. Although they do not focus on the fact that their children use gesture a great deal, like all parents, they respond to their children's gestures. By responding with either comprehension or noncomprehension to their children's gestures, the parents might have inadvertently shaped the structure of those gestures. We explore this very real possibility in two ways, first in an experimental study and then in a study of naturalistic data.

An Experimental Test

There is no grammatically correct or incorrect way of expressing a notion in gesture. However, certain gesture forms might be easier to understand than others. If so, these particular forms are likely to meet with communicative success and thus are likely to be used again and again. To determine whether English-speakers find certain types of gesture sentences easier to understand than others, we created a soundless videotape containing exemplars of the deaf children's most common two-gesture sentences (Goldin-Meadow & Mylander, 1984, 94–7). A child actress produced the gesture sentences while interacting with an adult playing the role of mother. Each gesture sentence was produced in two different orders, one following the order typically found in the deaf children's sentences (e.g., point at the bubbles, followed by a "blow" gesture), and the other violating that order (e.g., "blow" gesture, followed by a point at the bubbles). English-speaking adults were then asked to "translate" these gesture strings into English and rate their confidence in their responses.

Each adult saw six sentences that followed the deaf children's preferred orders (patient-act, patient-recipient, act-recipient) and six that violated these orders (act-patient, recipient-patient, recipient-act). No adult saw a given sentence in both the preferred and nonpreferred orders. The adults' responses were scored as correct if they contained a good spoken translation of the gestures in the videotape (e.g., for an "eat" gesture, words such as "chew," "eat," and "swallow" were all considered acceptable translations), and if they indicated comprehension of the predicating relation conveyed by the gesture sentence (e.g., for gesture sentences containing a point at the bubbles and a point at the table, sentences such as "please put the bubbles on the table" and "I will put the bubbles on the table"—i.e., sentences containing references to the bubbles, the table, and the transferring relation—were accepted as correct).

We found that adults were able to translate the gesture sentences equally well regardless of the orders in which the gestures were presented. Moreover, even the possibly more subtle index, confidence level, showed no differences between preferred and nonpreferred orders—and it wasn't because the adults weren't using the confidence scale consistently (they gave higher confidence ratings to their correct translations than to their incorrect translations).

Thus, gesture sentences following the deaf children's preferred orders are no more comprehensible to English-speaking adults than gesture sentences not following those orders—at least when those gestures are staged and shown on videotape. However, it is entirely possible that preferred orders *are* more comprehensible than nonpreferred orders, but that our measures of comprehension (translation and confidence) are just not subtle enough to capture this effect. In the actual give-and-take between mother and child, mothers might be more likely to reveal their true preferences. To explore this possibility, we returned to our videotapes of the naturalistic interactions between the hearing mothers and their deaf children.

A Naturalistic Test

In 1970, Brown and Hanlon used naturalistic data to test the hypothesis that "ill-formed constructions in a child's speech give way to well-formed constructions because there is selection pressure in communication which favors the latter" (Brown & Hanlon, 1970, 42). They looked at what they called "sequitur" responses—relevant and comprehending reactions—to children's grammatically correct and incorrect utterances. They expected parents to respond with sequiturs more often to grammatically correct than to grammatically incorrect child utterances. But what they actually found was that parents respond with sequiturs 45% of the time when the child's utterance is grammatically correct, and 45% of the time when the child's utterance is grammatically incorrect. In other words, the parents respond with sequiturs about half the time—whether or not the child's utterance is grammatically correct.

We did precisely the same analysis on our deaf children and their hearing parents (Goldin-Meadow & Mylander, 1984, 97–104). We first classified the deaf children's gesture sentences into grammatically correct (those that conformed to the child's own syntactic patterns) and grammatically incorrect (those that violated the child's patterns). We then calculated how often each mother responded with sequiturs to her child's grammatically correct versus incorrect gesture sentences. The data are presented in Table 5. We did the analysis looking at maternal responses both to children's gesture order patterns and to their production probability patterns (see Chapter 10 for descriptions of these patterns). Note that, like the hearing mothers in Brown and Hanlon's study, the hearing mothers in our study responded to their children's communications with sequiturs about half the time. And like the mothers in Brown and Hanlon's study, the mothers responded with sequiturs whether or not the child's gestures were (for that child) grammatically correct.

We tried looking at other types of maternal responses (e.g., approvals vs. disapprovals) and found the same result (Goldin-Meadow & Mylander, 1984, 100–2)—mothers react to the truth value of their children's gestures and not the form of those gestures. For example, if Mildred were to point at a

TABLE 5. Proportion of the Deaf Children's Gesture Sentences to Which Mothers Responded With Sequiturs

| | Gesture Order | | Production Probability | |
	Grammatically Correct	Grammatically Incorrect	Grammatically Correct	Grammatically Incorrect
Marvin	.46 (13)	.67 (3)	.53 (15)	.50 (2)
Abe	.69 (19)	(none)	.46 (26)	.54 (13)
Mildred	.46 (13)	.43 (7)	.36 (14)	.00 (1)
Karen	.46 (13)	.43 (7)	.50 (14)	.50 (2)

tambourine and then produce a "drum" gesture, her mother would likely respond with disapproval, shaking her head while saying, "No, you don't drum tambourines"—despite the fact that the form of Mildred's utterance follows the child's preferred patient-act order. Conversely, if Mildred were to produce a "shake" gesture and then point at the tambourine, mother would approve, nodding while saying, "Yes, you shake tambourines"—approval despite the fact that the gesture sentence follows Mildred's nonpreferred act-patient order. Thus, as we might have guessed, parents respond to the content of their children's gestures, not their form.

However, the children's gestures *are* iconic and, in fact, need to be iconic—if the children were to produce a gesture form that does not transparently reflect its meaning, no one would understand it. Thus, comprehensibility shapes the children's gestures at some level—but *not* at the level of grammatical form. Indeed, the overall iconicity of the gestures is what ensures that gesture order is *not* likely to affect whether a particular sentence is understood—mother can easily figure out that her child is describing apple-eating whether the child puts the point at the apple before the "eat" gesture, or the "eat" gesture before the point at the apple. Thus, although the children's gestures are quite comprehensible to the hearing individuals around them, there is no evidence that the *structural details* of each child's gesture system are shaped by the way in which the mothers respond to those gestures.

☐ Do Parents Provide a Gestural Model for Their Children's Gestures?

Hearing parents do gesture when they talk to young children (Bekken, 1989; Iverson, Capirci, Longobardi, & Caselli, 1999; Shatz, 1982) and the hearing parents of our deaf children are no exception. The deaf children's parents are committed to teaching their children to talk and therefore talk to them as often as they can. And when they talk, they gesture. These spontaneous gestures could serve as the model for the deaf children's gestural systems.

We selected six children (David, Dennis, Abe, Marvin, Karen, Mildred) whose mothers appeared often on their videotapes, and analyzed the gestures these mothers produced when they addressed their children. In each case, the mother was the child's primary caretaker. We used the analytic tools developed to describe the deaf children's gestures (see Chapter 7). We turned off the sound and coded the mothers' gestures as though they had been produced without speech. In other words, we attempted to look at the mothers' gestures through the eyes of a child who cannot hear.

The strong claim about the role of maternal gesture is that the mothers, already familiar with language, generate a structured gesture system that their deaf child then learns. There are essentially three different kinds of data that we might want to consider when arguing for or against this hypothesis. First we can look for similarities or differences in the regularities (if any) in the mothers' and children's gesture systems. If we find *qualitative* differences between the systems, we can reasonably argue that the children are not learning their gesture systems from their mothers. Finding similarities between the systems leaves open many possibilities—either the children learn their gestures from their mothers, their mothers learn them from their children, or mothers and children independently generate the same gesture system.

Second, we can look for similarities or differences in the timing or *onset* of gestural regularities between mothers and children. If mother and child generate the same pattern, but child develops the pattern several sessions before mother, we can reasonably assume that the child is not learning the pattern from mother. Conversely, if mother shows the pattern first, we assume that the child is learning from mother.

Finally, we can look for *quantitative* differences, instances where mother and child generate the same pattern but child either uses the pattern more frequently than mother, or applies the pattern to a wider range of instances than mother. Quantitative differences are the least persuasive of the three types of data as they are only differences of degree. Nevertheless, if we find that mother's rate of production of a given structure is much lower than her child's, at a minimum, we would have to conclude that the child is forming linguistic generalizations from a relatively sparse data base—one in which the structure occurs infrequently and without particular salience. If children are able to form linguistic generalization from such poor exemplars, it is likely that they were biased to make those generalizations in the first place.

Gestures

Not surprisingly, all six mothers use both pointing and iconic gestures when they talk to their children. Moreover, with only two exceptions (Marvin and

Mildred), mothers use pointing and iconic gestures in roughly the same distribution as their children (Goldin-Meadow & Mylander, 1984, 78). However, mothers produce fewer different types of iconic gestures than their children. They also use only a small subset of the gestures that their children use—only 22% of each child's gestures are used by that child's mother (range from 9% to 33%). So almost 80% of the children's gestures are novel, that is, forms that are not modeled by their mothers. Moreover, mothers use their iconic gestures as nouns (as opposed to verbs and adjectives) much less often than their children (Goldin-Meadow et al., 1994).

There are differences between mother and child even with respect to pointing gestures and modulators. The mothers use both pointing gestures and modulators in a more restricted way than their deaf children. For example, mothers do not use their pointing gestures to refer to non-present objects, but their children do. Not surprisingly, mothers rely on words to serve this function (Butcher et al., 1991). Moreover, as described in Chapter 8, mothers use the "flip" and "wait" gestures for a narrower range of meanings than their children. In fact, two of the children (Marvin and David) use novel modulators that are found nowhere in their mothers' gestural repertoires (Morford & Goldin-Meadow, 1997).

The Parts of Gestures: Morphology

Can the mothers' gestures be characterized by the same system of parts (i.e., the same morphological system) as their children's gestures? To address this question, we analyzed the gestures of four mothers in two different ways (Goldin-Meadow et al., 1995).

First, we ran the system we had devised for each child over his or her mother's gestures, asking whether mother's gestures fit her child's system. We found that each mother uses her gestures in a more restricted way than her child. She omits many of the morphemes that the child produces (or uses the ones she does produce more narrowly than the child). And she omits a very large proportion of the handshape-motion combinations that the child produces. In addition, there is good evidence that the gestures of each deaf child can be characterized in terms of handshape and motion components which map onto a variety of related objects and a variety of related actions, respectively (see Chapter 9). However, there is *no* evidence that the mothers ever go beyond mapping gestures as wholes onto entire events— that is, the mothers' gestures do *not* appear to be organized in relation to one another to form the same system of contrasts that their children display in their gestures.

Second, we analyzed the mother's gestures with the same tools that we used on the children's gestures, asking whether mother's gestures form a coherent system and, if so, whether that system matches her child's. We found that, although a morphological system can be imposed on the mothers' gestures, those systems lack coherence. For example, Marvin's mother uses the CMedium form for objects that are *narrower* in width than the objects for which she uses the OTouch form. The CMedium has a greater thumb-finger distance than the OTouch. If these handshape forms are being used to systematically capture differences between objects, we would expect the CMedium to be used for wider objects than the OTouch (as it is in all four of the children's systems, see Table 4 in Chapter 9). Given that the mothers' systems lack coherence, it is not surprising that they do not map easily onto their children's systems. The mothers' gestures don't even seem to be the source for the arbitrary differences that we find across the children's systems (see Table 4). These differences cannot be traced to the mothers' gestures, but seem instead to be shaped by the early gestures that the children themselves create. In other words, the differences across children can be more easily traced to the gestural input that the children provide for themselves, than to gestural input that their mothers provide for them (Goldin-Meadow et al., 1995).

Gesture Sentences, Simple and Complex: Syntax

Although the hearing mothers do indeed gesture, they produce relatively few gesture combinations—that is, like most English-speakers (McNeill, 1992), they tend to produce one gesture per spoken clause and thus rarely combine several gestures into a single, motorically uninterrupted unit.

Moreover, the few gesture combinations that the mothers do produce do *not* exhibit the same structural regularities as their children's. The mothers show no reliable order patterns in their gesture sentences (Goldin-Meadow & Mylander, 1983, 1984), and do not appear to be responsible for their children's gesture orders. The children were the first to produce instances of the gesture orders they ended up adhering to. For example, Dennis reliably used a patient-act order in his observation sessions overall, and produced his first patient-act gesture sentence in Session 1. His mother did not produce any patient-act gesture sentences until the 7th session, and even thereafter did not consistently abide by the order.

In addition, the production probability patterns in the mothers' gesture sentences are different from the production probability patterns in the children's strings (see Figure 18, which re-presents the data from the children of these six mothers along with the mothers' data). For the most part, mothers produce more gestures for patients than for transitive actors, thus distinguishing between the two, as do their children. However, it is where *intransitive actors* are situated relative to transitive actors and patients that determines the typology of a language, and here mothers and children differ: Mothers show no reliable patterning of intransitive actors, whereas children produce intransitive actors at a rate significantly different from transitive actors but not different from patients, thus displaying an ergative pattern.

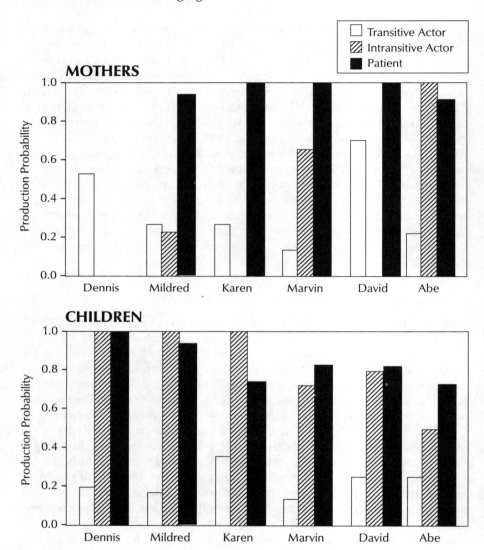

Figure 18. Hearing Mothers Do Not Use Gesture in the Same Way as Their Deaf Children. The figure displays the likelihood that the hearing mothers of six deaf children will produce a gesture for a transitive actor, a patient, or an intransitive actor in the spontaneous gestures that they produce along with their talk. The mothers' gesture production probability patterns did not match their children's, nor was there uniformity across the mothers' patterns. As a result, the mothers' gestures could not have served as a straightforward model for their deaf children to copy.

Abe's mother is the only mother to display an ergative pattern in her gestures (she produces gestures for patients and intransitive actors equally often, and more often than she produces gestures for transitive actors). But Abe is the only child *not* to display an ergative pattern in his gestures (i.e., he produces gestures for patients more than intransitive actors, and gestures for intransitive actors more than transitive actors). Thus, there is not a good fit between mothers and their children in how often they produce gestures for various thematic roles.

Finally, the mothers start to convey complex gesture sentences several sessions after their children, and they produce proportionally fewer complex gesture sentences than their children (Goldin-Meadow & Mylander, 1983, 1984). Moreover, not only do mothers produce few complex gesture sentences, but the complex sentences they do produce contain fewer propositions per sentence than their children's. On average, the mothers' maximum number of propositions per complex sentence is two, whereas the children's maximum number is 5.3. In addition, the children produce a wide variety of types of complex sentences—"and," "but," "or," "then," "which," "cause," and "while" complex sentences—but mothers tend to produce only one type, the "and" sentence. On average, the mothers produce 1.5 (range 0 to 4) types of complex sentences, whereas the children produce 4.8 (range 1 to 7). Mothers apply the recursive pattern to a narrower range of instances than do their children. Thus, there is little evidence to suggest that the children are learning to produce complex gesture sentences from their mothers, and a good deal of evidence to suggest that they are not.

Grammatical Categories

Do the mothers' gestures provide a model for their children's grammatical categories? Recall that we have thus far looked for grammatical categories only in David's data. We examined the gestures that David's mother produced with this question in mind, and found that she does not use the same morphological and syntactic devices in her gestures that David uses in his to distinguish among nouns, verbs, and adjectives (Goldin-Meadow et al., 1994). Indeed, David's mother does not use abbreviation at all, and does not use consistent gesture order patterns to distinguish among nouns, verbs, and adjectives. These devices are therefore likely to have been initiated by David. David's mother does use his third device, inflection. However, David's inflections pattern systematically with the predicate structure of the verb and consistently mark objects playing particular thematic roles in those predicates (see Chapter 10; Goldin-Meadow et al., 1994); that is, they function as part of a system—his mother's inflections do not.

The Functions Gesture Serves

Finally, examining the functions that gesture assumes in the hearing mothers' communications, we found that all of the mothers use their gestures to make requests and comments about the here-and-now. However, the mothers are far less likely than their children to use gesture to describe events that are spatially or temporally removed from the present (Morford & Goldin-Meadow, 1997). Moreover, the mothers do not tell stories in gesture, as their children do. In fact, as described in Chapter 13, the mothers very rarely incorporate gestures into the few verbal stories that they co-construct with their children (Phillips et al., 2001). Finally, we never observed the deaf children's mothers using gesture to refer to their own gestures; that is, they do not use gesture metalinguistically.

Thus, for the deaf children, gesture assumes a large number of the functions that language typically serves. However, it serves a very restricted range of functions for the hearing mothers—which is not all that surprising given that the mothers have a perfectly good spoken system that they can, and do, use for these functions.

☐ Summary: The Deaf Children Go Well Beyond Their Input

So, do the deaf children learn to structure their gesture systems from their mothers? Almost certainly, the answer is "no." The mothers' responses to their deaf children's gestures cannot account for the structure that we find in those gestures. Moreover, the gestures that the mothers use when talking to their children do not resemble the children's gestures and therefore cannot serve as a model for those gestures. The mothers share only a small percentage of iconic gestures with their children, and use their pointing and modulating gestures more narrowly than their children. The mothers' gestures do not conform to the children's morphology or syntax; in fact, the mothers' gestures do not conform to *any* morphological or syntactic structure, let alone their children's structure. The mothers' gestures do not have grammatical categories. And finally, the mothers use their gestures for a much more restricted range of functions than their children do. The hearing mothers' gestures are clearly not systematically structured when looked at with the same tools as we use to describe the deaf children's gestures. Their gestures may, however, be structured when looked at in relation to the speech they accompany, an issue to which we return in Part 3 of the book.

The important point to take from this chapter is that the deaf children's hearing parents are not responsible for their children's gesture systems. Neither the way the parents respond to the children's gestures, nor the gestures that the parents produce when talking to the children can explain the structure found in the deaf children's gestures. It may well be necessary for the deaf children to see hearing people gesturing in communicative situations in order to arrive at the idea that gesture can be appropriated for the purposes of communication. However, in terms of how the children *structure* their gestured communications, there is no evidence that this structure comes from the children's hearing parents. Although the children may be using hearing peoples' gestures as a communication starting point, they go well beyond that point, transforming the gestures they see into a structured system that looks very much like language.

Gesture Creation Across the Globe

The gestures that the hearing parents use with their deaf children don't resemble their children's gestures enough to serve as a full-blown model for those gestures. However, the parents might be influencing their children's gesture systems in other more subtle ways, perhaps through the patterns they adopt when interacting with their children. For example, a number of years ago, Bruner (1974/75) suggested that the structure of joint activity between mother and child might influence the structure of the child's communication. Perhaps the structure we find in the deaf children's gestures is a product of the way in which mothers and children jointly interact in their culture.

To explore this possibility, we sought a culture in which mothers are known to interact differently with their children than do American mothers. We settled on China. The salient differences in the way Chinese and American mothers interact with their children provide us with an excellent opportunity to examine the role that mother-child interaction plays in the development of the gestural communication systems of deaf children. If we find *similarities* between the gestural systems developed by deaf children in Chinese culture and deaf children in American culture, an increasingly powerful argument can be made for the non-effects of mother-child interaction patterns on the development of these gestural systems. In other words, we will have increasingly compelling evidence for the resilience of the linguistic properties found in the deaf children's gestural systems in the face of cultural variation. Conversely, if we find *differences*, an equally compelling argument can be made for the effects of cultural variation—as instantiated in mother-child interaction patterns—on the spontaneous gestural systems of deaf children.

☐ A Study of Chinese Deaf Children of Hearing Parents

We observed four deaf children living in middle-class families in Taipei, Taiwan. Their fathers owned their own small businesses and their mothers stayed at home to care for them and their siblings. Like the American deaf children, the Chinese children were congenitally deaf and had no other known physical or cognitive disabilities. In each case, the cause of deafness was unknown. All of the children attended oral programs for the deaf which were relatively common in Taipei when we collected our data. However, at the time of our observations, none of the Chinese children had made much progress in spoken Mandarin or Taiwanese. The children did vocalize some words, but these seemed to punctuate their gestured utterances in a manner somewhat like gestures punctuate speech for hearing speakers. They did not combine two or more spoken words within a single string. Moreover, none of the children had been exposed to a conventional sign system such as Mandarin or Taiwanese Sign Language or Signed Mandarin. Thus, the Chinese deaf children, like our American deaf children, had no knowledge of conventional language, either spoken or signed.

We had learned from the literature that Chinese mothers socialize their children differently (Miller, Mintz, & Fung, 1991; Young, 1972), and have different attitudes toward task-oriented activities (Smith & Freedman, 1982) and academic achievement (Chen & Uttal, 1988; Stevenson, Lee, Chen, Stigler, Hsu, & Kitamura, 1990) than do American mothers, particularly white, middle-class American mothers. We began our study by attempting to replicate the reported differences in mother-child interaction in our own sample of Chinese and American families—and we did (Wang, Mylander, & Goldin-Meadow, 1993). We found, first, that our Chinese mothers are very active in initiating interactions with their deaf children, whereas our American mothers tend to wait for their children to initiate interactions. Second, our Chinese mothers offer directives to their deaf children before the children have the opportunity to try out the task; our American mothers offer directives to their deaf children only after their children fail to accomplish the task or after their children request help. Third, when commenting on pictures or toys, our Chinese mothers not only label the objects but also supply additional information. For example, in reaction to a picture of a house, a Chinese mother says the Mandarin equivalent of "house, the house is very high; the roof is pointed; there are houses over there." In contrast, our American mothers do little more than label the picture, "house, that's a house."

In addition, we found a fourth difference, one that had not been documented in the literature. Chinese mothers gesture substantially more when they talk to their children than do American mothers (Goldin-Meadow &

Saltzman, 2000). In fact, there was *no overlap* in the distribution of gesture frequency between the two cultures—all of the Chinese mothers (whether interacting with a deaf or hearing child) produced many more gestures than the American mothers.

We might have expected otherwise. After all, the deaf children had limited abilities in understanding speech. Moreover, even hearing children grasp the message conveyed in speech better when it is accompanied by gesture than when it is not (Goldin-Meadow, Kim, & Singer, 1999). We might therefore expect hearing mothers to use a great deal of gesture when addressing their deaf children—particularly American mothers who typically try to accommodate to the needs of their children (Ochs & Schieffelin, 1984). Americans, for example, childproof their homes, provide toys and child-scaled objects for children, and adapt their speech to the limited language abilities of young children. But it turns out that they don't gesture more to their deaf children. It's the Chinese mothers, not the American mothers, who gesture a great deal with their children. The result, of course, is that the Chinese deaf children are exposed to substantially more gestural input than the American deaf children. The question is whether this quantitative difference, along with cultural differences in interactional style, has any effect on the gesture systems the deaf children generate.

☐ Lexical Differences

All four of the Chinese deaf children use gesture to communicate. Moreover, all four use the three types of gestures used by the American deaf children—pointing gestures, iconic gestures, and modulating gestures—and in precisely the same proportions (Wang et al., 1993). In fact, we found it easy to code the Chinese deaf children's gestures using the system we had devised for the American deaf children. It seemed like the same kind of communication.

Nevertheless, there were differences. The children's gestures capture salient aspects of their worlds and, not surprisingly, those salient aspects are not always the same in the two cultures. For example, to represent "eat" in gesture, the American deaf children move an O-handshape back and forth in a short arc at their mouths, as though placing food in the mouth (see Figure 19A). The Chinese deaf children also use the O-handshape gesture for "eat" but, in addition, they use a gesture that we do not find in our American sample—they move a V-handshape back and forth at their mouths as though their fingers were chopsticks (see Figure 19B). The children thus capture in their gestures objects and movements that make sense to the people in their worlds.

Recall from Chapter 9 that there are two types of iconic gestures in the

 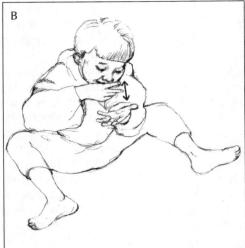

FIGURE 19. Lexical Gestures Can Differ Across Cultures. In panel A, an American deaf child jabs an "O" shaped hand toward his mouth as though eating food. In panel B, a Chinese deaf child holds one hand like chopsticks (in a "V" shape) and makes a bowl shape with the other hand (in a "C" shape) as though indicating eating Chinese-style. The deaf children thus capture in their gestures objects and movements that make sense to the people in their worlds.

American deaf children's repertoires. The first type is truly iconic—the form of the gesture is transparently related to its referent; the "eat" gesture is a good example. The second type is borrowed from hearing culture and is therefore often less transparent in form. For example, "thumbs-up" is a conventional gesture, or emblem, in American culture meaning "good" or "okay." Emblems are gestures that are recognized within hearing culture as particular symbols for a given meaning (Ekman & Friesen, 1969). They are often appropriated by the deaf children to serve as "words" within their gesture systems. "Break" and "give" shown in Figures 2A and 2B of Chapter 8 are emblems in American culture that have a more iconic base than "thumbs-up" and that become part of the American deaf children's gesture systems.

Like the American children, the Chinese children produce conventional as well as truly iconic gestures. As we might expect given that emblems tend to be culturally specific (McNeill, 1992), the Chinese children have different repertoires of conventional gestures than their American counterparts (Wang et al., 1993). The American deaf children use conventional gestures almost exclusively to make requests—for example, the "give" gesture, or the "beckon" gesture requesting someone to come near. They occasionally use conventional gestures to convey a number (e.g., an index finger held vertically to mean "one") or an emotion (e.g., eyebrows knitted and face scowling in an exaggerated fashion to mean "angry"). In contrast, the Chinese deaf children use conventional gestures for requests no more frequently than for other purposes. And, of course, their conventional gestures come from those they see hearing speakers produce; for example, a bent index finger used to mean "dead" (a state), and an index finger brushed against the cheek used to mean "shame" (an emotion)—gestures that the American deaf children never produce. Finally, the Chinese children use conventional gestures to evaluate—for example, an extended pinky meaning "bad." The American children never use conventional gestures for this purpose despite the fact that the evaluative "thumbs-up" is part of American culture.

Thus, the deaf children in the two cultures have different repertoires of conventional gestures—which, of course, is not all that surprising given that their hearing parents also have different repertoires of conventional gestures (Wang et al., 1993). What may be more surprising is that the deaf children fully incorporate these conventional gestures into their systems, treating them as though they were "just another gesture." For example, for the deaf children in both cultures, conventional gestures combine with other gestures, and can be abbreviated and displaced in space like other gestures. Moreover, when they become part of the children's systems, these conventional gestures often take on expanded meanings. For example, the "wait" gesture is used exclusively to request a brief delay or time-out by American hearing parents, but it takes on the added role of signaling the immediate future in their deaf children (see Chapter 8).

Children in both cultures take the gestures they see in their worlds and make them their own. Since the children see different gestures, they create different lexicons. Interestingly, however, they do not create different syntaxes, as we will see in the next section.

☐ Syntactic Similarities

Like the American deaf children, the Chinese deaf children combine their gestures into sentences, and those sentences are structured in language-like ways. Moreover, and more striking, the *particular* structures the Chinese deaf children use are identical to those found in the American deaf children's gestures.

Marking Thematic Roles

Like the American deaf children, the Chinese deaf children use a variety of different devices to indicate who does what to whom. The Chinese children use *production probability* to mark thematic roles, and three of the four children display the same ergative production probability pattern that we find

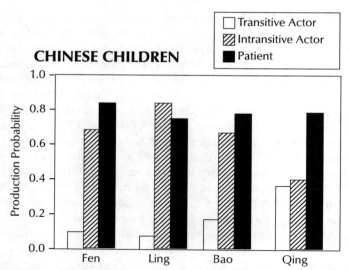

FIGURE 20. Chinese Deaf Children Follow the Same Ergative Pattern as American Deaf Children When They Omit and Produce Gestures for Different Semantic Elements. The figure displays the likelihood that four Chinese deaf children will produce a gesture for a transitive actor, a patient, or an intransitive actor in a two-gesture sentence. Three of the children produced gestures for intransitive actors as often as for patients, and more often than they produced gestures for transitive actors—that is, they displayed the same ergative pattern found in the American deaf children. The fourth child, Qing, displayed an accusative pattern; she treats intransitive actors like transitive actors and different from patients.

in the American deaf children's data (Goldin-Meadow & Mylander, 1998).[1] As Figure 20 shows, the children produce gestures far more often for patients (the *cheese* when describing a mouse eating cheese) and for intransitive actors (the *mouse* when describing a mouse going to its hole) than for transitive actors (the *mouse* when describing a mouse eating cheese)—Qing is the exception. Note, however, that, even though Qing's pattern is not

---

[1] It is important to note that this ergative pattern cannot be explained by how likely the Chinese children were to produce gestures for new versus old semantic elements. Like the American children, the Chinese children were less likely to produce gestures for transitive actors than for intransitive actors or patients, whether those elements were new to the discourse (0.39 for transitive actors, 0.75 for intransitive actors, 0.91 for patients) or old (0.14 for transitive actors, 0.94 for intransitive actors, 0.84 for patients). We did a statistical analysis on the data from these four Chinese deaf children and the four American deaf children whose data are shown in Figure 9 and found significant effects for both old semantic elements (F(2,14) = 20.65, $p < .0001$) and new semantic elements (F(2,8) = 6.55, $p = .02$; three of the eight children had some empty cells and were therefore excluded from the analysis for new elements). Transitive actors were produced reliably less often than intransitive actors ($p < .0001$ for old elements, $p = .03$ for new, Tukey hsd) and patients ($p < .0003$ for old elements, $p = .05$ for new, Tukey hsd), and patients were not reliably different from intransitive actors.

ergative, it is a pattern found in natural language—unlike the American hearing mothers, many of whom exhibit gesture patterns that cannot be found in any natural language (see Figure 18). In fact, Qing's gestures follow an accusative pattern characteristic of both Mandarin and English—she produces gestures for patients (eaten-cheese) far more often than she does for *both* intransitive actors (going-mouse) and transitive actors (eating-mouse). In other words, Qing has an actor category that cuts across transitive and intransitive utterances.

The Chinese children also use *gesture order* to indicate who does what to whom (Goldin-Meadow & Mylander, 1998). They produce gestures for patients before gestures for acts (cheese-eat), and gestures for intransitive actors before gestures for acts (mouse-go; Qing again is the exception for intransitive actors, see Figure 21). Thus, like the American deaf children, the Chinese deaf children place intransitive actors in the same (initial) position as patients. Deaf children who are exposed to conventional sign languages learn the ordering patterns of those languages. For example, children exposed to ASL learn SVO (Subject-Verb-Object) as the unmarked, or standard, order (Hoffmeister, 1978; Newport & Ashbrook, 1977); children exposed to the Sign Language of the Netherlands learn SOV as the unmarked order (Coerts, 2000). Given this variability across conventional sign languages, it is striking—and somewhat surprising—that the Chinese and American deaf children in our studies not only use a consistent order, but use the *same* order.

Like the American deaf children, the Chinese children not only produce gestures in neutral space but also in marked spaces near objects that play a role in the proposition conveyed by the gesture sentence. We have argued that these spatial displacements function like *inflections* for the American deaf children because they are primarily used to indicate a particular semantic role (patients). Our future work will explore whether the Chinese deaf children's spatial displacements also serve a marking function and, if so, whether they mark the same role as the American deaf children's inflections.

Recursion

All four of the Chinese deaf children produce complex gesture sentences conveying more than one proposition, and they do so in 43% of their gesture sentences (range 33% to 54%), much the same as the 37% (range 31% to 45%) for the American children (Goldin-Meadow & Mylander, 1998). For example, Bao produces the following gesture sentence to tell us that Christmas lights are put on trees (proposition 1) and they blink (proposition 2).

Christmas tree—BLINK—PUT ON

As another rather intricate example, Qing produces the following gesture sentence upon seeing a picture of a swordfish (see Figure 22 for examples of

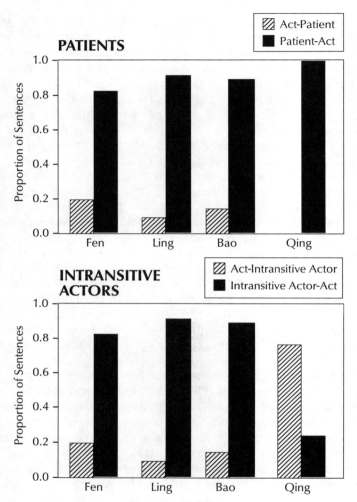

FIGURE 21. Chinese Deaf Children Follow the Same Consistent Gesture Orders as American Deaf Children When They Produce Patients and Intransitive Actors in Sentences with Acts. The figure displays the proportion of sentences in act-patient versus patient-act orders (top graph) and act-intransitive actor versus intransitive actor-act orders (bottom graph) that each Chinese deaf child produced. Like the American children, the Chinese children tended to produce both patients and intransitive actors before acts. The exception was Qing (intransitive actors).

each type of gesture). The "dead" gesture is one that Qing learned from Chinese hearing speakers—a bent index finger is an emblem for "dead" in Taiwan. With this long string of gestures, all produced before she relaxed her hands, Qing is indicating that swordfish can poke a person (proposition 1) so that the person becomes dead (proposition 2), that they have long, straight noses (proposition 3), and that they swim (proposition 4).

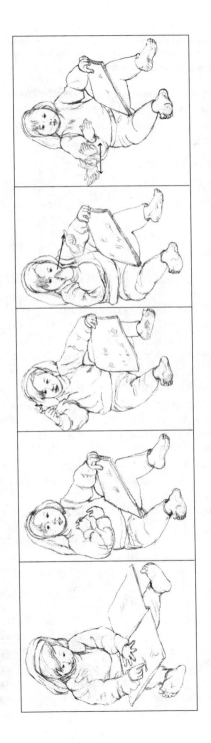

FIGURE 22. The Chinese Deaf Children Also Produce Complex Gesture Sentences. Qing produces five distinct gestures that she combines into a single complex gesture sentence (that is, she produces the string of gestures without breaking her flow of movement). The five gestures are illustrated in this figure: Qing points at a picture of a swordfish (= *swordfish*). She jabs at her own chest as though piercing her heart (= *poke-in-chest*). She crooks her index finger and holds it in the air (this is an emblem in Taiwan that hearing speakers use to mean *dead*). She holds her index finger on her nose and extends it outward (= *long-straight-nose*). She wiggles her palm back and forth (= *swim*).

[wave for attention]—swordfish—POKE IN CHEST—DEAD—
swordfish—LONG STRAIGHT NOSE—DEAD—POKE IN
CHEST—SWIM—POKE IN CHEST—DEAD

After this complex gesture sentence, Qing goes on to invent a fantasy—motivated perhaps by sibling rivalry—and produces the following gesture sentence to indicate that a swordfish could poke her sister who would then be dead.

POKE IN CHEST (produced toward her hearing sister's chest)—DEAD

Thus, like the American deaf children's gesture systems, the Chinese deaf children's gesture systems demonstrate generativity, an essential property of all natural languages.

Packaging Motion Events

A great deal of recent cross-linguistic work explores how children describe events that involve motion. As soon as hearing children begin to describe motion events, they demonstrate characteristics unique to the language they are learning (Berman & Slobin, 1994; Choi & Bowerman, 1991). These early differences in child language systems undoubtedly reflect the different language models to which the children are exposed. But the differences in child language might also reflect cultural differences. How can we possibly tell whether the differences across child language systems are due to cultural, as opposed to linguistic, differences in input?

The deaf children's gesture systems offer us a unique way to approach this question. We examined the gestures that four American and four Chinese deaf children used when describing motion events at ages 3;7 to 4;11, and compared them to the speech that four American and four Chinese hearing children used at a comparable age and in a comparable situation (Goldin-Meadow & Zheng, 1998; Zheng, 2000; Zheng & Goldin-Meadow, 1997, 2002). If the differences children display early in language-learning are there *only* because the children are exposed to different languages (and not because they experience different cultural worlds), those differences should *not* be found in our deaf children (who are not exposed to any language model whatsoever). If however, the differences children display early in language-learning reflect cultural as well as linguistic differences in input, we ought to find these same differences in our Chinese versus American deaf children.

We define a motion event as one in which an entity moves from one place to another. We include both transitive (I moved the duck to the cage) and intransitive (the duck moved to the cage) movements. Talmy (1985) has identified four components central to motion events in all languages: Figure (duck), Motion (moved), Path (into), and Ground (cage). A motion event can also have a Manner (the duck moved into the cage by *waddling*); and a transitive motion, by definition, involves an Agent (*the boy* moved the duck into its cage).

All 16 children in this analysis, deaf and hearing alike, conveyed these six semantic elements (not necessarily in the same utterance) when communicating about motion events (Zheng & Goldin-Meadow, 2002). Thus, children are able to isolate the essential elements of a motion event and include them in their communications whether or not they have a language model to guide them.

However, it's the packaging of semantic elements that differs across languages, and here we do find differences across the children. Figure 23 displays the proportion of utterances that the hearing and deaf children produce in each culture, Chinese children in the dark bars, American children in the striped bars. Each of the three graphs shows a different type of utterance. The graph on the left displays utterances containing only a single argument (typically the Figure, e.g., "duck"). The graph in the middle displays utterances containing a single verb or verb satellite (typically the Motion or Path, e.g., "move" or "into"). The graph on the right displays utterances containing a verb combined with one or more arguments (e.g., "duck move").

Note that, as expected, the language children hear influences how they package motion events in their early communications. Mandarin permits deletion of arguments, which licenses Chinese speakers to produce verbs on their own—and, indeed, the Chinese hearing children produce many more single verbs than the other three groups (middle graph in Figure 23). In contrast, English does *not* allow deletion of arguments, which prohibits English speakers from producing single verbs and thus requires them to produce verbs with arguments—and, in turn, the American hearing children produce many more verb + argument utterances than any of the other three groups (right graph in Figure 23).

In contrast, there are no differences between the Chinese and American deaf children. Both groups package the elements in their motion event utterances *in precisely the same way* in all three graphs. Whatever cultural differences there are in the deaf children's worlds appears to have had no impact on this aspect of their gesture systems.

We can think of the deaf children's packaging rates as a gold standard, and evaluate the impact of a language model relative to that standard. Having any language model (English or Mandarin) decreases production of single arguments (left graph). Having a language model that permits deletion of arguments (Mandarin) increases production of single verbs (middle graph). And having a language model that does *not* permit deletion of arguments (English) increases production of verbs and arguments (right graph) over the standard set by the deaf children. By observing deaf children generating their own gesture systems around the globe, we gain insight into the predispositions children bring to the language-learning situation, predispositions that are then shaped by the language model to which the child is exposed.

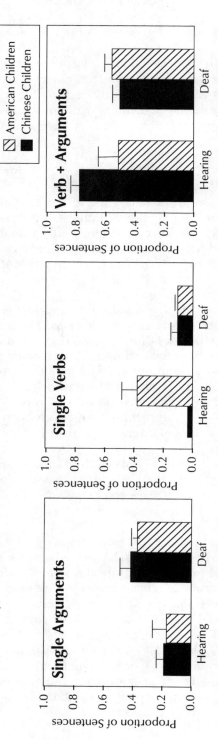

FIGURE 23. Chinese and American Deaf Children Concatenate Verbs and Arguments in the Same Way Despite Differences in the Cultures They Experience; Hearing Children in the Two Cultures Do Not. The figure displays the proportion of motion event utterances that contained a single argument, a single verb, or a verb + arguments produced by four groups of children: Chinese and American hearing children learning Mandarin or English, respectively; and Chinese and American deaf children creating their own gestures. The deaf children show no differences across cultures—the patterns are identical for the Chinese and American deaf children. In contrast, the hearing children are influenced by their language models: Mandarin permits deletion, which allows the children to produce a greater proportion of single verbs relative to the "standard" set by the deaf children; English does not permit deletion, which allows the children to produce a greater proportion of verb + arguments relative to the deaf children's standard. Error bars reflect standard errors.

☐ Generic Statements: Similarities in Rate and Distribution

We can use the same strategy to explore whether a language model influences how often and when children make generic statements. Gelman and Tardif (1998) found that English-speaking adults use generics more often than Mandarin-speaking adults. The question is whether this difference in rate has an impact on how often English-learning and Mandarin-learning children use generics of their own. To explore this question, we calculated the rate of generic production in eight American hearing children and eight Chinese hearing children (ages 3 to 4). To determine the gold standard for generic production—that is, the rate at which generics are produced in the absence of a language model—we calculated the rate of generic production in four American deaf children and four Chinese deaf children (ages 3 to 4). We used the coding system developed by Gelman and Tardif (1998) to identify generics in the hearing children's speech and the coding system described in Chapter 13 to identify generics in the deaf children's gestures.

We found that children in all four groups made generic statements (Goldin-Meadow, Gelman, & Mylander, 2003). Indeed, only one child in each group failed to produce generics. The rate at which children in each group produced generics (number of generics as a percentage of the total number of nouns produced) was: American hearing children 2.8% (SD = 2.5%); Chinese hearing children 2.9% (SD = 1.6%); American deaf children 1.4% (SD = 1.7%); Chinese deaf children 0.5% (SD = 0.5%). There were no significant effects of culture—no differences between the Chinese and American deaf children and, unexpectedly, no differences between the Chinese and American hearing children. American adults use generics more often than Chinese adults, but this difference seems to have little impact on how often hearing children in each culture use generics, at least at the early stages of language-learning.

However, the hearing children did produce significantly more generics than the deaf children in both cultures. The deaf children show us what the child's natural rate of generic production is—the gold standard against which to measure the impact of a language model. Having a language model—either English or Mandarin—seems to boost the rate at which children produce generics significantly above that standard.

We also investigated whether the deaf and hearing children in the two cultures showed the animacy bias first reported by Gelman and Tardif (1998). Both American and Chinese adults use generics more for animals than for artifacts. Gelman and Tardif suggest that this animacy bias reflects the essential difference between the two categories—animals are natural kinds, concepts with many similarities in common that promote rich inferences and could lead to generic statements; artifacts are not (Gelman, 1988).

Figure 24 presents the proportion of generics used for animals and artifacts in the hearing and deaf children in the two cultures. All four groups of children produced generics significantly more often for animals than for artifacts. Sixteen of the 20 children who produced generics showed this bias. The figure also shows the proportion of noncategoricals used for animals and artifacts in all four groups. Noncategoricals are words or gestures that refer to objects but are not produced to categorize those objects (e.g., *cat* and *table* in "the cat is on the table" for a hearing child, or in a point at a cat and point at a table for a deaf child). The children do *not* display an animacy bias with respect to noncategoricals—an important result because it makes it clear that the animacy bias in generics is not just a general disposition to talk about animals more than artifacts.

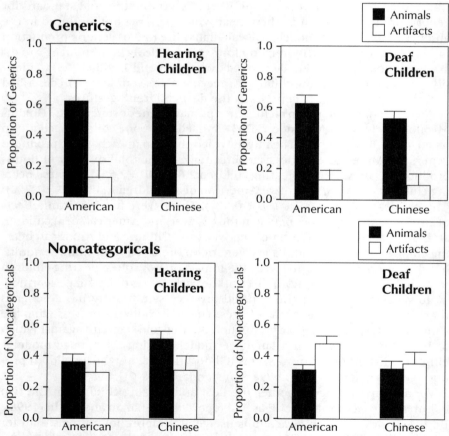

FIGURE 24.   Chinese and American Deaf Children and Hearing Children Produce More Generics for Animals Than for Artifacts. The figure displays the proportion of generics (top graphs) and noncategoricals (bottom graphs) that the American and Chinese hearing children (left graphs) and deaf children (right graphs) used for animals and artifacts. All four groups produced more generics for animals than artifacts. The children do not show this bias for noncategoricals. Thus, the animacy bias in generics does not reflect a propensity to talk about animals more than artifacts. Errors bars indicate standard errors.

All four groups of children thus exhibit precisely the same animacy bias. The absence of cultural differences between the American and Chinese deaf and hearing children suggests that this bias is a conceptual one, relatively impervious to whatever cultural differences exist between our samples of children. Moreover, the fact that the deaf children produce generics and display the animacy bias in those generics makes it clear that children do not need exposure to a conventional language to discover natural kinds. Nor, apparently, do they need a conventional language to encourage them to make generic statements about those kinds.

☐ Stories: Similarities in Structure, Cultural Differences in Content

Just as the American deaf children use their gestures to tell stories, so too do the Chinese deaf children (Phillips et al., 2001). In fact, the Chinese deaf children produce more narratives than their American counterparts, although they also gesture more overall. As in the American group, all four of the Chinese children produce narratives, but one in particular—Qing—produces many more narratives than the others. Nevertheless, all four Chinese children produce narratives containing *setting information* and *voluntary actions*. Three (all but Fen) produce narratives containing *complications*, and Qing produces narratives containing *temporal order*. By way of comparison, all four American deaf children include *setting information, voluntary actions*, and *complications* in their stories; three include *temporal order*, and only one (David) includes *orientation*. Note that the Chinese deaf children do not use *orientation* in their stories.

As an example of a relatively complex narrative, Qing produced the following story at age 5;3. The narrative was inspired by various unrelated pictures—a bear is driving a car at the top of the page; below this on the same page is a construction site with another bear's hard-hatted head peeking out of an open manhole.

Utterance 1: manhole

Utterance 2: DRIVE—FALL

Utterance 3: [tap Mom for attention]—DRIVE—FALL

Gloss: There's a manhole. Mom, the bear drives and falls in the manhole.

Qing's narrative gives *setting information* by indicating the manhole picture. The *voluntary action* is the bear's driving, and the *complication* is the bear's fall.

The Chinese children's narratives also focus on the same types of events as those recounted by the American deaf children—emotional gain in their positive narratives and physical harm in their negative narratives. Even the developmental pattern of building narratives feature-by-feature found in David is evident in Qing, the most prolific storyteller in our Chinese sample: When first observed, Qing was already producing narratives with both *setting information* and *voluntary actions*; she later began producing narratives containing *complications* and *temporal order*. Thus, the urge and capacity to share past experiences and conjecture on future ones in a narrative format appears to be robust across cultures, even if children are not exposed to storytelling models.

The narratives children hear across the globe not only provide them with models for how to tell stories, but also with cues as to how events and actions are to be viewed within their cultures. Chinese parents frequently take an evaluative stance in their narratives, using stories about children's past breaches to teach them how to behave. American parents rarely use stories for this purpose (Miller et al., 1997). Lacking the ability to hear oral narratives, deaf children do not have access to these differences. Will they pick up the cultural differences displayed in narrative nonetheless?

Interestingly, we found that they do. Chinese deaf children use evaluative gestures in their here-and-now communications far more frequently than their American counterparts, and even use these gestures in their narratives. For example, Qing produced the following narrative at age 4;2 to comment on what she considered to be inappropriate behavior on the part of her uncle who threw a ball at her while she was assembling a puzzle.

Utterance 1: uncle—THROW—uncle—THROW

Utterance 2: THROW

Utterance 3: uncle

Utterance 4: THROW—[nod]

Utterance 5: CROSS OUT (= not good)

Utterance 6: uncle—CROSS OUT—BAD—CROSS OUT

Gloss: Uncle threw a ball. That is not good. Uncle was not good; he was bad.

Thus, the Chinese deaf children use evaluative statements in their narratives to condemn a transgression. The American deaf children do not. This difference mirrors, albeit at a reduced level, differences between the stories Chinese and American hearing children tell (Miller et al., 1997).

In addition, although the deaf children in both cultures produce stories about themselves and others, there are differences in how elaborate these two types of stories are. The narratives that the children produce about themselves focus on events that they have personally experienced or plan to experience. The narratives about others are of two types. Some are prompted by pictures and objects in the room and are stories about mythical characters (e.g., Santa Claus, animals in a picture book). Others are about actual events that the children witnessed but did not participate in. Qing produced structurally elaborate narratives about others, but only simple narratives about herself (a structurally elaborate narrative contains a *complication, temporal order*, and/or *orientation*): 13 (37%) of her 35 stories about others were complex, compared to 2 (13%) of her 16 stories about herself. Elaborating stories about others (but not about self) is reminiscent of the other-centered, as opposed to self-centered, worldview frequently attributed to Eastern cultures (Markus & Kitayama, 1991).

Interestingly, David, Qing's counterpart who is not growing up in an Eastern culture, displayed no such disparity in his narratives about others versus himself: 7 (37%) of his 19 stories about others were complex, as were 8 (35%) of his 23 stories about himself. These two deaf children have thus incorporated very subtle cultural differences in self-presentation into their narratives without ever having heard a narrative that would include this kind of frame. The differences may, of course, reflect nothing more than idiosyncratic tendencies particular to these two children. The intriguing possibility, however, is that the deaf children are picking up on nonverbal cues to presentation of self within their cultures, either in the narratives told to them or in the nonverbal behavior they see in other contexts. Although this orientation can be (and is, in the case of hearing children) transmitted to a child through talk, our findings suggest that there are additional routes that a child can take to arrive at these cultural stances. Indeed, our findings point to the aspects of a culture that are so central to that culture that they are instantiated, not only in talk, but also in nonverbal practices.

☐ Summary: Gesturing Across the Globe— Some Differences but Many Similarities

We have examined deaf children who are creating their own gestural communication systems without the benefit of a conventional language model in two very different cultures. What have we learned from this comparison about gesture creation in particular and language-learning in general? Not surprisingly, we find both similarities and differences between the gesture systems created by Chinese and American deaf children. Interestingly, however, the similarities far outweigh the differences.

Moreover, the differences are in just the places we would expect—in the lexicon and in the content of stories, places where culture ought to have a large impact on the children's gestures. Although many of the lexical items that the deaf children use are the same across the two cultures, each group also uses iconic gestures that are particular to its world (see Figures 19A and B) and its own set of "emblems"—conventionalized gestures that hearing speakers use and that tend to vary from culture to culture. The children see their hearing parents use these emblems and they learn them. More interesting, the children incorporate the emblems they learn into the gesture systems they are generating—the emblems function just like any of the gestures that the children create.

But emblems carry with them aspects of culture that are sufficiently important to be codified not only verbally but also nonverbally. A good example is the evaluative emblem in Chinese cultures. Chinese speakers have a large store of evaluative emblems that they use routinely with and without talk. The Chinese deaf children learn these emblems and use them in their everyday conversations and in their stories. As a result, their gestural communications have an evaluative tone that is reminiscent of the tone found in the spoken communications of Chinese hearing children and adults—a tone that is missing from the American deaf children's gestural communications (and from the spoken communications of American hearing children and adults).

In general, the differences that we find in the gesture systems developed by deaf children growing up in two cultures are important because they reflect cultural differences that can be transmitted *without talk*. As Vygotsky (1934; 1978) has noted, language carries culture. When children learn a language, they are not only learning a formal symbolic system, they are also learning about the cultural world in which that language is used. How far can children go in understanding the culture within which they live without knowledge of their culture's language? The deaf children we study do not have access to verbal cues about how the world is viewed in their culture. But they do have access to the nonverbal cues to culture that members of that culture produce. To the extent that the deaf children display cultural differences—and the gesture system is one place in which those differences can be displayed—we can be certain that those aspects of culture can be passed onto children without talk. But to the extent that aspects of cultural knowledge are *only* available through the codified linguistic system that the members of the culture share, the deaf children are at a disadvantage. Our long-term plan is to observe deaf children generating gesture systems across the globe with an eye toward figuring out which aspects of a culture are so central to that culture that they will be instantiated not only in talk but also in gesture, artifacts, actions, and so on. In other words, our goal is to determine which aspects of culture are accessible to the deaf children (and thus do not rely on language to be transmitted to the next generation) and which are not.

In contrast to the differences between the Chinese and American deaf children's gesture systems which are few, the similarities between the systems are many.[2] The children in both cultures develop gesture systems that have similar syntactic structures. They both have devices for marking thematic roles, for introducing recursion, and for packaging motion events. Not only do the children in both cultures introduce the same kinds of syntactic regularities into their respective systems, but the specific patterns that they introduce are often the same. For example, the American and Chinese children not only display production probability and ordering regularities in their gestures, but they display precisely the same production probability and ordering patterns—patterns that are reminiscent of those found in certain natural languages, ergative languages. The children in both cultures also use their gestures to make generic statements about the same kinds of objects, and they use their gestures to tell stories that have the same structural foundations.

As mentioned earlier, we can think of the similarities that we find across the deaf children's gesture systems as a gold standard—the linguistic patterns children will exhibit in the absence of a conventional language model. This standard can then be used to assess the impact of a language model. We saw that having some language model—English or Mandarin—boosts the rate at which young children make generic statements, and decreases the rate at which they refer to single arguments. Having a particular language model that permits deletion of arguments (Mandarin) boosts production of verbs on their own. Having a particular language model that does not permit deletion of arguments (English) boosts production of verb + argument sentence combinations. All of this is relative to the standard set by the deaf children.

In the third and final section of the book, I pull together our findings on the deaf children's gestures systems, and consider what those gesture systems can tell us about how all children go about the process of learning language.

---

[2]Of course, it is possible that deaf children inventing gesture systems in other cultures will display more differences than we have found between our Chinese and American deaf children. We are currently pursuing this possibility by examining the gesture systems invented by deaf children in a Spanish culture and in a Turkish culture. We have chosen Spanish and Turkish cultures because the gestures that hearing speakers produce in these cultures look in many respects quite different from the gestures produced by hearing speakers in American and Chinese cultures (Kita, 2000; McNeill, 1998; McNeill & Duncan, 2000; Ozyurek & Kita, 1999). For example, the gestures Spanish- and Turkish-speakers use—and therefore the gestural models they present to their deaf children—seem to be richer (with gestures for more different types of semantic elements), but also more variable than the gesture models presented by English- and Mandarin-speakers. *A priori* this variability might be expected to provide deaf children with a stepping stone to a more complex linguistic system. Alternatively, variability could make it *harder* to abstract the essential elements of a semantic relation and thus result in a less language-like system. By comparing different gesture models that speakers of Spanish and Turkish versus English and Mandarin present to the deaf child, we will have an ideal paradigm within which to observe the relation between adult input and child output—and a unique opportunity to observe the child's skills as language-maker.

THE CONDITIONS THAT FOSTER LANGUAGE AND LANGUAGE-LEARNING

How Do the Resilient Properties of Language Help Children Learn Language?

The linguistic properties that appear in the deaf children's gesture systems are resilient—they crop up in a child's communications whether or not that child is exposed to a conventional language model. Having identified a number of properties of language as resilient, what then can we say about how children learn language? I tackle this question in this chapter. To remind us of where we are, I first pull together in a single list the linguistic properties that we have identified as resilient. I then consider what these properties tell us about the language-making skills of the children who created them. Finally, I consider how these skills might play a role in language-learning under typical circumstances.

In the remaining chapters of this third and final section of the book, I begin to explore the conditions under which gesture becomes language. We ask hearing adults to create a gestural language and look at how many (if any) of the resilient properties of language they are able to invent (Chapter 17). I then explore a central, and nagging, question about language that the study of gesture-creation in deaf children seems tailor-made to address: Is language innate (Chapter 18)? I end with a discussion of both sides of the resilience of language, the properties of language that are fragile in the face of environmental variation and those that are robust (Chapter 19).

☐ Properties of Language That Are Resilient

Table 6 lists the properties of language that we have found in the deaf children's gesture systems. There may, of course, be many others—the list of

TABLE 6. The Resilient Properties of Language

The Resilient Property	as Instantiated in the Deaf Children's Gesture Systems
Words	
Stability	Gesture forms are stable and do not change capriciously with changing situations (Ch. 8)
Paradigms	Gestures consist of smaller parts that can be recombined to produce new gestures with different meanings (Ch. 9)
Categories	The parts of gestures are composed of a limited set of forms, each associated with a particular meaning (Ch. 9)
Arbitrariness	Pairings between gesture forms and meanings can have arbitrary aspects, albeit within an iconic framework (Ch. 9)
Grammatical Function	Gestures are differentiated by the noun, verb, and adjective grammatical functions they serve (Ch. 12)
Sentences	
Underlying Frames	Predicate frames underlie gesture sentences (Ch. 10, 11)
Deletion	Consistent production and deletion of gestures within a sentence mark particular thematic roles (Ch. 10, 15)
Word Order	Consistent orderings of gestures within a sentence mark particular thematic roles (Ch. 10, 15)
Inflections	Consistent inflections on gestures mark particular thematic roles (Ch. 10)
Recursion	Complex gesture sentences are created by recursion (Ch. 11, 15)
Redundancy Reduction	Redundancy is systematically reduced in the surface of complex gesture sentences (Ch. 11)
Language Use	
Here-and-Now Talk	Gesturing is used to make requests, comments, and queries about the present (Ch. 13)
Displaced Talk	Gesturing is used to communicate about the past, future, and hypothetical (Ch. 13)
Generics	Gesturing is used to make generic statements, particularly about animals (Ch. 13, 15)
Narrative	Gesturing is used to tell stories about self and others (Ch. 13, 15)
Self-Talk	Gesturing is used to communicate with oneself (Ch. 13)
Metalanguage	Gesturing is used to refer to one's own and others' gestures (Ch. 13)

resilient properties of language could well be much longer than what you see in Table 6. The table lists properties at the word- and sentence-levels, as well as properties of language use, and details how each property is instantiated in the deaf children's gesture systems (and in which chapter the property was described). The table thus serves as a summary guide to Part 2 of the book.

Words

The deaf children's gesture words have five properties that are, in fact, found in all natural languages. The gestures are *stable* in form, although they needn't be. It would be easy for the children to make up a new gesture to fit every new situation. Indeed, that appears to be just what hearing speakers do when they gesture along with their speech (McNeill, 1992). But that's not what the deaf children do. They develop a stable store of forms which they use in a range of situations—they develop a lexicon, an essential component of all languages.

Moreover, the gestures they develop are composed of parts that form *paradigms*, or systems of contrasts. When the children invent a gesture form, they do so with two goals in mind—the form must not only capture the meaning they intend (a gesture-to-world relation), but it must also contrast in a systematic way with other forms in their repertoire (a gesture-to-gesture relation). In addition, the parts that form these paradigms are *categorical*. The manual modality can easily support a system of analog representation, with hands and motions reflecting precisely the positions and trajectories used to act on objects in the real world. But, again, the children don't choose this route. They develop categories of meanings that, although essentially iconic, have hints of *arbitrariness* about them (the children don't, for example, all share the same form-meaning pairings for handshapes).

Finally, the gestures the children develop are differentiated by *grammatical function*. Some serve as nouns, some as verbs, some as adjectives. As in natural languages, when the same gesture is used for more than one grammatical function, that gesture is marked (morphologically and syntactically) according to the function it plays in the particular sentence.

Sentences

The deaf children's gesture sentences have six properties found in all natural languages. Underlying each sentence is a *predicate frame* that determines how many arguments can appear along with the verb in the surface structure of that sentence. Indeed, according to Bickerton (1998), having predicate frames is what distinguishes language from its evolutionary precursor, proto-language.

Moreover, the arguments of each sentence are marked according to the thematic role they play. There are three types of markings that are resilient: (1) *deletion*—the children consistently produce and delete gestures for arguments as a function of thematic role; (2) *word order*—the children consistently order gestures for arguments as a function of thematic role; and (3) *inflection*—the children mark with inflections gestures for arguments as a function of thematic role.

In addition, *recursion*, which gives natural languages their generative capacity, is a resilient property of language. The children form complex gesture sentences out of simple ones. They combine the predicate frames underlying each simple sentence, following systematic, and language-like, principles. When there are semantic elements that appear in both propositions of a complex sentence, the children have a systematic way of *reducing redundancy*, as do all natural languages.

Language Use

The deaf children use their gestures for six central functions that all natural languages serve. They use gesture to make requests, comments, and queries about things and events that are happening in the situation—that is, to communicate about the *here-and-now*. Importantly, however, they also use their gestures to communicate about the non-present—*displaced* objects and events that take place in the past, the future, or in a hypothetical world.

In addition to these rather obvious functions that language serves, the children use their gestures to make category-broad statements about objects, particularly about natural kinds—to make *generic* statements. They use their gestures to tell stories about themselves and others—to *narrate*. They use their gestures to communicate with themselves—to *self-talk*. And finally, they use their gestures to refer to their own or to others' gestures—for *metalinguistic* purposes.

The resilient properties of language listed in Table 6 are found in all natural languages, and in the gesture systems spontaneously generated by deaf children. But, interestingly, they are *not* found in the communication systems of nonhumans. Even chimpanzees who have been explicitly taught a communication system by humans do not display the array of properties seen in Table 6. In fact, a skill as simple as communicating about the non-present seems to be beyond the chimpanzee. For example, Kanzi, the Cole Porter of language-learning chimps, uses his symbols to make requests 96% of the time (Greenfield & Savage-Rumbaugh, 1991, 243)—he very rarely comments on the here-and-now, let alone the distant past or future. The linguistic properties displayed in Table 6 are resilient in humans, but not in any other species—indeed, there are *no* conditions under which other species will develop the set of properties listed in Table 6.

The deaf children do not develop all of the properties found in natural languages. We call the properties that the deaf children don't develop the "fragile" properties of language. For example, the deaf children have not developed a system for marking tense. The only property that comes close is the narrative marker that some of the children use to signal stories (essentially a "once upon a time" marker). But these markers are lexical, not grammatical, and don't form a system for indicating the timing of an event relative to the act of speaking. As a second more subtle example, the deaf children do not organize their gesture systems around a principle branching direction. They show neither a bias toward a right-branching nor a left-branching organization, unlike children learning conventional languages who display the bias of the language to which they are exposed (see Chapter 11).

We are, of course, on more shaky ground when we speculate about the fragile properties of language than the resilient ones. Just because we haven't found a particular property in the deaf children's gesture systems doesn't mean it's not there (and it doesn't mean that the children won't develop the property later in development). The negative evidence that we have for the fragile properties of language can never be as persuasive as the positive evidence that firmly supports the resilient properties of language. Nevertheless, the data from the deaf children can lead to hypotheses about the fragile properties of language that can then be confirmed in other paradigms.

☐ Language-Making Skills That Do Not Require a Language Model

Children who are exposed to conventional language models can learn the resilient properties of language from those models. They apply whatever language-learning skills they have to the linguistic inputs they receive, and the product is a linguistic system that includes the resilient properties of language.

There is no reason to believe that deaf children who are *not* exposed to a conventional language model have a different set of language-learning skills. However, they apply these skills to a very different input. Despite this radical difference in input, their product is also a set of linguistic properties.

What kind of language-learning skills can create such a product in the absence of linguistically structured input? The properties listed in Table 6 offer hints as to what these skills might be, skills that might be more aptly called language-*making* than language-*learning*. I focus first on *processes* that children apply in a communication situation even if not exposed to a language model; I then turn to particular *structures* that children construct for communication even if not exposed to a language model (see Table 7).

Processes

One of the most striking aspects of the deaf children's gestures is that it is not mime. The children could easily (and effectively) convey information by producing continuous and unsegmentable movements in mime-like fashion. For example, a child could elaborately pantomime a scene in which she is given a jar, twists off the lid, and blows a bubble in order to request the jar and comment on what she'll do when she gets it. But the deaf children don't behave like mimes. They produce discrete gestures concatenated into

---

TABLE 7. Language-Making Skills That Do Not Require a Language Model

---

Processes that do not require a language model to be activated

I. Segmenting
   • Words are segmented into morphemes
   • Sentences are segmented into words

II. Constructing paradigms ⇒ morphology
   • Setting up systems of contrasts

III. Constructing Sequences ⇒ syntax
   • Building the sequence around an underlying frame
   • Marking thematic roles within the sequence:
     By whether they occur or fail to occur in the sequence
     By the order in which they occur in the sequence
     By an inflection on a word in the sequence
   • Combining propositions to generate new sequences

Structures that do not require a language model to be constructed

I. One-, two-, and three-argument predicate frames
II. Nouns, verbs, and adjectives
III. Ergative constructions

---

sentences—their gestures resemble beads on a string rather than one continuous strand. The basic process underlying the deaf children's gesture system (and all languages) appears to be *segmentation* and *combination* (Table 7).

Interestingly, the process of *segmentation* operates at two levels in the deaf children's gesture systems (and at many levels in natural languages). The deaf children segment their gesture-words into smaller units reminiscent of morphemes, and they segment their gesture-sentences into smaller units reminiscent of words. The discrete units that result from this process of segmentation are categorical. As such, they do not map onto their referents in analog fashion—a fact which opens the way for a relatively arbitrary mapping between symbol and referent (note that in order for a child's gesture system to be truly arbitrary, the child would need a partner willing to enter into a shared system of communication—none of the deaf children was in such a situation). Once segmented, the units become stable, maintaining the same form across a range of communicative acts. Thus, many of the resilient properties at the word level appear to fall out of the process of segmentation into categories.

In addition, once segmented into smaller units, those newly segmented units need to be related to one another within a larger *combination*. At the word level, the children's solution to the combination problem is to construct paradigms—systems in which a sub-word component derives its meaning by the way it contrasts with other sub-word components in the grid (Table 3 in Chapter 9 presents examples of contrasting morphemes for one of the deaf children). Paradigm-construction is a process that all natural languages employ to deal with the problem of how sub-word components (morphemes) relate to one another.

At the sentence level, the children's solution to the combination problem is to construct sequences. But just stringing elements together is not enough. Imagine that a mime for the bubble-blowing scene is segmented into many discrete gestures. Although the gestures may adequately refer to the elements in the scene, they do not convey how those elements relate to one another. This relation, which is conveyed iconically in a mime, must be conveyed through other processes in sequences of discrete elements.

One such process builds sequences around underlying organizations that determine which elements can appear in a sequence (predicate frames). A second process marks the elements in a sequence according to thematic role, using three syntactic devices—deletion, order, and inflection—devices that are found in all natural languages. These processes are necessary to tell who is doing what to whom. But propositions also need to be related to one another, and the third process does just that—it conjoins into a single sequence two or more propositions (recursion) in a systematic way. At the underlying level, elements that appear in both propositions are allotted only one slot in the conjoined predicate frames. At the surface level, redundant elements that appear in both propositions are reduced (appear less often or with less weight) relative to nonredundant elements.

Freyd (1983) has suggested that the very act of transmitting information to another mind will force that information to take a discrete and segmented form. Freyd argues that even if knowledge is truly represented in a continuous form, in the process of imparting that knowledge to another individual, the knowledge must go through a discrete filter and, as a result, its representation ends up looking discrete. Under this view, it is the communication of information to another that encourages the child to activate the process of segmentation.

Once having segmented a chunk into pieces, an obvious next step is to combine those pieces into some sort of larger unit. However, it is less obvious why children should invoke *these particular* processes of combination—constructing paradigms (which leads to a morphology), and constructing sequences by building on underlying frames, marking roles, and introducing recursion (which leads to a syntax). Of all the cognitive processes that children have at their disposal, why should these particular processes be the ones invoked when the task is communication?

Indeed, the deaf children do *not* co-opt all cognitive structures for the purposes of communication. For example, we might guess that a gesture system would be particularly amenable to grammaticizing Euclidean-geometric concepts (fixed distance, size, contour, angle, etc.). But the deaf children don't grammaticize these notions in their gestures, nor apparently does any natural language (Talmy, 1988, 171). That the children choose to co-opt the particular combinatorial processes listed in Table 7 over others is therefore significant. Even if we are completely comfortable saying that these processes reflect general cognitive operations (as opposed to specifically linguistic operations), we still need to explain why *this set* has been co-opted. For the child learning language from a model, the answer is obvious—the language model tells the child that these processes are relevant to communication. But what tells the deaf children? Why should the deaf children invoke just these processes for the purposes of communication? It may be that the communicative situation itself demands not only segmentation, but also combinatorial processes of this sort—a hypothesis to which we return in Chapter 17.

Structures

In addition to a set of processes that do not require a language model to be activated, there is also a set of structures that does not require a language model to be constructed (Table 7).

Not only do the deaf children build their gesture sentences around underlying predicate frames, but the particular frames they rely on are fundamental constructions found in all natural languages. The children construct three-argument predicate frames (an act plus actor, patient, and recipient); two-argument frames (an act plus actor and patient; or an act plus actor and recipient); and one-argument frames (an act plus actor). It is, at some level, not at all surprising that children choose to parse events into these particular components—they seem like the most natural way of viewing events of this sort. However, it is worth noting that events do *not* come pre-parsed. It is the children themselves who take the unsegmented scene, parse it into just the units that languages exploit, and then package those units into linguistic frames. Moreover, there are other distinctions that the children could impose but don't; for example, the gender of the participants, their size, their agility, the timing and placement of their actions. The striking result is that children need no guidance from a language model to do the parsing and packaging that results in the core set of predicate frames.

In addition, the children incorporate into their gestures grammatical distinctions between nouns, verbs, and adjectives. Following Sapir (1921), we based our initial criteria for dividing gestures into nouns, verbs, and adjectives on discourse function—gestures that focus attention on a discourse topic (nouns) versus those that comment on a topic (verbs and adjectives). We found a host of formal distinctions (morphological and syntactic) that, over time, come to be correlated with these uses. But our initial distinction was based in discourse, which may be precisely where the impetus for such divisions comes from, not only in conventional language systems (cf. Hopper & Thompson, 1984, 1988; Sapir, 1921), but also in nonconventional systems invented by children. Whatever their source, these are distinctions that are fundamental to language but do not require a language model for their construction.

Finally, the children's gestures assumed an ergative pattern in many constructions. Unlike the predicate frames we have identified in the deaf children's gesture systems and their noun-verb distinctions, ergative constructions are not universal. Indeed, ergative languages are relatively rare across the globe. Thus, it may be somewhat surprising that these particular constructions are the ones that children come up with in the absence of linguistic input. However, although it may be counterintuitive to speakers of English (which is not an ergative language), the ergative pattern may be the default organization—it may require input to structure language in any other way. We return to this point below.

Slobin (1997b, 276) has suggested that certain grammatical forms and constructions may be more accessible than others to children. However, it is not a simple matter to determine which notions are more, or less, accessible. Slobin argues quite convincingly that accessibility hierarchies cannot be discovered by surveying the array of languages that are spoken across the globe by adults. We need to look at children. If a child gives grammatical expression to a notion early in development, that notion is a good candidate for being high on the accessibility hierarchy. However, the age at which a construction appears in a child's language is affected by many factors, not the least of which is the language model to which the child is exposed.

Deaf children inventing their own gesture systems offer the most straightforward data on this question. If a child is able to produce a grammatical construction without any guidance from a language model, that grammatical construction must be very high on the accessibility hierarchy. Thus, the constructions listed in Table 7—predicate frames consisting of one, two, and three arguments; grammatical distinctions among nouns, verbs, and adjectives; ergative constructions—can be said to be highly accessible to children and may well serve as the conceptual "starting points" for grammatical notions (Slobin, 1997b, 276).

Language Uses

Note that, in Table 7, I have listed only language-making skills that result in word- and sentence-level structure. What is the relation between these language-making skills and the language uses that are listed as resilient in Table 6?

One possibility is that these uses provide the impetus for the language-making skills—that the particular skills listed in Table 7 are activated in order to solve the problems generated by talking about the non-here-and-now, making generic statements, telling stories, or talking about talk. In fact, just such a hypothesis has been suggested to explain how creole languages become structurally more complex—as their communicative uses expand, so too do their linguistic devices (Sankoff & Brown, 1976).

Another possibility is that these word- and sentence-level structures are needed in order to use language in this way—that the structures precede, and are necessary for, the expanded language uses. As we increase the number of children, and cultures, in our study we may be able to tackle this question. If there is variability across children, with some children failing to develop either particular linguistic structures or particular linguistic functions, we can use this variability to determine whether there is a conditional relation between the two. Will, for example, a child who fails to use recursive devices in gesture also fail to use gesture to narrate?

☐ What Happens When Language-Making Skills Meet a Language Model?

We have used the properties of language listed in Table 6 to generate a set of language-making skills that all children can be expected to bring to the task of language-learning. The deaf children run these skills over nonlinguistic input and arrive at what we've called the resilient properties of language. What happens when these language-making skills meet a language model?

In Chapter 3, we identified commonalities in the early stages of language-learning that children across the globe display despite differences in the languages to which they are exposed—a set of privileged meanings and forms that crop up in children's language even if there is no explicit model for them in the language the children are learning. On the basis of the cross-linguistic literature, we identified word order, predicate frames, and paradigms as privileged forms in early child language—all forms that the language-making *processes* listed in Table 7 ought to generate. Children look for ordering relations and underlying organizations across words within a sentence, and regularities of form across words in their lexicons. They will impose regularities of this sort even if there is no explicit model for those regularities, as in the deaf children's case or, less dramatically, in the case of children whose language happens not to have exemplars of such constructions.

What about the particular *structures* listed in Table 7? Some of these structures—the predicate frames and the distinction between nouns and verbs—are found in all languages and thus are universal (although, of course, the details of how nouns and verbs behave, or which verbs belong to which predicate frames, differ across languages). Children who are exposed to a language model may display these structures either because they themselves bring them to the language-learning situation, or because they see them instantiated in the language to which they are exposed. Their presence in early child language is overdetermined.

But ergative constructions are not universal and, indeed, ergative languages are not even frequent across the globe. What happens then when children are exposed to a non-ergative language? The data that we collected on Chinese and American deaf and hearing children (Zheng, 2000; Zheng &

Goldin-Meadow, 2002) are relevant here. Recall from Chapter 15 that we examined four groups of children at approximately 4 years of age: Chinese and American deaf children, and Chinese and American hearing children, all interacting with their hearing parents. Both English and Mandarin are accusative rather than ergative languages. However, the languages differ in that Mandarin permits deletion of arguments, whereas English does not (see Figure 23 in Chapter 15). We examined how often the children produced words (or gestures) for actors and patients in transitive sentences, and actors in intransitive sentences. The grouped data are presented in Figure 25, with data for hearing children on the left and deaf children on the right.

Note first the robustness of the ergative pattern in the deaf children across cultures. Both the Chinese and American deaf children produce gestures for patients and intransitive actors at the same high rate, and gestures for transitive actors at a much lower rate. The question is what happens when a hearing child, who presumably is equipped with this same ergative tendency, meets an accusative language model.

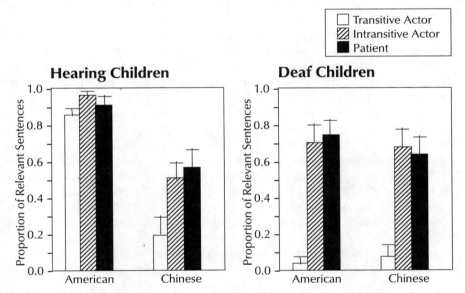

FIGURE 25. When the Language They Are Learning Permits, Hearing Children Structure Their Language Like the Deaf Children. The figure displays the proportion of utterances in which the Chinese and American deaf and hearing children produced words or gestures for a transitive actor, a patient, or an intransitive actor. As in Figure 23, the deaf children show no differences across cultures—both groups display an ergative pattern (intransitive actors are treated like patients and different from transitive actors). Again, the hearing children are influenced by their language models. English does not permit deletion, and the American children do not delete—all three elements are produced almost all of the time. Mandarin does permit deletion. Interestingly, when the Chinese hearing children delete, they too follow an ergative pattern, despite the fact that Mandarin is not an ergative language. Error bars reflect standard errors.

English does not permit deletion of arguments and, as the figure shows, the American children are good English-speakers in this respect—they produce words for all three arguments at the same high rate. The Chinese children are interesting, however. Mandarin permits deletion, and the Chinese hearing children delete a great deal. And when they do, they delete according to an ergative pattern. Thus, the ergative structuring that we see in the deaf children crops up in hearing children wherever their language does not rule it out. It's even found in very young English-learners who can only produce two words at a time (Goldin-Meadow & Mylander, 1984, 62–64), and in children learning Korean, which is also not an ergative language (Choi, 1999; Clancy, 1993).

Recall that in Chapter 3, in addition to identifying privileged forms on the basis of the cross-linguistic literature, we also identified privileged meanings. A focus on *results* was one such meaning. In a sense, ergative patterns can be thought of as focusing on results—when intransitive actors are marked like patients, their properties as affected object (i.e., the properties that result from the action) are highlighted in preference to their properties as initiator or agent.

Interestingly, the focus on results is not limited to children. Recent findings on adults suggest that focusing on the patient may be a default way of viewing an action. Griffin and Bock (2000) monitored eye movements under several conditions: adults described a simple event shown in a picture (speech condition); they viewed the picture with the goal of finding the person or thing being acted on in each event (patient condition); they viewed the picture without any specific task requirements (inspection condition). The interesting result from our perspective is that the adults' eye movements were skewed toward the patient early in the viewing, not only in the patient condition, but also in the inspection condition. When given no instructions, the adults' first inclination was to focus on the patient—the semantic element around which many constructions in the deaf children's gesture systems revolve. In contrast, when asked to describe the scene in speech, the adults skewed their eye movements to the agent, the semantic element that typically occupies the subject position of an English sentence.

Our data, in conjunction with Griffin and Bock's findings (2000), suggest that focusing on patients may be a default bias found in both processing and acquisition tasks. When asked only to view a scene, adults focus their attention on the patient. This attentional bias is abandoned when the adult is asked to talk about the scene in a conventional language whose syntactic structure does not match the bias. In a similar fashion, when not exposed to a usable conventional language model, children display a patient bias in their self-generated communication systems. This bias is abandoned when a hearing child is exposed to a language model whose syntactic structures do not match the bias.

If a patient-focus is such a natural way of taking in a scene, why don't most of the world's languages design their structures to take advantage of what would appear to be an easily processed format? Slobin (1977) has outlined a number of pressures that language faces—pressures to be clear, processible, quick and easy, and expressive. Importantly, Slobin points out that these pressures do not necessarily all push language in the same direction. Thus, for example, the pressure to be semantically clear may come into conflict with pressures to be processed quickly or to be rhetorically expressive. The need to be clear may pressure languages to adopt structures that reinforce the patient-bias. However, at the same time, the need to be quick and expressive may pressure languages toward structures that do not have a patient focus. If the bias toward patients is as fundamental as Griffin and Bock's (2000) and the spontaneous gesture data suggest, there may be a cognitive cost to overriding it—for example, there may be greater cognitive costs involved in processing sentences that do not organize around the patient than sentences that do. This would be an intriguing direction for future research, one that we are currently pursuing.

☐ The Deaf Children Provide Empirical Evidence on the Child's Initial Grammatical State

The way the deaf children instantiate an ergative pattern in their gesture systems is to omit gestures for transitive actors, which are typically subjects in conventional languages. Conventional languages vary according to whether they permit deletion of subjects (i.e., null subjects). Italian does (it's a null-subject language), English does not. As described in Chapter 2, the theory of *Universal Grammar* (UG) formulates the knowledge children bring to language-learning in terms of principles and parameters that determine the set of possible human languages. Some principles of UG do not account exhaustively for properties of grammars; they are underspecified, leaving several options open. Input from a given language is needed for learners to "set" the parameters of that language. Null subjects is one such parameter. Children need input to determine whether or not the language they are learning is a null-subject language.

Do children come to language-learning with a default setting on the null-subject parameter and, if so, how do we determine what that default is? On the basis of empirical data, Hyams hypothesized in 1986 that all children start out with a grammar that licenses null subjects. Recently, however, she has become convinced that the properties of the child's initial state prior to experience may have to be determined logically, rather than empirically, simply because linguistic input begins to alter the child's initial state almost immediately (Hyams, 1994, 297–8).

I suggest that the deaf children's gesture systems can provide important empirical data on children's initial grammatical state prior to linguistic experience. And the data support Hyams' view that children come to the language-learning situation with the expectation that subjects (transitive actors in the deaf children's gesture systems) can be omitted (note that they really are omitted, or more accurately not lexicalized, as opposed to never being there in the first place—otherwise we could not explain the systematic actor production probability patterns we find in relation to underlying predicate frames, see Figure 7 in Chapter 10). Children need a language model to teach them that subjects ought to be given expression.

In some domains, children may come to the language-learning situation *without* a bias or default setting—and the deaf children can provide useful data here as well. Recall from Chapter 3 that children discover relatively early that they are learning either a right-branching (English) or a left-branching (Japanese) language. Discovering the branching direction of the language they are learning has ramifications throughout the children's linguistic system. Do children have a bias toward right- versus left-branching systems before being exposed to linguistic input? No—at least not according to the data on the deaf children's complex gesture sentences presented in Chapter 11. The deaf children show no bias of any sort, suggesting that the initial grammatical state may be neutral on this dimension.

These constructions—obligatoriness of explicit subjects, and dominant branching organization (left vs. right)—are places where Slobin (1997a, 3) has hypothesized that children learn a general format or "solution" from the syntax of the language model to which they are exposed. Our findings suggest that a language model is indeed essential to obligatorily produce subjects and to have a branching direction, thus providing empirical support for Slobin's claim. However, our findings go one step farther—they make it clear that these two cases are *not* identical. In one case (branching direction), the child does not appear to come to the language-learning situation with a bias. In the other case (obligatoriness of subjects), the child does—a bias to omit subjects (or at least agents, cf. Zheng & Goldin-Meadow, 2002).

To summarize, the deaf children's gestures provide evidence, as direct as we can possibly hope for, on the properties of language that are resilient. These resilient properties of language inform us not only about how children tackle communication in atypical environments but also how they learn language in typical environments. The resilient properties listed in Table 6 thus constitute a set of (testable) hypotheses that we can take to the cross-linguistic literature—they are just the meanings and forms that we would expect to be robust across linguistic variation at the earliest stages of language-learning (the conceptual starting points for language-learning). Moreover, the deaf children's gestures provide what might be the only empirical evidence on the child's initial grammatical state prior to linguistic experience. Finally, the gestures provide fodder for our speculations about the language-making skills that all children bring to the task of communication.

CHAPTER

When Does Gesture Become Language?

What is it that leads gesture to assume language-like structure in the deaf children but not their hearing parents? This question is important as it can provide insight into the factors that are necessary for language-like structure to appear in human communication. I believe we have an answer to the question. I suggest that it is only when gesture is called upon to carry the full burden of communication (as opposed to playing an adjunct role) that it assumes language-like structure. In this chapter, I describe a series of studies on hearing adults that test this hypothesis.

☐ When Gesture Does or Does Not Assume the Full Burden of Communication

The deaf children's hearing parents produce all of their gestures while talking—their goal is, after all, to teach their children to speak, not to gesture. When gesture is used along with speech, it shares the burden of communication with that speech. Gesture and speech form a single, integrated system in which the two modalities work together both semantically and temporally. When gesture is produced with speech, its form is constrained by the framing that speech provides and it becomes global and imagistic (McNeill, 1992). The gestures that accompany speech are not composed of parts but are instead noncompositional wholes. Since the gesture must be a good representation of its referent, the addition of semantic information to a spontaneous gesture always increases its iconicity. If, for example, an act is thought of as very slow, the gesture for that act must also be very slow. In other words, when the manual modality shares the burden of communication with speech, it mimetically depicts events as global wholes.

In direct contrast to the global synthetic form that gesture assumes when used with speech, when the manual modality takes on the full burden of communication—as it does in conventional sign languages—global representation is abandoned. In its stead, we find representation by hierarchically arranged parts—morphemes combine to form signs which, in turn, combine to form sentences. Thus, for example, the ASL sign for "slow" is made by moving one hand across the back of the other hand; when the sign is modified to mean "very slow," it is produced *more rapidly* since this is the particular modification of movement associated with an intensification meaning (Klima & Bellugi, 1979). Unlike the spontaneous gestures that accompany speech, modifying the meaning of a sign in ASL can *reduce* its iconicity simply because the meaning of the sign as a whole is, in rule-governed fashion, made up of the meanings of the components that comprise it.

The hypothesis here is that segmented representation arises in sign language (and not in the spontaneous gestures that accompany speech) precisely because, in sign language (but not in the gestures that accompany speech), the manual modality assumes the primary burden of communication. Gesture becomes increasingly interpretable when seen in the context of the speech it accompanies. When there is no speech, gesture must "do it all" and, in assuming this responsibility, can no longer afford its former unsegmented form.

But is it really the fact that the manual modality is assuming the primary burden of communication that matters? Sign languages differ from spontaneous gesture not only in function (serving the full burden of communication versus not), but also in codification. Sign languages have histories and are passed down from one generation of users to the next (Frishberg, 1975). They are codified linguistic systems. The gestures that accompany speech are not.

The gesture systems created by deaf children become relevant at this point in the argument. The deaf children's gesture systems are not codified and, in this sense, are like the gestures that accompany speech. However, the deaf children's gestures do serve the full burden of communication and thus, in this respect, are like conventional sign languages. Where do they fall in this argument? Importantly, we find that the deaf children's gesture systems are structurally more similar to conventional sign languages than to the gestures that accompany speech. Thus, the function to which the manual symbols are put, rather than the extent to which they are codified, appears to be critical in fostering language-like structure. We put this hypothesis to experimental test in the next sections.

☐ Gestures With and Without Speech

When produced along with speech, gestures do not and (I claim precisely because of the constraints imposed by speech) *cannot* assume the segmented form of the words they accompany. One might suspect that if the deaf children's hearing mothers had merely refrained from speaking as they gestured, their gestures would have become more language-like in structure, assuming the segmented and combinatorial form characteristic of their children's gestures. In other words, the mothers would have been more likely to use gestures that mirrored their children's if they kept their mouths shut.

To test this hypothesis, we have conducted a series of experiments in which hearing adults are asked to describe scenes with and without speech. We predicted that the gestures the adults would produce *without* speech would be segmented and combined into sentence-like strings and, as such, would be distinct from the gestures these same adults would produce spontaneously when they describe the scenes *with* speech.

This experiment attempts to simulate the deaf child's language-creating situation. However, we use hearing adults not deaf children as creators. There are two, very obvious differences between the adults and the deaf children. First, the adults already know a conventional language (English) and thus their created gestures could be heavily influenced by the particular language that they know. Second, the adults are not children and thus are well beyond whatever critical period there is for language-learning (and perhaps for language-creating as well). To the extent that we find differences between the gestures that the adults and the deaf children create, age and language-knowledge become likely candidates for causing those differences. But to the extent that the gestures created by the adults and deaf children resemble one another, we have evidence that the created structures do *not* reflect a childlike way of organizing the world—and that they may well reflect the effect of gesture assuming the primary burden of communication. Adults, even those who already have a language, may organize their manual-only communications in precisely the same ways as the deaf children, raising the possibility that the language-like properties found in the deaf children's systems result from trying to get information from one human mind to another in real time.

We asked English-speakers who had no knowledge of sign language to participate in the study (Goldin-Meadow, McNeill, & Singleton, 1996). We showed the adults videotaped vignettes of objects and people moving in space from the test battery designed by Supalla, Newport, and their colleagues (2003) to assess knowledge of ASL. Half the scenes contained only one moving object (e.g., a porcupine wandering across the screen) while the other half contained one moving object and one stationary object (e.g., a girl jumping into a hoop, a donut-shaped object arcing out of an ashtray). The adults were asked to describe each event depicted on the videotape twice, first using speech and then in a second pass through the scenes, using only their hands. We examined whatever gestures the adults produced in their first pass through the events (the Gesture + Speech condition) and compared them to the gestures they produced in their second pass (the Gesture condition). What happened?

As predicted, we found that the adults' gestures resembled the deaf children's in the Gesture condition but not the Gesture + Speech condition. Specifically, in the Gesture condition, the adults produced clearly articulated gestures that were often combined into connected strings. Moreover, the strings were reliably ordered, with gestures for certain semantic elements occurring in particular positions. Interestingly, all of the adults used the same gesture order and that order did *not* follow canonical English word order. For example, in one scene, the adults saw a donut-shaped object rising on its own in an arc out of an astray and landing on a nearby table. To describe this scene in the Gesture alone condition, one adult produced a string of four gestures. Each gesture was crisp (with clearly formed handshapes and motions) and segmented, and the string of four was produced without any pause or break in the flow of motion.

> The adult brought his right hand shaped in a "V" to his lips as though smoking a cigarette (= ashtray);
> He cupped his left hand in a large "C" with the fingers spread forming a dishlike shape and bounced his right hand with his fingers bunched into a squashed "O" as though stubbing out a cigarette (= ashtray);
> He drew a circle in the air with his right hand in a well-formed point (= donut-shaped object);
> He formed his right hand into a round "O" shape and arced it out of his left, still in the shape of the dish (= arc-out).

The adult's gestures thus followed the order "ashtray donut arc-out" (stationary object—moving object—action), rather than the typical English order "donut arc-out ashtray". The "stationary object—moving object—action" order is typical of adults creating their own gestures on the spot (Goldin-Meadow et al., 1996; Gershkoff-Stowe & Goldin-Meadow, 2002).[1]

In contrast, in the Gesture + Speech condition, although the adults did produce gestures that convey information about actions and objects, they rarely combined those gestures into strings. Moreover, their handshapes were loosely formed and sloppy. For example, the same adult who produced the "ashtray donut arc-out" sequence in the Gesture condition, followed typical English word order when describing the scene in the Gesture + Speech condition. He said, "a crooked circular donut shape moved from out. . . . from within a yellow ashtray." The gestures he produced were timed along with these words and followed roughly the same English order. Importantly, however, the gestures were *not* connected to one another—each gesture was followed by a pause and relaxation of the hands.

---

[1]When the deaf children describe events of this type, they typically put gestures for the moving object (intransitive actor) before gestures for the action. Thus, the adult gesturers' ordering pattern in the Gesture condition mirrors the deaf children's, with the exception that the children rarely include gestures for the stationary object in their gesture sentences.

The adult made a small arcing motion away from his body with his left
  hand in no particular shape (= arc).
[He paused and returned his hands to his lap].
He made a larger arcing motion that crossed space, this time with his
  hand in a loose "O" shape (= arc-out).
[He paused and returned his hands to his lap].
He indicated the spot where his arc had begun with a sloppy point and
  rotated his hand twice in the air (= ashtray)

The adult's gestures were loosely constructed and did not cohere into a uni-
fied string. In this sense, they were very different from the deaf children's
gestures, and very different from the gestures this same adult produced when
called upon to speak with his hands.

In short, when gesture accompanies speech in ordinary conversation, the
imagistic information it conveys is clearly an important part of the communication (Goldin-Meadow, 1999a, 2003c; McNeill, 1992). However, this function can be sacrificed (although not completely lost) when gesture is called
upon to carry the full burden of communication. When gesture is the *only*
modality available, it is no longer purely driven by imagery. Instead, it assumes the segmented and combinatorial form required for symbolic human
communication—and it does so whether the gesturer is an adult or a child.

☐ Ergative Structure Crops Up Again

All of the vignettes in our initial study involved objects and people moving
about in space, events that elicit intransitive sentences. With only intransitive sentences as stimuli, we cannot determine whether the adults use ergative
constructions in their gestures, as do the deaf children. We therefore conducted a second study (albeit a preliminary one since only two adults have
participated to date) with vignettes involving some events that elicit intransitive sentences and others that elicit transitive sentences (Goldin-Meadow,
Yalabik, & Gershkoff-Stowe, 2000). We included only a Gesture condition
in this study (there was no Gesture + Speech condition): The adults were
asked to describe each scene using their hands and not their mouths. Because we were interested in whether there would be changes in the gestures
over time, we arranged for the two adults to meet twice a week for several
weeks.

We used the same system of analysis for the adults as we did for the deaf
children. We looked at gesture strings that could have contained three semantic elements but, in fact, only contained two (e.g., transitive sentences
with an underlying predicate frame of actor-act-patient, and intransitive
sentences with an underlying predicate frame of actor-act-recipient). Both
adults produced gestures for intransitive actors as often as they produced

gestures for patients, and far more often than they produced gestures for transitive actors. In other words, they displayed the same ergative pattern seen in the deaf children's gestures. And they did so immediately—the ergative pattern was evident in the adults' initial sessions and did not change over time (Figure 26; Goldin-Meadow, 2003b; Goldin-Meadow et al., 2000).

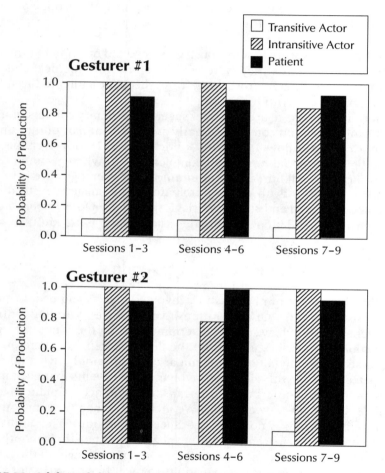

FIGURE 26. Adult English Speakers, Asked to Gesture Without Speaking, Follow the Same Pattern as the Deaf Children When They Omit and Produce Gestures for Different Semantic Elements. The figure displays the likelihood that two adult gesturers will produce a gesture for a transitive actor, a patient, or an intransitive actor in a two-gesture sentence. The data are divided into three parts: the first three sessions in which the two gesturers participated, the second three, and the last three. Both gesturers produced gestures for intransitive actors as often as for patients, and more often than they produced gestures for transitive actors—that is, they displayed the same ergative pattern found in the Chinese and American deaf children.

In terms of gesture order, both adults produced gestures for intransitive actors in first position of their two-gestures sentences (e.g., "mouse go"). This result is hardly surprising as the pattern parallels typical word order for intransitive actors in English. Neither adult produced many gestures for transitive actors, which made it impossible to determine an order preference for this semantic element. More interestingly, both gesturers also produced gestures for patients in first position of their two-gesture sentences ("cheese eat"; see also Hammond & Goldin-Meadow, 2002). Not only is this pattern identical to the deaf children's gesture order for patients, but it is also different from the pattern typically found in English (i.e., "eat cheese").

The patient-first pattern is particularly interesting in the adults. The deaf children often (although not always) used pointing gestures to convey patients. The adults were not able to take advantage of this pointing strategy simply because there were no objects in the room to point at. The adults were forced to invent an iconic gesture for their patients—for example, a smoking movement at the mouth to refer to an ashtray, which was then followed by a gesture representing the action that was done on that ashtray (e.g., a throwing action). Despite the fact that they used iconic rather than pointing gestures to refer to patients, the adults followed the same (non-English) ordering patterns as the deaf children.

Thus, when asked to describe a series of action vignettes using their hands rather than words, English-speaking adults invent an ergative structure identical to the one developed by the deaf children, rather than the accusative pattern found in their own spoken language. Ergative structure is *not* unique to child language-creators and therefore cannot reflect a childlike way of organizing information for communication. Rather, the ergative pattern may reflect a robust solution to the problem of communicating information from one mind to another, be it an adult or child mind. If the ergative pattern is indeed an outgrowth of communicative pressures, altering aspects of the communication situation might be expected to have an impact on the way these self-generated gesture systems are structured. We explore this possibility in the next section.

☐ The Importance, or Nonimportance, of the Communication Situation

We chose to explore the effect of variations in the communication situation on one particularly salient aspect of language—word order. Every language has a way to talk about objects and actions and a method to specify the relations among them. Word order is one device that serves this purpose in all languages (Greenberg, 1966; Hawkins, 1983). Although languages vary in how much they rely on surface order, all languages have some basic canonical arrangement. Why is word order so robust?

Our data allow us to rule out historical convention as a factor necessary for word order. The deaf children we have observed are not exposed to a language that has had its word order patterns passed down from generation to generation. Nonetheless, they invent gesture systems with consistent ordering patterns. Children do not need a language model to introduce word order into their communication systems.

We can also rule out age as a factor necessary for word order. When asked to rely solely on gesture, hearing adults generate a non-English gesture order, thus making it clear that adults can introduce a novel order not found in their first language when generating a second "language." The fact that both adults and children exploit order when learning or creating a first or second language suggests that word order is not solely the product of a young mind.

Two other, not mutually exclusive, factors might play a role in encouraging communicators to rely on word order—*communicative* and *cognitive* factors. Word order may be essential in conveying information effectively to another person. If so, aspects of the communication situation itself might make it more, or less, likely that speakers will rely on order in their communications. Under this hypothesis, it is the *communicative* relationship speakers and listeners hold to one another that makes ordering an essential strategy in communication. Alternatively, speakers may naturally parse events into a sequence of elements when apprehending those events. If so, order in communications may reflect this *cognitive* processing strategy. Under this hypothesis, it is qualities of the speaker that make ordering an inevitable component of communication.

Using our gesture-creation paradigm, we first asked whether consistent ordering is robust across a variety of communicative arrangements, arrangements that might be expected to shape how communication is structured (Gershkoff-Stowe & Goldin-Meadow, 2002). We asked adults to describe scenes in gesture under a variety of communicative conditions—we varied whether the listener could give feedback; we varied whether the information to be communicated was present in the context that the gesturer and listener shared; and we varied whether the gesturer assumed the role of gesture-receiver as well as gesture-producer. We found that, not only was consistent ordering of semantic elements robust across the range of communication situations, but the *same non-English* order appeared in all contexts.

We then went on to explore whether this non-English order is bound to a communication context at all—that is, whether it arises *only* when a person attempts to share information with another, or whether it crops up in noncommunicative contexts as well. We asked adults to reconstruct scenes using transparent pictures that could be stacked on top of one another. In one condition, the adults were asked to reconstruct the scene while describing what they were doing in English to the experimenter. In the other condition, the experimenter was blocked from view and the adults were instructed only to reconstruct the scene. Unbeknownst to them, what we were really interested in was whether they used a consistent order when

creating the stack. We found that adults in both conditions did indeed reconstruct the scenes in an ordered fashion. Interestingly, however, the particular orders they used were quite different depending on the experimental
condition. The adults who talked while reconstructing the scene, perhaps
not surprisingly, often placed their pictures in the stack following English
word-order—the picture for the donut came first, then the picture for the
action (a cartoon-like directional sweep), and finally the picture for the ashtray. In contrast, the adults who reconstructed the scenes in the
noncommunicative context used the same order that we found in our adult
gesture-creation study—the picture for the ashtray came first, then the gesture for the donut, and finally the gesture for the action. Finding the same
non-English order in a noncommunicative context suggests that the order is
not driven solely by communication in the manual modality, but may be a
more general property of human thought.

Thus, in two studies—one in which adults were asked to create a "language"
to describe a scene to another, and a second in which adults were asked to
reconstruct a scene for themselves—we find that it is completely natural for
humans to sequence symbols that represent semantic roles according to a
consistent order. Whether or not adults are communicating, they place symbols for particular semantic roles in particular sequential positions. The reli-
ance on ordering devices found in all natural languages appears to reflect
general processing strategies that are not necessarily specific to language.

In addition to this general predisposition to sequence symbols for semantic roles according to a consistent order, we also find a *specific* order that
appears to serve as a default for sequencing semantic roles (stationary object—moving object—action). This order is used when adults reconstruct an
event for themselves, and when they communicate the event to another in
gesture without talking. However, this order is *not* the canonical order that
most conventional languages offer their speakers to describe such events—
many conventional languages, including English, override the default order
(whether there is a cognitive cost to doing so, as mentioned in Chapter 16, is
an open question). Thus, although ordering itself is a general cognitive skill
that all languages exploit, the particular orders that languages adopt are
quite specific to language. They do not necessarily reflect a general (i.e.,
nonlanguage) way of viewing the world, but instead may be arbitrary out-
growths of the many pressures that conspire to make language what it is
(see Slobin, 1977).

☐ Grammatical Properties and the Conditions of Language Creation

The emergence of segmentation and combination (including ordering) in
the experimental paradigms we have used with adults underscores the

resilience of these grammatical properties in symbolic human communication. With little time for reflection, the adults in our studies constructed a set of gestures characterized by segmentation and combination. However, our simple experimental paradigm was not sufficient to support the emergence of all of the grammatical properties that we find in the deaf children's gesture systems. The adults' gestures were not systematically organized into a system of internal contrasts, that is, into a morphology.

When the hearing adults generated a gesture, their goal was to produce a handshape that adequately represented the object, and their choice of handshapes appeared to be constrained *only* by their imaginations and the physical limitations imposed by their hands (that is, how the gesture relates to the world). For example, a hearing adult might produce a different handshape for each of the five airplanes on the test, with each handshape capturing an idiosyncratic property of the airplane pictured in that event. In contrast, when the deaf children in our studies generate a gesture, their choice of handshapes is guided not only by how well the handshape captures the features of the object, but also by how well that handshape fits into the set of handshapes allowed in their individual gesture systems (that is, how the gesture relates to other gestures in the set). Thus, they use the same handshape for all airplanes (indeed, for all vehicles), regardless of their individual idiosyncracies, and this handshape contrasts with the handshape used to represent, say, curved objects (see Chapter 9).

The fact that adults instantly invent a gesture system with segmentation and combination but without a system of internal contrasts suggests that some properties of language may be more resilient than others. It may therefore be possible to classify grammatical properties according to the types of conditions that support their creation, and we may be able to use our experimental paradigm to help us do the classification. By altering aspects of the paradigm, we can explore the effects of various circumstances on the emergence of grammatical properties.

For example, using the experimental paradigm as is, we discovered that a system of contrasts is not an *immediate* consequence of symbolically communicating information to another human. The fact that the deaf children did develop a system of contrasts suggests that continued experience with a set of gestures may be required for a system of contrasts to emerge in those gestures. However, it is also possible that even with continued experience with their own gestures, *adults* may not be able to develop a system of contrasts within those gestures. In other words, it may be that the creator must be a child in order for a system of contrasts to emerge. Our experimental paradigm can be adapted to address this issue. Adults and children can be asked to participate in the study over an extended period, thus allowing each creator the time that appears to be necessary (but may not be sufficient) to develop a system of contrasts.

Alternatively, it may be that what is crucial for a system of contrasts to evolve in a symbolic communication system has more to do with the recipient than the creator. We have thus far examined morphological structure only in the conditions where the gesturers were not given feedback by their "listeners." Because the adults received no feedback as to how well they communicated the characteristics of each vignette, the grammatical properties that appeared in their gestures had to reflect the creators' intuitive sense of what their recipient would find comprehensible, not what the recipient actually understood. In order to explore the role of the recipient in shaping morphologic structure, both gesturer and receiver must be subjects in the study, and the nature (e.g., child vs. adult) or number (e.g., one vs. many) of recipients can be systematically varied. For example, an adult asked to communicate with the same recipient might, over time, generate a set of arbitrary symbols. These arbitrary symbols may or may not form a system of contrasts. Indeed, it might even be better to have many recipients rather than one if a *system* is the goal. Thus, when asked to communicate with a *variety* of recipients, the adult might generate gestures that are relatively iconic but those gestures may be systematized to accommodate the variability across receivers.

As a final example, our study is a single generation deep. Passing a conventional communication system down from generation to generation tends to alter the structure of that system, creating language change over historical time. This interesting phenomenon can be explored over a shorter time period by again adapting our experimental paradigm along a different dimension. After two adults have developed a gesture system, they may be asked to share that system with a third person (an adult or perhaps a child) who is new to the task. The third person, experiencing the system for the first time, may introduce changes into the system, changes that may come about only when a novice views the system as a whole (cf. Kegl, 1994; Singleton & Newport, 2003).

Thus, our experimental paradigm can be adapted to probe language creation over the short term, providing us with a technique to explore the effects of various environments on the structure of symbolic human communication. Note, however, that our gesture-creation paradigm, while useful to explore aspects of language creation, does not simulate the conditions that existed when language was created for the first time. Nevertheless, our findings provide us with grounds for speculation about language evolution, and we turn to this topic in the final section of this chapter.

☐ Why Doesn't Gesture Become Language More Often?

Signed languages (as well as our gesture creation data in children and adults) make it clear that the manual modality *can* assume a segmented and combinatorial form. Why then did language become the province of the oral modality? Why is speech the most common form of linguistic behavior in human cultures when it could just as easily have been gesture?

David McNeill and I (Goldin-Meadow & McNeill, 1999) have gone out on a limb and proposed an (undoubtedly untestable) hypothesis to explain this situation. We speculate that, having segmented structure in the oral modality, as we currently do, leaves the manual modality free to co-occur with speech and to capture the mimetic aspects of communication *along with* speech. Thus, our current arrangement allows us to combine, in a single stream of communication, the imagistic aspects of the mimetic that are so vital to communication along with a segmented representation.

We argue that the alternative arrangement—in which the manual modality would serve language-like functions and the oral modality would serve the mimetic functions—won't work because it forces the oral modality to be unnaturally imagistic in form (although see Haiman, 1985, for evidence that the oral modality does exhibit some iconic properties). Consider this compelling example from Huttenlocher (1973, 1976). Try to describe the East Coast of the United States in words and then in gesture. A verbal description of the shape of the coastline is likely not only to be very cumbersome but also to leave out important information about the coastline—information that could easily be captured in a mimetic gesture tracing the outline of the coast.

Because gesture allows one to represent an image as a whole without breaking it into parts, gesture offers a better vehicle for encoding imagistic information than does speech (Goldin-Meadow, Alibali, & Church, 1993). The manual modality is therefore the natural choice to encode mimetic information, leaving information that is better captured in a discrete and segmented form to the oral modality.

Under this scenario, speech did not become the predominant medium of human language because it is so well suited to the linear and segmented requirements of symbolic human communication—the manual modality is equally suited to the job, as the deaf children's gesture systems suggest and sign languages make clear. Rather, speech became the medium of human communication because it is *not* particularly good at capturing the imagistic components of human communication—a task at which the manual modality excels. McNeill and I speculate that language is the province of speech because it's the only job the oral modality can do well.

This speculation about the importance of maintaining a vehicle for mimetic representation along with speech raises an interesting question with respect to sign language. In sign, it is the manual modality that assumes the segmented and combinatorial form essential to human language. Can the manual modality at the same time also be used for global and mimetic expression? In other words, do signers gesture along with their signs and, if not, how is the global and mimetic function filled? One possibility is that sounds or mouth movements might assume the mimetic function for signers. Sandler (2003) describes the way the mouth works in Israeli Sign Language (ISL), and finds that some mouth movements are independent of the lexical and grammatical system and vary from signer to signer, as do the gestures that accompany speech. For example, one signer produced a sentence translated as "he carried a suitcase," while puffing out his right cheek (he was signing with his right hand). The signer thus indicated that the suitcase was full with his mouth gesture, and only with his mouth gesture. Thus, mouth movements (and perhaps other behaviors as well, cf. Liddell & Metzger, 1998) may serve the mimetic function for sign that gesture serves for speech.

We end by returning to the question with which we began this chapter—when and why does gesture become language? One requirement seems to be that gesture must assume the *full burden of communication* in order to abandon its global and imagistic form and take on the linear and segmented form associated with natural language. In addition, a number of other dimensions are likely to have an impact on when and how gesture takes on language-like properties; for example, *who the creator is*—child or adult. Thus far, we have found that adults can create gesture systems on the spot, but those systems exhibit fewer linguistic properties than the gesture systems created by children (in particular, the gestures are segmented and combined into ordered strings for adults, but they do not exhibit a system of contrasts as the children's gestures do). However, a second dimension—*time*—may be the issue. Perhaps with more time adults would generate a gesture system with all of the resilient properties of language. Or perhaps the *social structure* within which the creator sits, or the *creator's motivation*, is essential to the blossoming of resilient properties.

The experimental gesture-creation paradigm that we have developed allows us to explore the effect on language-creation of these and other dimensions—who the recipient is and how many of them must there be; whether the system is passed on to a novice who might then, in learning the system as a whole, totally reorganize it. Although we obviously cannot re-create the conditions under which language evolved, we can simulate some of those conditions in order to explore when it is more, or less, likely that a human will create more, or less, language.

18
CHAPTER

Is Language Innate?

The fact that all known human groups (even those incapable of hearing) have developed language is reason enough to consider the possibility that language-learning is innate. And, of course, the fact that human children can invent components of language even when not exposed to language makes it more likely still that language-learning ought to be considered innate. The problem in even beginning to address this issue is finding a comfortable definition of "innate" and of "language."

One might naively think that, if learning is involved in the development of a behavior, the behavior cannot be considered innate. However, we'd like our definition of innate to be more subtle than that—some learning is involved in the acquisition of all human skills, even one as basic as walking (Thelen & Ulrich, 1991). The issue is not whether learning has occurred but whether learning is guided by the organism as much as, if not more than, by the environment. A study by Peter Marler (1990) best exemplifies the point. Two closely related species of sparrows were raised from the egg in identical environments and exposed to a collection of songs containing melodies typical for each species. Despite their identical input, the two species learned different songs. Each species learned only the songs in the collection that adult members of its species typically sing. Similarly, Locke (1990) argues that to a certain extent human infants select the sounds they learn preferentially, often learning frequently heard phonemes relatively late and infrequently heard phonemes quite early. Birds and children both learn from the input they receive, but their learning is selective.

Another way of saying this is that the range of possible outcomes in the learning process is narrowed, and the organism itself does the narrowing. This narrowing, or "canalization," is often attributed to genetic causes (cf. Waddington, 1957). However, canalization can also be caused by the environment. For example, exposing a bird to a particular stimulus at one point early in its development can narrow the bird's learning later on: The bird becomes particularly susceptible to that stimulus, and buffered against responding to other stimuli, at later points in development (Gottlieb, 1991). Thus, for any given behavior, we need to investigate the causes of canalization rather than assume a genetic base. In human studies, one cannot freely engineer organisms and environments, and developmental histories are quite complex. It is therefore difficult to attribute canalization to either genetic or environmental causes. Does this difficulty render the notion "innate" meaningless?

☐ Innateness: Evolutionary and Ontogenetic Timespans

In his recent book, Pinker (1994, 18) calls language an "instinct." By this he means that "people know how to talk in more or less the sense that spiders know how to spin webs. . . . spiders spin spider webs because they have spider brains, which give them the urge to spin and the competence to succeed." Pinker's approach to the language-learning question is best situated on the evolutionary timespan (rather than the ontogenetic). His use of the term "instinct" aligns him with European ethologists, and he is indeed interested in the possibility that language has a genetic base. Pinker (1994, 324–5) believes that we now have suggestive evidence for grammar genes—not for a single gene responsible for all the circuitry underlying grammar but for a set of genes whose effects seem most specific to the development of the circuits underlying parts of grammar. Pinker fully admits that the chromosomal loci of these genes is, at present, completely unknown, as is their effect on the structure of the brain.

Having said that language has a genetic base, where do we go from here if our interest is in language-learning, that is, in language over the ontogenetic and not evolutionary timespan? We could leave it to researchers who study twins, both fraternal and identical, to explore the phenomenon of language-learning. In this regard, it is important to note that, in twin studies conducted to explore the genetic basis of *intelligence* (i.e., IQ), the focus is on differences among individuals relative to a normative scale. In arguing that *language* is genetically based, there is no obvious claim that two individuals who are genetically related have linguistic systems that are more alike than two individuals who are not genetically related. As Pinker (1994, 428) himself states, "All claims about a language instinct . . . are claims about the commonalities among all normal people. They have virtually nothing to do with possible genetic differences between people." In fact, Pinker's claim is that all humans who are genetically intact have, at base, comparable linguistic systems, comparable in the same way that all human bodies have two arms and two legs. The details of the arms of any two unrelated individuals (their length, width, definition, etc.) are likely to differ (and those differences may or may not be grounded at the genetic level) but the basic twoness and structure of the arm is constant across all genetically intact humans—so too for language.

What then do we know about how children acquire language over the ontogenetic timespan from the claim that human language is genetically encoded? At some level, this claim is vacuous in that whatever we humans are capable of developing is made possible by the genetic hand we are dealt. The goal at this level must be to isolate the particular set of genes responsible for language in humans—a goal from which we are a long way off as I write this chapter. Must we wait until the genes are identified before we can begin our exploration of language-learning over the ontogenetic timespan? Clearly not. So why then (assuming we are not geneticists) should we care about the genetic base of a behavior?

Perhaps we shouldn't. Of all of the very large number of definitions and criteria that have, over the years and over the disciplines, been applied to the term "innate," Wimsatt (1986) argues that the one that is *least* central to the notion's core is having a genetic base (see also Block, 1979, 1995). Nativist explanations need not imply genetic determination (Spelke & Newport, 1998). For example, recent research in developmental neurobiology has isolated a number of epigenetic processes through which neural structures develop. These processes follow a species-typical, seemingly inevitable, plan; however, the plan is neither shaped by specifics in the environment, nor guided by details in the genetic instructions (e.g., the development of neural connectivity in the visual system; Shatz, 1992). The definition of "innate" need not be anchored in genetic mechanisms. Indeed, I suggest that the definition is more usefully anchored in the notion of developmental resilience.

☐ Language Is Resilient on the Ontogenetic Timespan

A behavior that is developmentally resilient is one whose development is, if not inevitable, certainly one that each organism in the species is predisposed to develop under widely varying circumstances. I claim that language is such a behavior.

Resilience in the Face of External Variation

Predispositions are often phrased in terms of how easy it is, or how little environmental support is needed, to develop a particular behavior (Seligman & Hager, 1972). One way to explore the human organism's predisposition for language then is to determine the range of environments that can support language development in the human child. To the extent that the range of environments is large and varied, language can be considered developmentally resilient or robust in humans (cf. Alcock, 1988; Goldin-Meadow, 1982). To the extent that the range is narrow, language appears relatively fragile.

For obvious ethical reasons, we cannot deliberately degrade the conditions under which language is acquired. However, as has been made abundantly clear in this book, we can take advantage of variations in language-learning conditions that occur naturally in order to explore the boundary conditions under which language development is possible.

In Chapter 5, we considered the effects of variability in the way adults speak to children within a culture. Adults in each culture tend to use a distinct register of speech with their children. There is, however, variability across adults in how much they talk to their children and in the frequency with which certain constructions are used. Variability in the amount of talk a child hears has been shown to affect that child's rate of vocabulary growth, and variability in how often a particular construction is used in speech to a child has been shown to affect how quickly the child develops that construction. However, despite the effects of input on the pacing of language-learning, there is no evidence that the particular way in which an adult speaks to a child affects whether or not language is ultimately learned by that child.

Indeed, the amount of input a child receives can be quite minimal and still the child will learn language. For example, hearing children born to deaf parents often get very minimal exposure to speech. But it turns out that they don't need much—5 to 10 hours a week of exposure to hearing speakers is typically sufficient to allow language-learning to proceed normally (Schiff-Myers, 1988). As another example, twins "share" their language-learning situation with one another, making the typical adult-twin situation triadic rather than dyadic. Nonetheless, language-learning proceeds along a normal trajectory, although often with mild delays (Mogford, 1988). A child may develop language more or less quickly, but almost all intact children in almost all linguistic environments eventually develop language.

The resilience of language-learning in the face of across-culture variability is even more impressive (see Chapter 3). Cultures hold different beliefs about the role that parents need to play to ensure the child's acquisition of language. Not surprisingly then children across the globe differ in how much, when, and what types of language they receive—not to mention the fact that, in each culture, the child is exposed to a model of a different language. Indeed, many children are exposed to input from two different languages and must learn both at the same time (de Houwer, 1995). Despite the broad range of inputs, children in all corners of the earth learn language and at approximately the same pace.

Resilience in the Face of Internal Variation

Language-learning is also resilient in the face of many organic variations from the norm, variations that alter the way children process whatever input they receive. For example, intermittent conductive hearing losses from repeated middle-ear infections can cause a child's "intake" of linguistic input to vary over time in amount and pattern. Despite this variability, spoken language development for the most part proceeds normally in children with this type of hearing loss (Klein & Rapin, 1988; Paradise et al., 2000). As a second example, blind children live in a nonvisual world that is obviously different from the sighted child's world, and that offers a different spectrum of contextual cues to meaning. However, this difference has little impact on language-learning in the blind child (Landau & Gleitman, 1985).

Organic variation can be much more severe and still result in relatively intact language-learning. For example, grammar-learning in the earliest stages can proceed in a relatively normal manner and at a normal rate even in the face of unilateral ischemic brain injury (Feldman, 1994). As a second example, children with Down syndrome have numerous intrinsic deficiencies that complicate the process of language acquisition. Nevertheless, most Down syndrome children acquire some basic language reflecting the fundamental grammatical organization of the language they are exposed to (the amount of language that is acquired is in general proportion to their cognitive capabilities, Rondal, 1988; Fowler, Gelman, & Gleitman, 1994). Finally, and strikingly given the social impairments that are at the core of the syndrome, autistic children who are able to learn language are not impaired in their grammatical development, either in syntax or in morphology, although they do often have deficits in the communicative, pragmatic, and functional aspects of their language (Tager-Flusberg, 1994).

Interestingly, even when children do have trouble learning language, many of the resilient properties of language are spared. For example, a basic understanding of predicate frames appears to be intact in children with Specific Language Impairment (children who have neither hearing impairment, cognitive deficit, nor neurological damage yet fail to develop language normally). However, these children have difficulty with morphological constructions (Fletcher, 1999)—precisely the property that our adult language-creators have thus far failed to incorporate into their newly invented gesture systems. As another example, children who are not exposed to a usable language until adolescence have no trouble mastering word order when learning language late in life, but do have difficulty with morphology (Newport, 1991). Some properties of language appear to be robust, and some fragile, across a variety of circumstances and internal states.

There may be no greater testament to the resilience of language in humans than the example we have explored in this book. A combination of internal and external factors together create the unusual language-learning circumstances in which the deaf children we study find themselves. Deaf children with profound hearing losses are prevented from taking in the spoken language input that surrounds them. In addition, the deaf children we study have not been exposed to input from a sign language. We might expect such children to fail to communicate—or to communicate in non-language-like ways. But, in fact, deaf children in these circumstances do communicate with those around them and they use gesture to do so. Moreover, the deaf children's gestures are structured more like the spoken language they can't hear than like the gestures they can see. The lack of a usable language model does not prevent the human child from communicating with self and other, in the here-and-now and in the non-present, using the segmented and combinatorial representational format that is the hallmark of human language.

Thus, language development can proceed in humans over a wide range of environments and a wide range of organic states, suggesting that the process of language development may be buffered against a large number of both environmental and organic variations. No one factor seems to be ultimately responsible for the course and outcome of language development in humans, a not-so-surprising result given the complexity and importance of human language.

☐ What Types of Mechanisms Can Lead to Resilience?

The deaf children apply their language-making skills to a completely atypical input and arrive at a product that looks like human language. How did they end up at a language-like system given their starting point? It looks as though there is a basic, resilient form that human communication naturally gravitates toward, and a variety of developmental paths that can be taken to arrive at that form. In this sense, language development in humans can be said to be characterized by "equifinality"—a term coined by the embryologist Driesch (1908, as reported in Gottlieb, 1996) to describe a process by which a system reaches the same outcome despite widely differing input conditions. No matter where you start, all roads lead to Rome.

Are there any implications for the mechanisms of development that we can draw once having identified language as a trait characterized by equifinality? Two types of systems seem possible:

1. A system characterized by equifinality can rely on a *single* developmental mechanism that not only can make effective use of a wide range of inputs (both external and internal) but will not veer off track in response to that variability; that is, a mechanism that is not sensitive to large differences in input. The gross image that comes to mind here is a sausage

machine that takes inputs of all sorts and, regardless of the type and quality of that input, creates the same product.

2. A system characterized by equifinality can rely on *multiple* developmental mechanisms, each activated by different conditions but constrained in some way to lead to the same end-product (cf. Miller, Hicinbothom, & Blaich, 1990). The analogy here is to several distinct machines, each one designed to operate only when activated by a particular type of input (e.g., a chicken, pig, cow, or turkey). Despite the different processes that characterize the dismembering operations of each machine, the machines result in the same sausage product. At first glance, it may seem improbable that a variety of developmental mechanisms would be constrained to arrive at precisely the same outcome. However, it is relatively easy to imagine that the *function* served by the mechanisms—a function that all of the developmental trajectories would share—might have been sufficient to, over time, constrain each of the mechanisms to produce the same product. Communicating via symbols with other humans might be a sufficiently constraining function to result in several mechanisms, each producing language-like structure.

Which of these scenarios characterizes what actually happens when children learn language is an open question, one that we are very far from answering. But what is clear is that language-like structure is overdetermined in human children. Many paths lead to the same outcome, and whatever developmental mechanism we propose to explain language-learning is going to have to be able to account for this "equifinality."

☐ Language Is Not a Unitary Phenomenon When It Comes to Resilience

We have been discussing language as though it were a unitary phenomenon, as though it were completely obvious what the appropriate unit of analysis for language is. However, it is clear that language is not a unitary whole, particularly when it comes to issues of resilience and innateness.

The deaf children do not produce in their gesture systems all of the properties found in natural human languages. Thus, the absence of a conventional language model appears to affect some properties of language more than others. Even when linguistic input is present, it is more likely to affect rate of acquisition for certain properties of language than for others (Newport et al., 1977). Further, when language is acquired "off-time" (i.e., relatively late in the ontogenetic timespan), certain properties of language are likely to be acquired and others are not (Curtiss, 1977; Newport, 1991). Thus, some properties of language are relatively resilient, while others are relatively fragile. Moreover, there is some evidence that the *same* properties of language are resilient across many different circumstances of acquisition—acquisition without a conventional language model, acquisition with varying input from a language model, and acquisition late in development after puberty (Goldin-Meadow, 1978, 1982).

Thus, language *as a whole* need not be said to be innate. Before tackling questions of innateness, we have to decide what the appropriate unit of analysis is and, of course, we have to decide what it means to be innate. I have suggested that innate is best viewed as meaning "developmentally resilient" or "developmentally buffered against certain kinds of experience." This notion operationalizes innateness by specifying the range of environments in which language-learning can take place. There clearly are limits on the process of language development—children raised without human interaction do not develop language. But, as we have seen throughout this book, the process of language development can proceed even in the face of a radical deviation from the typical learning environment—children raised in the company of humans but not exposed to conventional linguistic input can, on their own, develop a communication system with many of the properties of language. What we have seen in exploring this resilience is that certain aspects of language are central to humans—so central that their development is virtually guaranteed, not necessarily by a particular gene but by a variety of combinations of genetic and environmental factors. In this sense, language is innate.

19
CHAPTER

The Resilience of Language

We have seen that even without guidance from a conventional language model, children can fashion a communication system that incorporates the fundamental properties of language. The deaf children we study cannot make use of the spoken language that surrounds them and have not yet been exposed to sign language. Nevertheless, they fashion a gesture system that looks like natural language at both word and sentence levels and that acts like natural language in its functions. In this final chapter, I begin by examining the fragile properties of language—that is, the properties of language that the deaf children *don't* develop—and consider what they tell us about language-learning. I then take one final look at the resilient properties of language, the linguistic properties that children expect to find in their input and will invent if they are not there.

☐ The Fragile Properties of Language: What Do Children Need to Develop Them?

Not surprisingly given the minimal input they have at their disposal, the deaf children in our studies do not incorporate into their gesture systems all of the properties found in natural human languages. Indeed, the absence of a particular linguistic property in the deaf child's gesture system can be taken as indirect evidence of that property's relative lack of resilience. Such a property is likely to need exposure to a conventional linguistic system in order to be developed (for example, a system for marking tense; see also Chapter 11 and Goldin-Meadow, 1987). In general, these *fragile* properties of language need a more specified and particular set of environmental circumstances within which to develop than do resilient properties of language.

What do children require to develop the more fragile properties of language? A language model will clearly suffice. But are there other less optimal circumstances that would also permit the fragile properties of language to flourish? Perhaps having a community of speakers or signers or, at the least, a willing communication partner would allow the fragile properties of language to emerge even without a language model. Recall from Chapter 6 that the deaf children's families chose to educate them through an oral method, and their emphasis was on their children's verbal abilities. The families did not treat the children's gesture as though it were a language. In other words, they were not equal partners in the gestural communication that the children used.

I have often wondered how far a deaf child could move toward arbitrariness and a more complex system without a conventional language as a model but *with* a willing communication partner who could enter into and share an arbitrary system with the child. But the circumstance that would allow me to address this question—two deaf children inventing a gestural system with no input from a conventional sign language—has not presented itself.

However, this question has been addressed on a much broader scale. Due to unusual political circumstances, a group of home-signers in Nicaragua were brought together to form a community in 1980. Over the course of two decades, a sign language appearing to have much of the grammatical complexity of well-established sign languages has evolved out of this set of home-sign systems (Kegl, Senghas, & Coppola, 1999). This newly emergent language is referred to as Lengua de Signos Nicaraguense, Nicaraguan Sign Language, and it appears far more complex than any of the home-sign systems out of which it was formed—and far more complex than the gesture systems of the deaf children I have described here. The considerable distance between the deaf children's gesture systems and the newly formed Nicaraguan Sign Language highlights the importance of a community of signers, and generations of signers, in constructing a full-blown linguistic system (see box on page 223).

An alluringly similar phenomenon has been reported in birds. Young chaffinches, when taken from the nest at five days and reared by hand in auditory isolation, each develops its own song and each of those songs lacks the normal features of chaffinch song (Thorpe, 1957). However, if the young chaffinches are reared together *as a group*, albeit still in auditory isolation, the group develops a uniform community song—one that is unlike anything recorded in the wild but one that does have a tendency toward the division into phrases characteristic of typical chaffinch song (Thorpe, 1957). In other words, developing song without a model but in a group leads to a more structured output than does developing song without a model and on one's own. Note that the deaf child's relative performance appears to be much closer to the norm than the isolated chaffinch's—the deaf children develop a gesture system that has many structural properties characteristic

Nicaraguan Sign Language: Transforming Gesture Into Home Sign and Home Sign Into Sign Language

Nicaraguan Sign Language offers us a unique opportunity to watch a sign language become increasingly complex over generations of creators. The initial step in the creation process took place when deaf children in Managua were brought together for the first time in an educational setting. The deaf children had been born to hearing parents and, like the deaf children described in this book, were likely to have invented gesture systems in their individual homes. When they were brought together, they needed to develop a common sign language. Not surprisingly, we see many of the resilient properties of language in the sign system created by this first cohort of signers. For example, unlike the gestures that Spanish-speakers use when they talk, the signs that this first cohort uses are segmented, with each semantic primitive represented as an independent element. Like our American deaf children (see Figure 3), the signers are more likely to convey manner and path in separate signs than in a single sign (e.g., the hand makes a circular movement *followed by* a downward movement, rather than the hand making a circular movement *simultaneously with* the downward movement; Senghas, Ozyurek, & Kita, 2003). Moreover, the signers combine their signs as do our American deaf children, adhering to consistent word orders to convey who does what to whom (Senghas, Coppola, Newport, & Supalla, 1997).

But Nicaraguan Sign Language has not stopped there. Every year, new students enter the school and learn to sign among their peers. This second cohort of signers has as its input the sign system developed by the first cohort and, interestingly, changes that input so that the product becomes more language-like. For example, although first cohort signers do describe events using individual manner and path signs presented sequentially, second cohort signers do it more often (Senghas et al., 2003). Similarly, first cohort signers produce verbs with two or more arguments, but second cohort signers use them more often (Senghas, 1995). Given this additional complexity, it seems quite natural that second cohort signers go beyond the small set of basic word orders used by the first cohort, introducing new orders not seen previously in the language (Senghas et al., 1997). Moreover, the second cohort begins to use spatial devices invented by the first cohort, but they use these devices consistently and for contrastive purposes (Senghas et al., 1997; Senghas & Coppola, 2001).

The second cohort, in a sense, stands on the shoulders of the first. They do not need to invent the resilient properties of language—

those properties are already present in their input. They can therefore take the transformation process one step farther. The Nicaraguan home signers (and the deaf children we study) take the first, and perhaps the biggest, step: They transform their hearing parents' gestures, which are *not* structured in language-like ways, into a language-like system that contains the resilient properties of language (Coppola, Newport, Senghas, & Supalla, 1997; see also Singleton, Goldin-Meadow, & McNeill, 1995). The first and second cohort of Nicaraguan signers are then able to build on these properties, creating a system that looks more and more like the natural languages of the world.

There is, however, another interesting wrinkle in the language-creation story—it matters how old the creator is. Second cohort signers who began learning Nicaraguan Sign Language relatively late in life (after age 10) do not exhibit these linguistic advances and, in fact, use sign systems that are no different from those used by late-learning first cohort signers (Senghas, 1995; Senghas & Coppola, 2001). It looks like you may have to be a child to take full advantage of the input provided by the first cohort and continue the process of language creation. Thus, we see in Nicaraguan Sign Language that language creation depends not only on what the creator has to work with, but also on who the creator is.

of human language even without the benefit of a group. However, unlike the isolated chaffinch, the deaf children in our studies are not deprived of all social stimulation. Although lacking a partner who might willingly enter into a joint gesture system, the deaf children produce gestures in order to communicate with others and thus, in this important sense, are isolated from a language model but not from the social world.

We cannot intentionally vary the social situation in which language-creators live. We can, however, use the paradigm introduced in Chapter 17 to begin to explore experimentally the impact of social factors on language creation. For example, we can examine the type of gesture system adults create when they are in a group versus on their own. Or we can observe what happens to a gesture system when it is learned by a novice; that is, when it is passed down from the original creators to the next generation. We can even attempt to simulate the deaf child's unusual communicative situation. The deaf children produce one type of gesture (their language-like gesture system) but see another (their hearing parents' gestures which are not language-like in structure, see Chapter 14). The children are thus not producers and receivers of the same system, a situation that could be simulated by allowing an adult to assume only one role in the dyad (the role of either gesture producer or gesture receiver). Although contrived, experimental manipulations of this sort can provide useful data to supplement the insights we glean from studies of naturally occurring situations such as those in Nicaragua.

☐ The Resilient Properties of Language

I have focused in this book on the properties of language that are robust—properties that are sufficiently central to human communication that they will be reinvented by a child who has not been exposed to a conventional language. The number and extent of these properties is impressive (see Table 6).

Deaf children who are not exposed to a usable conventional language model will invent gestures to communicate. This, by itself, is not striking. What is striking is that the gesture systems the children create are structured just like natural languages. Indeed, all of the structures that we have identified in the deaf children's gesture systems can be found in natural language systems that have evolved over generations. This is an important result as it indicates the naturalness of these kinds of structures to human communication.

The children develop a lexicon of gestures that form the basic building blocks of the system. These gesture "words" are stable in form and do not change capriciously with changing situations. They themselves are composed of smaller parts (akin to morphemes) that form paradigms and can be combined to produce new gestures with different, and predictable, meanings. These parts are, for the most part, iconic but the pairings between form and meaning do have arbitrary aspects and differ subtly across children. Finally, the gestures serve noun, verb, and adjective functions that are marked morphologically and syntactically.

The children produce gesture "sentences" characterized by underlying predicate frames that determine how likely it is that a given semantic element will be lexicalized in the sentence. Thematic roles within these sentences—who does what to whom—are marked by three devices: deletion, word order, and inflections. Just as words are created by combining gesture morphemes, complex sentences are created by combining simple sentences—the system is characterized by recursion. Finally, the redundancy that is introduced into complex gesture sentences by combining propositions is systematically reduced in the surface form of those sentences, thus distinguishing redundant from nonredundant elements.

In all these senses, the children have invented a *linguistic system.*

Moreover, the children use their structured gesture systems for many of the basic and not-so-basic functions of language. They make requests, comments, and queries about the present. They communicate about the past, future, and hypothetical. They make generic statements. They tell stories. They talk to themselves. And they refer to their own and others' gestures.

Do the deaf children's gesture systems serve all of the roles that conventional languages serve, and are they equally effective? The deaf children in our studies do use their gestures to communicate, one of the most important functions language serves, and are relatively effective in doing so. However, the act of communicating using an *un*shared system is not at all seamless. Communicating with a young child (and perhaps with all listeners) is always a process of negotiation, but the negotiation becomes that much more cumbersome when every word requires some interpretation—nothing is automatic. Even interpreting pointing gestures is not straightforward. For example, recall from Chapter 8 that David pointed at the dining-room chair to refer to his non-present father, a speech act that worked only because his communication partners (his mother and I) were willing and able to figure out a sensible meaning for the chair-point in that particular context. As I have mentioned several times, the deaf children must keep their gestures grounded in the here-and-now and relatively transparent, or no one will understand them. Whatever arbitrariness the children introduce into their systems must stay within the bounds of iconicity. And it's hard to represent abstract ideas iconically—it's doable, but it's hard.

It's also hard to talk about objects and events that are not on the scene, as the pointing example illustrates. The deaf children do manage to participate in conversations about events that are displaced in time and space, but they do so far less often than their peers who are learning conventional languages. Eventually, this difference in opportunity for conversation about the non-here-and-now is going to take its toll. Talk is one very important way that children learn about and broaden their worlds. They hear stories about objects and events that they have not witnessed and those stories inform and shape their lives—they learn, for example, to fear spiders simply from having heard about Little Miss Muffet's encounters. The deaf children's access to such conversation is extremely limited, leaving them with relatively few opportunities to learn about their worlds in this way.

Language also offers us tools for thinking (e.g., Gentner & Goldin-Meadow, 2003). Having a word for a particular notion (e.g., a quark) may make it easier to manipulate that notion in thought and relate it to other notions. The deaf children lack the codified names and structures that come with a conventional language. To the extent that the children's homemade gesture systems can substitute for the conventional codes they lack, they will be able to use those gestures as tools for thought. However, to the extent that their gesture systems cannot substitute for the codes and constructions found in conventional language, the children may suffer the consequences, not only in communication (i.e., in what they can say), but also in nonlinguistic tasks (cf. Whorf, 1956).

For example, I have argued here that children come to language-learning biased to focus on results and patients, a bias that encourages children to organize their communications around ergative patterns (see also Goldin-Meadow, 2003b). To deviate from an ergative pattern and adopt an accusative pattern in their communications, children seem to require a language model. Since the deaf children in our studies have no such model, they do not adopt an accusative organization in communication. More interestingly, they may also not adopt an accusative organization in noncommunicative tasks—for example, they may not think to group actors of intransitive events (running mice) with actors of transitive events (eating mice) in a single category. It seems obvious to us as English speakers that mice acting as runners or eaters ought to be part of the same category. But it may be obvious simply because our language encourages this particular alignment. If the deaf children do, in fact, have difficulty seeing the similarities between runners and eaters, this would be a good example of how language structure can encourage a particular pattern of thought—without such encouragement, the pattern is less likely to appear.

☐ How Do Children Learn Language?

We have isolated a list of linguistic properties that crop up in a child's communication system even when that child is not exposed to a conventional language. The list tells us about the properties of language that are most robust. Indeed, the properties of language that the deaf children develop are just those properties that all linguists take for granted—the ones they never fight over. The list also gives us insight into how language is learned and, as a result, may even have implications for situations in which language-learning has gone awry (see box on page 229). In this final section, I review the fundamental lessons that we have learned about language-learning from the resilient properties of language.

- We learn first about the *importance of the organism*. The list of properties that the deaf children develop is particularly impressive when compared to the linguistic accomplishments of chimpanzees who have been exposed to models of human language. Other than word order (Savage-Rumbaugh & Rumbaugh, 1993), the chimps display none of the structural properties that the deaf children exhibit in their gesture systems (see Table 6). Nor do the chimps use whatever language they do have for the full range of linguistic functions—most of their productions are here-and-now requests, not comments on the present or the non-present or on talk itself (Greenfield & Savage-Rumbaugh, 1991). Moreover, the chimps' relatively sparse accomplishments need to be evaluated in terms of the input the chimps are getting. These chimpanzees are supported in extremely rich environments from a language-learning point of view—far richer, at least in terms of a potentially accessible language model, than the environments in which the deaf children find themselves. The chimpanzees are extensively exposed to a model of a human language yet, despite this exposure, develop almost none of the resilient properties of language that the deaf children develop without a language model. Whatever gains chimps make in learning language, they appear to do so at great cost and with much effort. In contrast, language comes naturally to human children—even when they lack an adequate model for language. The point here is that the most simple of human language systems (like the deaf children's gesture systems) is still much richer than the most complex chimpanzee system, despite massive attempts at enriching the linguistic environment of one and the relative impoverishment of the linguistic environment of the other. Language is resilient in people, not in chimps.

- We learn next about the *relative unimportance of a conventional language model* in the development of the resilient properties of language. The claim is not that the environment is irrelevant. Some environmental conditions undoubtedly play a role in the development of these most basic properties of language. For example, children do not generate a communication system of any sort in the absence of people. Moreover, it is likely that those people have to make some effort to communicate, and perhaps do so using gesture, in order for children to even contemplate exploiting gesture as a medium for communication. Certain aspects of the environment are going to turn out to be crucial for the development of the resilient properties of language in young children. What our studies show is that a conventional language model is *not* one of them. The studies thus underscore an important point—resilient properties of language are not maintained as universal aspects of language solely by historical tradition. These properties are sufficiently fundamental to human communication that, in a supportive social environment, children can invent them *de novo*.

- We learn also about the *initial grammatical state* that children are in prior to linguistic experience. It is difficult to determine whether children exposed to language models bring their own biases to language-learning because the children are influenced very early on by those models. In contrast, the biases that the deaf children exhibit, or fail to exhibit, are not tainted by exposure to a language model. The deaf children thus offer us a unique perspective on the biases that all children bring to language-learning. For example, we learn from the deaf children that children come to language-learning with a bias to omit subjects, but without a bias for either a right- or left-branching system. In general, Slobin (1997b, 276) has suggested that certain grammatical forms and meanings may be more accessible to

When a Language Model Is Not Enough: Language-Learning That Goes Awry

The findings from the deaf children make it clear that children come to language-learning equipped with ideas and structures that are relevant to language. Most children have no trouble applying these ideas and structures to the task and learning the language to which they have been exposed. But some children do have trouble. Have we learned anything from studying deaf children that can help us think about language-learning when it goes awry?

We do know that children who have intact language-making skills can use those skills to construct pieces of language out of gesture. To the extent that a child's difficulty with language-learning has nothing to do with his or her language-making skills, that child ought to be able to create language through gesture. Thus, we might expect that children who use gesture to compensate for a language-learning problem might have a better prognosis than children who do not compensate in this way. And, indeed, there is some evidence that gesture can serve as a diagnostic for success in later language-learning.

For example, Thal and her colleagues (Thal & Tobias, 1992; Thal, Tobias, & Morrison, 1991) have found that gesture can be an excellent predictor of later language development in children who are delayed language-learners. Late talkers who performed poorly on gesture tasks, and who made little use of gesture for the purposes of communication, continued to exhibit delays in language development one year later. In contrast, late talkers who performed relatively well on the gesture tasks and used communicative gestures extensively "caught up" with their age-matched controls and spoke at appropriate age levels one year later (the so-called "late-bloomers"). Similarly, Evans, Alibali, and McNeil (2001) found that children diagnosed as Specific Language Impaired (i.e., children who fail to acquire age appropriate language skills yet have no other identifiable problems) are able to express in gesture ideas that they are unable to express in speech. Gesture is a medium within which children can display their linguistic knowledge. It is therefore an ideal place to look for skills that children have but may have difficulty expressing in the verbal modality. I am suggesting that, in certain cases, we can use gesture to discover linguistic capabilities that, for whatever reason, a child is unable to display in speech.

Can we also use gesture to develop the child's language skills? Adults who are sensitive to the gestures that a child produces may be able to provide speech input that is finely tuned to that child's level—and, for children who are having trouble with language-learning, finely tuned input could be particularly helpful. We do know that that the gestures *adults* produce can affect vocabulary learning in young children (Goodwyn, Acredolo, & Brown, 2000; Namy, Acredolo & Goodwyn, 2000). Thus, gesture can play a role in effecting linguistic change. There is consequently good reason to hypothesize that gesture might be able to serve not only as an excellent tool for diagnosis, but also as a tool for remediation.

At the least, gesture ought to be exploited in teaching deaf children language, be it signed or spoken. As described in Chapter 6, deaf children born to deaf parents are exposed to sign language at birth and learn it without explicit instruction. But deaf children born to hearing parents are not likely to be exposed to sign until their hearing losses have been discovered and arrangements for their education made. Moreover, their hearing parents are not likely to know sign language and therefore can't use it fluently at home. Thus, deaf children of hearing parents are going to have to get explicit instruction in sign language at school. And, of course, all deaf children need explicit instruction in spoken language if they are to learn it. Devising adequate instructional programs is the key. I suggest that instructional programs be constructed to take advantage of, and build on, the foundational language skills deaf children bring to language-learning—the resilient properties of language.

children than others. Deaf children inventing their own gesture systems offer the most straightforward way of identifying those forms and meanings. If a child is able to produce a grammatical construction without guidance from a language model, that grammatical construction must be very high on the accessibility hierarchy. Thus, the resilient properties of language displayed in Table 6 ought to be highly accessible to all children—the conceptual starting points for grammatical notions.

- We learn finally about the *language-making skills* that all children bring to communication (see Table 7). Language-creating deaf children come to the communication situation with language-making skills that are no different from the skills other children bring to the task. The difference is that the deaf children apply these skills to an input that has no linguistic structure. The fact that the outcome of this process is a communication system characterized by the resilient properties of language makes it clear that the structuring behind these properties comes, not from linguistic input, but from the child's own language-making skills. Recently, Slobin

(1997b, 296) has suggested that children are endowed with "sufficient flexibility to discern and master the particular organization of the exposure language." This hypothesis is correct as far as it goes. But flexibility is just not enough of an endowment. Children certainly do need sufficient flexibility to discern the organization of the language they are learning, but, in the event that they are not exposed to a language, they need sufficient *direction* that they can make language-like structure out of relatively impoverished input. Children have to be able not only to see patterns that are there in their input, but also to ferret those patterns out if their input is impoverished.

The deaf children incorporate many of the most basic properties of natural languages into their gesture systems. But they don't include all of the properties found in natural languages. Some properties of language undoubtedly require the presence of a conventional language model to develop. Others don't. The gesture systems that the deaf children generate offer an ideal paradigm within which to discover which properties are which. And, in the process, we not only gain a unique perspective on how children learn language, but we also discover just how resilient language is.

REFERENCES

Acredolo, L. P., & Goodwyn, S. W. (1985). Symbolic gesture in language development: A case study. *Human Development, 28,* 40–49.

Acredolo, L. P., & Goodwyn, S. W. (1988). Symbolic gesturing in normal infants. *Child Development, 59,* 450–466.

Akmajian, A., Demers, R. A., Farmer, A. K., & Harnish, R. M. (1995). *Linguistics* (4th edition). Cambridge, MA: MIT Press.

Aksu-Koc, A. A., & Slobin, D. I. (1985). The acquisition of Turkish. In D. I. Slobin (Ed.), *A cross-linguistic study of language acquisition, Vol. 1* (pp. 839–878). Hillsdale, NJ: Erlbaum.

Alcock, J. (1988). Singing down a blind alley. *Behavioral and Brain Sciences, 11,* 630–631.

Anderson, S. R. (1985). Typological distinctions in word formation. In T. Shopen (Ed.), *Language typology and syntactic description, Volume III: Grammatical categories and the lexicon* (pp. 3–56). New York: Cambridge University Press.

Antinucci, F., & Miller, R. (1976). How children talk about what happened. *Journal of Child Language, 3,* 167–189.

Barnes, S., Gutfreund, M., Satterly, D., & Wells, G. (1983). Characteristics of adult speech which predict children's language development. *Journal of Child Language, 10,* 65–84.

Bates, E. (1976). *Language and context: The acquisition of pragmatics.* New York: Academic.

Bekken, K. (1989). *Is there "Motherese" in gesture?* Unpublished doctoral dissertation, University of Chicago.

Bellugi, U., & Studdert-Kennedy, M. (Eds.). (1980). *Signed and spoken language: Biological constraints on linguistic form.* Deerfield Beach, FL: Verlag Chemie.

Berko, J. (1958). The child's learning of English morphology. *Word, 14,* 150–177.

Berman, R. A. (1985). The acquisition of Hebrew. In D. I. Slobin (Ed.), *A cross-linguistic study of language acquisition, Vol. 1* (pp. 256–371). Hillsdale, NJ: Erlbaum.

Berman, R. A., & Slobin D. I. (1994). *Relating events in narrative: A cross-linguistic developmental study.* Hillsdale, NJ: Erlbaum.

Bickerton, D. (1990). *Language and species.* Chicago: University of Chicago Press.

Bickerton, D. (1998). Catastrophic evolution: The case for a single step from protolanguage to full human language. In J. R. Hurford, M. Studdert-Kennedy, & C. Knight (Eds.), *Approaches to the evolution of languages* (pp. 341–358). Cambridge, UK: Cambridge University Press.

Bickerton, D. (1999). Creole languages, the language bioprogram hypothesis, and language acquisition. In W. C. Ritchie & T. K. Bhatia (Eds.), *Handbook of child language acquisition* (pp. 195–220). New York: Academic.

Block, N. (1979). A confusion about innateness. *Behavioral and Brain Sciences, 2,* 27–29.

Block, N. (1995). How heritability misleads about race. *Cognition, 56,* 99–128.

Bloom, L. (1970). *Language development: Form and function in emerging grammars.* Cambridge, MA: MIT Press.

Bloom, L. (1973). *One word at a time.* The Hague, The Netherlands: Mouton.

Bloom, L., Lahey, M., Hood, L., Lifter, K., & Fiess, K. (1980). Complex sentences: Acquisition of syntactic connectives and the semantic relations they encode. *Journal of Child Language, 7*, 235–262.

Bloom, L., Lifter, K., & Hafitz, J. (1980). Semantics of verbs and the development of verb inflections in child language. *Language, 56*, 386–412.

Bloom, L., Lightbown, P., & Hood, L. (1975). Structure and variation in child language. *Monographs of the Society for Research in Child Development, 40* (Serial No. 160).

Bloom, L., Miller, P., & Hood, L. (1975). Variation and reduction as aspects of competence in language development. In A. Pick (ed.), *Minnesota Symposium on Child Psychology, Vol. 9* (pp. 3-55). Minneapolis: University of Minnesota Press.

Bloom, P. (1990). *Semantic structure and language development.* Unpublished doctoral dissertation, Massachusetts Institute of Technology.

Bloom, P. (2000). *How children learn the meanings of words.* Cambridge, MA: MIT Press.

Bonvillian, J. D., Orlansky, M. O., & Novack, L. L. (1983). Developmental milestones: Sign language acquisition and motor development. *Child Development, 54*, 1435–1445.

Bonvillian, J. D., & Folven, R. J. (1993). Sign language acquisition: Developmental aspects. In M. Marschark & M. D. Clark (Eds.), *Psychological perspectives on deafness* (pp. 229–265). Hillsdale, NJ: Erlbaum.

Bowerman, M. (1973a). *Early syntactic development: A cross-linguistic study with special reference to Finnish.* Cambridge, UK: Cambridge University Press.

Bowerman, M. (1973b). Structural relationships in children's utterances: Syntactic or semantic. In T. Moore (ed.), *Cognitive development and the acquisition of language* (pp. 197–213). New York: Academic.

Bowerman, M. (1979). The acquisition of complex sentences. In P. Fletcher & M. Garman (Eds.), *Language acquisition* (pp. 285–306). Cambridge, UK: Cambridge University Press.

Bowerman, M. (1982a). Starting to talk worse: Clues to language acquisition from children's late speech errors. In S. Strauss (Ed.), *U-shaped behavioral growth.* New York: Academic.

Bowerman, M. (1982b). Reorganizational processes in lexical and syntactic development. In E. Wanner & L. R. Gleitman (Eds.), *Language acquisition: The state of the art.* New York: Cambridge University Press.

Braine, M. D. S. (1976). Children's first word combinations. *Monographs of the Society for Research in Child Development, 41* (Serial No. 164).

Brentari, D. (1998). *A prosodic model of sign language phonology.* Cambridge, MA: MIT Press.

Brown, R. (1957). Linguistic determinism and the part of speech. *Journal of Abnormal and Social Psychology, 55*, 1–5.

Brown, R. (1958). *Words and things.* New York: The Free Press.

Brown, R. (1973). *A first language.* Cambridge, MA.: Harvard University Press.

Brown, R., & Hanlon, C. (1970). Derivational complexity and order of acquisition in child speech. In J. R. Hayes (Ed.), *Cognition and the development of language* (pp. 11–53). New York: Wiley.

Bruner, J. (1974–75). From communication to language: A psychological perspective. *Cognition, 3*, 255–287.

Bruner, J. (1986). *Actual minds, possible worlds.* Cambridge, MA: Harvard University Press.

Burger, L. K., & Miller, P. J. (1999). Early talk about the past revisited: Affect in working-class and middle-class children's co-narrations. *Journal of Child Language, 26*, 133–162.

Butcher, C., & Goldin-Meadow, S. (2000). Gesture and the transition from one-to two-word speech: When hand and mouth come together. In D. McNeill (Eds.), *Language and gesture: Windows into thought and action* (pp. 235–257). Cambridge, UK: Cambridge University Press.

Butcher, C., Mylander, C., & Goldin-Meadow, S. (1991). Displaced communication in a self-styled gesture system: Pointing at the non-present. *Cognitive Development, 6*, 315–342.

Bybee, J. L. (1985). *Morphology: A study of the relation between meaning and form.* Philadelphia: John Benjamins.

Carey, S. (1978). The child as word learner. In M. Halle, J. Bresnan, & G. Miller (Eds.), *Linguistic theory and psychological reality* (pp. 264–293). Cambridge, MA: MIT Press.

Chamberlain, C., & Mayberry, R. I. (2000). Theorizing about the relation between American Sign Language and reading. In C. Chamberlain, J. P. Morford, & R. I. Mayberry (Eds.), *Language acquisition by eye* (pp. 221–259). Mahwah, NJ: Erlbaum.

Chen, C., & Uttal, D. H. (1988). Cultural values, parents' beliefs, and children's achievement in the United States and China. *Human Development, 31*, 351–358.

Choi, S. (1999). Early development of verb structures and caregiver input in Korean: Two case studies. *The International Journal of Bilingualism, 3*, 241–265.

Choi, S., & Bowerman, M. (1991). Learning to express motion events in English and Korean: The influence of language-specific lexicalization patterns. *Cognition, 41*, 83–121.

Chomsky, N. (1959). A review of B.F. Skinner's *Verbal Behavior. Language, 35*, 26–58.

Chomsky, N. (1982). *Lectures on government and binding: The Pisa lectures*. Holland: Foris.

Chomsky, N. (1999). On the nature, use, and acquisition of language. In W. C. Ritchie & T. K. Bhatia (eds.), *Handbook of child language acquisition* (pp. 33–54). New York: Academic.

Clancy, P. M. (1993). Preferred argument structure in Korean acquisition. In E. Clark (Ed.), *The proceedings of the twenty-fifth annual child language research forum* (pp. 307–314). Stanford University: Center for the Study of Language and Information.

Clark, E. (1973). How children describe time and order. In C. A. Ferguson & D. I. Slobin (Eds.), *Studies in child language development* (pp. 585–606). New York: Holt, Rinehart & Winston.

Clark, E. (1985). The acquisition of Romance, with special reference to French. In D. I. Slobin (Ed.), *A cross-linguistic study of language acquisition, Vol. 1* (pp. 687–782). Hillsdale, NJ: Erlbaum.

Coerts, J. A. (2000). Early sign combinations in the acquisition of Sign Language of the Netherlands: Evidence for language-specific features. In C. Chamberlain, J. P. Morford, & R. Mayberry (Eds.), *Language acquisition by eye* (pp. 91–109). Mahwah, NJ: Erlbaum.

Cohen, E., Namir, L., & Schlesinger, I. M. (1977). *A new dictionary of Sign Language*. Hague: Mouton.

Conrad, R. (1977). Lip-reading by deaf and hearing children. *British Journal of Educational Psychology, 47*, 60–65.

Conrad, R. (1979). *The deaf child*. London: Harper & Row.

Coppola, M., Newport, E. L., Senghas, A., & Supalla, T. (1997, November). The emergence of grammar: Evidence from family-based sign systems in Nicaragua. Paper presented at the Boston University Conference on Language Development.

Coulter, G. R. (1986). One aspect of ASL stress and emphasis: Emphatic stress. Presented at the Conference on Theoretical Issues in Sign Language Research, Rochester, NY.

Crago, M. B. (1988). *Cultural context in communicative interaction of Inuit children*. Unpublished doctoral dissertation, McGill University.

Curtiss, S. (1977). *Genie: A psycholinguistic study of a modern-day "Wild-Child."* New York: Academic.

deBoysson-Bardies, B. (1999). *How language comes to children: From birth to two years*. Cambridge, MA: MIT Press.

deBoysson-Bardies, B., Sagart, L., & Durand, C. (1984). Discernable differences in the babbling of infants according to target language. *Journal of Child Language, 8*, 511–524.

de Houwer, A. (1995). Bilingual language acquisition. In P. Fletcher & B. MacWhinney (eds.), *The handbook of child language* (pp. 219–250). Oxford, UK: Blackwell.

DeMatteo, A. (1977). Visual imagery and visual analogues in American Sign Language. In L. Friedman (Ed.), *On the other hand: New perspectives on American Sign Language*. New York: Academic.

de Villiers, J. G., Roeper, T., & Vainikka, A. (1990). The acquisition of long distance rules. In L. Frazier & J. G. de Villiers (Eds.), *Language processing and acquisition*. Dordrecht: Kluwer.

Dik, S. C. (1968). *Coordination*. Amsterdam: North-Holland Publishing.

Dixon, R. M. W. (1979). Ergativity. *Language, 55,* 59–138.

Dixon, R. M. W. (1994). Adjectives. In R. E. Asher (Ed.), *The encyclopedia of language and linguistics.* New York: Pergamon Press.

Dougherty, R. C. (1970). A grammar of coordinate conjoined structures: I. *Language, 46,* 850–898.

Dougherty, R. C. (1971). A grammar of coordinate conjoined structures: II. *Language, 47,* 298–339.

Driesch, H. (1908/1929). *The science and philosophy of the organism.* London: A. & C. Black.

Dromi, E. (1987). *Early lexical development.* New York: Cambridge University Press.

DuBois, J. W. (1987). The discourse basis of ergativity. *Language, 63,* 805–855.

Ekman, P., & Friesen, W. (1969). The repertoire of nonverbal behavioral categories. *Semiotica, 1,* 49–98.

El'konin, D. B. (1973). General course of development in the child of the grammatical structure of the Russian language (according to A. N. Gvozdev). In C. A. Ferguson & D. I. Slobin (Eds.), *Studies in child language development* (pp. 565–583). New York: Holt, Rinehart & Winston.

Elman, J. L. (1993). Learning and development in neural networks: The importance of starting small. *Cognition, 48,* 71–99.

Evans, J. L., Alibali, M. W., & McNeil, N. M. (2001). Divergence of embodied knowledge and verbal expression: Evidence from gesture and speech in children with Specific Language Impairment. *Language and Cognitive Processes, 16,* 309–331.

Fant, L. J. (1972). *Ameslan: An introduction to American Sign Language.* Silver Springs, MD: National Association of the Deaf.

Farwell, R. (1976). Speech reading: A research review. *American Annals of the Deaf, 121,* 19–30.

Feldman, H. M. (1994). Language development after early unilateral brain injury: A replication study. In H. Tager-Flusberg (Ed.), *Constraints on language acquisition: Studies of atypical children* (pp. 75–90). Hillsdale, NJ: Erlbaum.

Feldman, H., Goldin-Meadow, S., & Gleitman, L. (1978). Beyond Herodotus: The creation of language by linguistically deprived deaf children. In A. Lock (Ed.), *Action, symbol, and gesture: The emergence of language.* New York: Academic.

Fischer, S., & Gough, B. (1978). Verbs in American Sign Language. *Sign Language Studies, 18,* 17–48.

Fisher, C., Hall, D. G., Rakowitz, S., & Gleitman, L. (1994). When it is better to receive that to give: Syntactic and conceptual constraints on vocabulary growth. In L. Gleitman & B. Landau (Eds.), *The acquisition of the lexicon* (pp. 333–376). Cambridge, MA: MIT Press.

Fletcher, P. (1999). Specific language impairment. In M. Barrett (Ed.), *The development of language* (pp. 349–371). East Sussex, UK: Psychology Press.

Fortescue, M., & Olsen, L. L. (1992). The acquisition of West Greenlandic. In D. I. Slobin (Ed.), *A cross-linguistic study of language acquisition, Vol. 3* (pp. 111–219). Hillsdale, NJ: Erlbaum.

Fowler, A. E., Gelman, R., & Gleitman, L. R. (1994). The course of language learning in children with Down Syndrome: Longitudinal and language level comparisons with young normally developing children. In H. Tager-Flusberg (Ed.), *Constraints on language acquisition: Studies of atypical children* (pp. 91–140). Hillsdale, NJ: Erlbaum.

Freyd, J. J. (1983). Shareability: The social psychology of epistemology. *Cognitive Science, 7,* 191–210.

Frishberg, N. (1975). Arbitrariness and iconicity: Historical change in American Sign Language. *Language, 51,* 696–719.

Fromkin, V., Krashen, S., Curtiss, S., Rigler, D., & Rigler, M. (1974). The development of language in Genie: A case of language acquisition beyond the "Critical Period." *Brain and Language, 1,* 81–107.

Furrow, D., Nelson, K., & Benedict, H. (1979). Mothers' speech to children and syntactic development: Some simple relationships. *Journal of Child Language, 6,* 423–442.

Gee, J. P., & Goodhart, W. (1985). Nativization, linguistic theory, and deaf language acquisition. *Sign Language Studies, 49,* 291–342.

Gelman, S. A. (1988). The development of induction with natural kind and artifact categories. *Cognitive Psychology, 20,* 65–95.

Gelman, S. A., & Tardif, T. (1998). A cross-linguistic comparison of generic noun phrases in English and Mandarin. *Cognition, 66,* 215–248.

Gentner, D. (1982). Why nouns are learned before verbs: Linguistic relativity versus natural partitioning. In S. A. Kuczaj (Ed.), *Language development: Syntax and semantics.* Hillsdale, NJ: Erlbaum.

Gentner, D., & Goldin-Meadow, S. (Eds.). (2003). *Language in mind: Advances in the study of language and thought.* Cambridge, MA: MIT Press

Gershkoff-Stowe, L., & Goldin-Meadow, S. (2002). Is there a natural order for expressing semantic relations. *Cognitive Psychology, 45*(3), 375–412.

Givon, T. (1979). *On understanding grammar.* New York: Academic.

Gleitman, L. R. (1965). Coordinating conjunctions in English. *Language, 41,* 260–293.

Gleitman, L. R. (1990). The structural sources of verb meanings. *Language Acquisition, 1,* 3–55.

Gleitman, L. R., & Newport, E. L. (1995). The invention of language by children: Environmental and biological influences on the acquisition of language. In L. R. Gleitman & M. Liberman (Eds.), *An invitation to cognitive science: Language, Vol. 1,* 2nd edition (pp. 1–24). Cambridge, MA: MIT Press.

Gleitman, L. R., Newport, E. L., & Gleitman, H. (1984). The current status of the motherese hypothesis. *Journal of Child Language, 11,* 43–79.

Goldin-Meadow, S. (1978). A study in human capacities. *Science, 200,* 649–651.

Goldin-Meadow, S. (1979). Structure in a manual communication system developed without a conventional language model: Language without a helping hand. In H. Whitaker & H. A. Whitaker (Eds.), *Studies in neurolinguistics* (Vol. 4). New York: Academic.

Goldin-Meadow, S. (1982). The resilience of recursion: A study of a communication system developed without a conventional language model. In E. Wanner & L. R. Gleitman (Eds.), *Language acquisition: The state of the art* (pp. 51–77). New York: Cambridge University Press.

Goldin-Meadow, S. (1985). Language development under atypical learning conditions: Replication and implications of a study of deaf children of hearing parents. In K. Nelson (Ed.), *Children's Language, Vol. 5* (pp. 197–245). Hillsdale, NJ: Erlbaum.

Goldin-Meadow, S. (1987). Underlying redundancy and its reduction in a language developed without a language model: The importance of conventional linguistic input. In B. Lust (Ed.), *Studies in the acquisition of anaphora: Applying the constraints, Vol. 2* (pp. 105–133). Boston, MA: D. Reidel.

Goldin-Meadow, S. (1993). When does gesture become language? A study of gesture used as a primary communication system by deaf children of hearing parents. In K. R. Gibson & T. Ingold (Eds.), *Tools, language, and cognition in human evolution* (pp. 63–85). New York: Cambridge University Press.

Goldin-Meadow, S. (1999a). The role of gesture in communication and thinking. *Trends in Cognitive Science, 3,* 419–429.

Goldin-Meadow, S. (1999b). The development of gesture with and without speech in hearing and deaf children. In L. Messing & R. Campbell (eds.), *Gesture, speech and sign* (pp. 117–132). Oxford: Oxford University Press.

Goldin-Meadow, S. (2003a). Lexical development without a language model. To appear in G. Hall & S. Waxman (Eds.), *Weaving a lexicon.* Cambridge, MA: MIT Press.

Goldin-Meadow, S. (2003b). Thought before language: Do we think ergative? In D. Gentner & S. Goldin-Meadow (eds.), *Language in mind: Advances in the study of language and thought.* Cambridge, MA: MIT Press.

Goldin-Meadow, S. (2003c). *Hearing gesture: How our hands help us think.* Cambridge, MA: Harvard University Press.

Goldin-Meadow, S., Alibali, M. W., & Church, R. B. (1993). Transitions in concept acquisition: Using the hand to read the mind. *Psychological Review, 100*(2), 279–297.

Goldin-Meadow, S., & Butcher, C. (2003). Pointing toward two-word speech in young children. In S. Kita (ed.), *Pointing: Where language, culture, and cognition meet* (pp. 85–107). NJ: Erlbaum.

Goldin-Meadow, S., Butcher, C., Mylander, C., & Dodge, M. (1994). Nouns and verbs in a self-styled gesture system: What's in a name? *Cognitive Psychology, 27,* 259–319.

Goldin-Meadow, S., & Feldman, H. (1977). The development of language-like communication without a language model. *Science, 197,* 401–403.

Goldin-Meadow, S., Gelman, S. A., & Mylander, C. (2003). Expressing generic concepts with and without a language model. Under review.

Goldin-Meadow, S., Kim, S., & Singer, M. (1999). What the teacher's hands tell the student's mind about math. *Journal of Educational Psychology, 91,* 720–730.

Goldin-Meadow, S., & Mayberry, R. (2001). How do profoundly deaf children learn to read? *Learning Disabilities Research and Practice* (special issue: Emergent and early literacy: Current status and research directions), *16,* 221–228.

Goldin-Meadow, S., & McNeill, D. (1999). The role of gesture and mimetic representation in making language the province of speech. In M. C. Corballis & S. Lea (Eds.), *The descent of mind* (pp. 155–172). Oxford: Oxford University Press.

Goldin-Meadow, S., McNeill, D., & Singleton, J. (1996). Silence is liberating: Removing the handcuffs on grammatical expression in the manual modality. *Psychological Review, 103,* 34–55.

Goldin-Meadow, S., & Morford, M. (1985). Gesture in early child language: Studies of deaf and hearing children. *Merrill-Palmer Quarterly, 31,* 145–176.

Goldin-Meadow, S., & Mylander, C. (1983). Gestural communication in deaf children: The non-effects of parental input on language development. *Science, 221,* 372–374.

Goldin-Meadow, S., & Mylander, C. (1984). Gestural communication in deaf children: The effects and non-effects of parental input on early language development. *Monographs of the Society for Research in Child Development, 49,* 1–121.

Goldin-Meadow, S., & Mylander, C. (1990). The role of a language model in the development of a morphological system. *Journal of Child Language, 17,* 527–563.

Goldin-Meadow, S. & Mylander, C. (1998). Spontaneous sign systems created by deaf children in two cultures. *Nature, 91,* 279-281.

Goldin-Meadow, S., Mylander, C., & Butcher, C. (1995). The resilience of combinatorial structure at the word level: Morphology in self-styled gesture systems. *Cognition, 56,* 195–262.

Goldin-Meadow, S., & Saltzman, J. (2000). The cultural bounds of maternal accommodation: How Chinese and American mothers communicate with deaf and hearing children. *Psychological Science, 11,* 311–318.

Goldin-Meadow, S., Seligman, M. E. P., & Gelman, R. (1976). Language in the two-year-old. *Cognition, 4,* 189–202.

Goldin-Meadow, S., Yalabik, E., & Gershkoff-Stowe, L. (2000). The resilience of ergative structure in language created by children and by adults. *Proceedings of Boston University Conference on Language Development, 24,* 343–353.

Goldin-Meadow, S., & Zheng, M-Y. (1998). Thought before language: The expression of motion events prior to the impact of a conventional language model. In P. Carruthers & J. Boucher (Eds.), *Language and thought: Interdisciplinary essays* (pp. 26–54). New York: Cambridge University Press.

Goodhart, W. (1984). *Morphological complexity, ASL and the acquisition of sign language in deaf children.* Unpublished doctoral dissertation, Boston University.

Goodman, M. (1984). Are creole structures innate? *Behavioral and Brain Sciences, 7,* 193–194.

Goodwyn, S. W., Acredolo, L. P., & Brown, C. A. (2000). Impact of symbolic gesturing on early language development. *Journal of Nonverbal Behavior, 24,* 81–103.

Gopnik, A., & Choi, S. (1995). Names, relational words, and cognitive development in English and Korean speakers: Nouns are not always learned before verbs. In M. Tomasello & W. E. Merriman (Eds.), *Beyond names for things: Young children's acquisition of verbs* (pp. 83–90). Hillsdale, NJ: Erlbaum.

Gopnik, A., & Meltzoff, A. N. (1997). *Words, thoughts, and theories.* Cambridge, MA: MIT Press.

Gottlieb, G. (1991). Experiential canalization of behavioral development: Results. *Developmental Psychology, 27,* 35–39.

Gottlieb, G. (1996). A systems view of psychobiological development. In D. Magnusson (ed.), *The lifespan development of individuals: Behavioral, Neurobiological, and psychosocial perspectives: A synthesis* (pp. 76–103). New York: Cambridge University Press.

Greenberg, J. (1966). Some universals of grammar with particular reference to the order of meaningful elements. In J. Greenberg (Ed.), *Universals of language* (pp. 73–113). Cambridge, MA: MIT Press.

Greenfield, P. M., & Savage-Rumbaugh, E. S. (1991). Imitation, grammatical development, and the invention of protogrammar by an ape. In N. A. Krasnegor, D. M. Rumbaugh, R. L. Schiefelbusch, & M. Studdert-Kennedy (Eds.), *Biological and behavioral determinants of language development* (pp. 235–262). Hillsdale, NJ: Erlbaum.

Griffin, Z. M., & Bock, K. (2000). What the eyes say about speaking. *Psychological Science, 11,* 274–279.

Haiman, J. (1985). *Iconicity in syntax.* Amsterdam: John Benjamins.

Hammond, A. J., & Goldin-Meadow, S. (2002). The robustness of non-English sequences in created gesture systems. *Proceedings of Boston University Conference on Language Development, 26,* 278–289.

Harris, M. (1992). *Language experience and early language development: From input to uptake.* Hillsdale, NJ: Erlbaum.

Hauser, M. D., Chomsky, N., & Fitch, W. T. (2002). The faculty of language: What it is, who has it, and how did it evolve? *Science, 289,* 1569–1579.

Hawkins, J. A. (1983). *Word order universals.* New York: Academic.

Hawkins, J. A. (1988). Explaining language universals. In J. A. Hawkins (Ed.), *Explaining language universals* (pp. 3–28). Cambridge, MA: Blackwell.

Heath, S.B. (1983). *Ways with words: Language, life and work in communities and classrooms.* Cambridge: Cambridge University Press.

Hirsh-Pasek, K., & Golinkoff, R. M. (1991). Language comprehension: A new look at some old themes. In N. A. Krasnegor, D. M. Rumbaugh, R. L., Schiefelbusch, & M. Studdert-Kennedy (Eds.), *Biological and behavioral determinants of language development* (pp. 301–320). Hillsdale, NJ: Erlbaum.

Hirsh-Pasek, K., Golinkoff, R. M., & Naigles, L. (1996). Young children's use of syntactic frames to derive meaning. In K. Hirsh-Pasek & R. M. Golinkoff (Eds.), *The origins of grammar: Evidence from early language comprehension* (pp. 123–159). Cambridge, MA: MIT Press.

Hockett, C. F. (1960). The origin of speech. *Scientific American, 203*(3), 88–96.

Hockett , C. F. (1977). *The view from language: Selected essays 1948–1974.* Athens, GA: University of Georgia Press.

Hoff-Ginsberg, E. (1985). Some contributions of mothers' speech to their children's syntactic growth. *Journal of Child Language, 12,* 367–385.

Hoff-Ginsberg, E., & Shatz, M. (1982). Linguistic input and the child's acquisition of language. *Psychological Bulletin, 92,* 3–26.

Hoffmeister, R. (1978). *The development of demonstrative pronouns, locatives, and personal pronouns in the acquisition of American Sign Language by deaf children of deaf parents.* Unpublished doctoral dissertation, Univ. of Minnesota.

Hoffmeister, R., & Wilbur, R. (1980). Developmental: The acquisition of sign language. In H. Lane & F. Grosjean (Eds.), *Recent perspectives on American Sign Language.* Hillsdale, NJ: Erlbaum.

Hopper, P. J., & Thompson, S. (1980). Transitivity. *Language, 56,* 251–299.

Hopper, P. J., & Thompson, S. A. (1984). The iconicity of the universal categories "noun" and "verb" In J. Haiman (Ed.), *Iconicity in syntax* (pp. 151–183). Philadelphia, PA: John Benjamins.

Hopper, P. J., & Thompson, S. A. (1988). The discourse basis for lexical categories in universal grammar. *Language, 60*(4), 703–752.

Hsu, J. R., Cairns, H. S., Eisenberg, S., & Schlisselberg, G. (1989). Control and coreference in early child language. *Journal of Child Language, 16,* 599–622.

Hudson, J. A., & Shapiro, L. R. (1991). From knowing to telling: the development of children's scripts, stories, and personal narratives. In A. McCabe & C. Peterson (Eds.), *Developing Narrative Structure.* Hillsdale, NJ: Erlbaum.

Huttenlocher, J. (1973). Language and thought. In G. A. Miller (Ed.), *Communication, language and meaning: Psychological perspectives* (pp. 172–184). New York: Basic Books.

Huttenlocher, J. (1976). Language and intelligence. In L. B. Resnick (Ed.), *The nature of intelligence* (pp. 261–281). Hillsdale, NJ: Erlbaum.

Huttenlocher, J., & Smiley, P. (1987). Early word meanings: The case of object names. *Cognitive Psychology, 19,* 63–89.

Huttenlocher, J., & Smiley, P. (1989). *An emerging lexicon: Acquiring words for events.* Unpublished manuscript, University of Chicago.

Huttenlocher, J., Haight, W., Bryk, A., Seltzer, M., & Lyons, T. (1991). Early vocabulary growth: Relation to language input and gender. *Developmental Psychology, 27,* 236–248.

Huttenlocher, J., Vasilyeva, M., Cymerman, E., & Levine, S. (2002). Language and syntax. *Cognitive Psychology, 45,* 337–374.

Hyams, N. (1986). *Language acquisition and the theory of parameters.* Boston: Reidel.

Hyams, N. (1994). Commentary: Null subjects in child language and the implications of cross-linguistic variation. In B. Lust, G. Hermon, & J. Kornfilt (Eds.), *Syntactic theory and first language acquisition: Cross-linguistic perspectives, Vol. 2, Binding, dependencies and learnability* (pp. 287–299). Hillsdale, NJ: Erlbaum.

Iverson, J. M., Capirci, O., & Caselli, M. S. (1994). From communication to language in two modalities. *Cognitive Development, 9,* 23–43.

Iverson, J. M., Capirci, O., Longobardi, E., & Caselli, M. C. (1999). Gesturing in mother-child interaction. *Cognitive Development, 14,* 57–75.

Johnston, J. R., & Slobin, D. I. (1979). The development of locative expressions in English, Italian, Serbo-Croatian, and Turkish. *Journal of Child Language, 6,* 529–545.

Jusczyk, P. W. (1993). From general to language specific capacities: The WRAPSA model of how speech perception develops. *Journal of Phonetics, 21,* 3–28.

Kantor, R. (1980). The acquisition of classifiers in American Sign Language. *Sign Language Studies, 28,* 193–208.

Kantor, R. (1982). Communicative interaction: Mother modification and child acquisition of American Sign Language. *Sign Language Studies, 36,* 233–282.

Karmiloff-Smith, A. (1979). *A functional approach to child language: A study of determiners and reference.* New York: Cambridge University Press.

Karmiloff-Smith, A. (1992). *Beyond modularity: A developmental perspective on cognitive science.* Cambridge, MA: MIT Press.

Kegl, J. (1985). *Locative relations in ASL.* Unpublished doctoral dissertation, Massachusets Institute of Technology.

Kegl, J. (1994). The Nicaraguan Sign Language project: An overview. *Signpost, 7,* 24–31.

Kegl, J., Senghas, A., & Coppola, M. (1999). Creation through contact: Sign language emergence and sign language change in Nicaragua. In M. DeGraff (Ed.), *Language creation and language change: Creolization, diachrony, and development* (pp. 179–237). Cambridge, MA: MIT Press.

Keil, F. C. (1989). *Concepts, kinds, and cognitive development.* Cambridge, MA: MIT Press.

Kita, S. (2000). How representational gestures help speaking. In D. McNeill (Ed.), *Language and gesture: Window into thought and action* (pp. 162–185). Cambridge: Cambridge University Press.

Klein, S. K., & Rapin, I. (1988). Intermittent conductive hearing loss and language development. In D. Bishop & K. Mogford (Eds.), *Language development in exceptional circumstances* (pp. 96–109). New York: Churchill Livingstone.

Klima, E. S., & Bellugi, U. (1966). Syntactic regularities in the speech of children. In J. Lyons & R. J. Wales (Eds.), *Pyscholinguistics papers* (pp. 183–208). Edinburgh: Edinburgh University Press.

Klima, E., & Bellugi, U. (1979). *The signs of language.* Cambridge, MA: Harvard University Press.

Krifka, M., Pelletier, F. J., Carlson, G. N., ter Meulen, A., Chierchia., G., & Link, G. (1995). Genericity: An introduction. In G. N. Carlson & F. J. Pelletier (Eds.), *The generic book.* Chicago: University of Chicago Press.

Kuhl, P., Williams, K. A., Lacerda, F., Stevens, K. N., & Lindblom, B. (1992). Linguistic experience alters phonetic perception in infants by 6 months of age. *Science, 255,* 606–608.

Kulochova, J. (1972). Severe deprivation in twins: A case study. *Journal of Child Psychology and Psychiatry, 13,* 107–114.

Labov, W., & Waletzky, J. (1967). Narrative analysis: oral versions of personal experience. In J. Helm (Ed.), *Essays on the verbal and visual arts: Proceedings from the 1966 annual spring meeting of the American Ethnological Society.* Seattle: American Ethnological Society.

Lakoff, G., & Peters, S. (1969). Phrasal conjunction and symmetric predicates. In D. A. Reibel & S. A. Schane (Eds.), *Modern studies in English.* Englewood Cliffs, NJ: Prentice-Hall.

Landau, B., & Gleitman, L. R. (1985). *Language and experience: Evidence from the blind child.* Cambridge, MA: Harvard University Press.

Lane, H. (1977). *Wild boy of Aveyron.* New York: Bantam Books.

Lane, H., Boyes-Braem, P., & Bellugi, U. (1976). Preliminaries to a distinctive feature analysis of handshapes in American Sign Language. *Cognitive Psychology, 8,* 263–289.

Lane, H., & Grosjean, F. (1980). *Recent perspectives on American Sign Language.* Hillsdale, NJ: Erlbaum.

Lenneberg, E. H. (1964). Capacity for language acquisition. In J. A. Fodor & J. J. Katz (Eds.), *The structure of language: Readings in the philosophy of language.* Englewood Cliffs, NJ: Prentice-Hall.

Leopold, W. F. (1939–49). *Speech development of a bilingual child: A linguist's record, vols. 1–4.* Evanston, IL: Northwestern University Press.

Liddell, S. (1980). *American Sign Language syntax.* The Hague: Mouton.

Liddell, S. (1984). "Think" and "believe": Sequentiality in American Sign Language. *Language, 60,* 372–399.

Liddell, S. & Johnson, R. (1986). American Sign Language compound formation processes, lexicalization, and phonological remnants. *Natural Language and Linguistic Theory, 4,* 445-513.

Liddell, S. K., & Metzger, M. (1998). Gesture in sign language discourse. *Journal of Pragmatics, 30,* 657–697.

Lieven, E. V. M. (1994). Crosslinguistic and crosscultural aspects of language addressed to children. In C. Gallaway & B. Richards (Eds.), *Input and interaction in language acquisition* (pp. 56–73). Cambridge, UK: Cambridge University Press.

Lillo-Martin, D. (1986). Two kinds of null arguments in American Sign Language. *Natural Language and Linguistic Theory , 4,* 415–444.

Lillo-Martin, D. (1999). Modality effects and modularity in language acquisition: The acquisition of American Sign Language. In W. C. Ritchie & T. K. Bhatia (Eds.), *The handbook of child language acquisition* (pp. 531–567). New York: Academic.

Limber, J. (1973). The genesis of complex sentences. In T. Moore (Rd.), *Cognitive development and the acquisition of language* (pp. 169–186). New York: Academic.

Livingston, S. (1983). Levels of development in the language of deaf children. *Sign Language Studies, 40,* 193–286.

Locke, J. L. (1990). Structure and stimulation in the ontogeny of spoken language. *Developmental Psychobiology, 23,* 621–643.

Lou, M. W-P. (1988). The history of language use in education of the Deaf. In M. Strong (Ed.), *Language learning and deafness* (pp. 75–98). Cambridge, UK: Cambridge University Press.

Lucy, J. A. (1993). Reflexive language and the human disciplines. In J. Lucy (Ed.), *Reflexive language: Reported speech and metapragmatics* (pp. 9–32). New York: Cambridge University Press.

Lust, B. (1977). Conjunction reduction in child language. *Journal of Child Language, 4,* 257–288.

Lust, B. (1981). Constraints on anaphora in child language: A prediction for a universal. In S. L. Tavakolian (Ed.), *Language acquisition and linguistic theory* (pp. 74–96). Cambridge, MA: MIT Press.

Lust, B. (1983). On the notion "principle branching direction": A parameter of universal grammar. In Y. Otsu, K. H. Van Riemsdijk, K. Inoue, A. Kamio, & N. Kawasaki (Eds.), *Proceedings of the Thirteenth International Congress of Linguistist* (pp. 1127–1130). Tokyo: Gakushuin.

Lust, B., & Mervis, C. A. (1980). Development of coordination in the natural speech of young children. *Journal of Child Language, 7,* 279–304.

Lust, B., & Wakayama, T. K. (1979). The structure of coordination in children's first language acquisition of Japanese. In F. R. Eckman & A. J. Hastings (Eds.), *Studies in first and second language acquisition* (pp. 134–152). Rowley, MA: Newbury House.

Lyons, J. (1977). *Semantics: I.* Cambridge, UK: Cambridge University Press.

MacKay, D. M. (1972). *Formal analysis of communicative processes. Nonverbal communication.* New York: Cambridge University Press.

Macnamara, J. (1982). *Names for things.* Cambridge, MA: MIT Press.

MacWhinney, B. (1977). Starting points. *Language, 53,* 152–168.

MacWhinney, B. (1978). The acquisition of morphophonology. *Monographs of the Society for Research in Child Development, 43* (serial no. 174), 1–22.

MacWhinney, B. (1995). *The CHILDES project: Tools for analyzing talk* (2nd ed.). Hillsdale, NJ: Erlbaum.

Marcus, G. (1995). Children's overregularization of English plurals: A qualitative analysis. *Journal of Child Language, 22,* 447–459.

Markman, E. M. (1991). The whole-object, taxonomic, and mutual exclusivity assumptions as initial constraints on word meanings. In S. A. Gelman & J. P. Byrnes (Eds.), *Perspectives on language and thought: Interrelations in development* (pp. 72–106). Cambridge, UK: Cambridge University Press.

Markman, E. M. (1994). Constraints on word meaning in early language acquisition. In L. Gleitman & B. Landau (Eds.), *The acquisition of the lexicon* (pp. 199–229). Cambridge, MA: MIT Press.

Markus, H., & Kitayama, S. (1991). Culture and the self: Implications for cognition, emotion, and motivation. *Psychological Review, 98,* 224–253.

Marler, P. (1990). Innate learning preferences: Signals for communication. *Developmental Psychobiology, 23,* 557–568.

Marmor, G., & Petitto, L. (1979). Simultaneous communication in the classroom: How well is English grammar represented? *Sign Language Studies, 23,* 99–136.

Masataka, N. (1992). Motherese in a signed language. *Infant Behavior and Development, 15,* 453–460.

Masataka, N. (2000). The role of modality and input in the earliest stage of language acquisition: Studies of Japanese Sign Language. In C. Chamberlain, J. P. Morford, & R. I. Mayberry (Eds.), *Language acquisition by eye* (pp. 3–24). Mahwah, NJ: Erlbaum.

Mayberry, R. I. (1992). The cognitive development of deaf children: Recent insights. In F. Boller & J. Graffman (Series Eds.), S. Segalowitz & I. Rapin (Vol. Eds.), *Child Neuropsychology: Vol. 7. Handbook of Neuropsychology* (pp. 51–68). Amsterdam: Elsevier.

McCabe, A. & Peterson, C. (1991). Getting the story: a longitudinal study of parental styles in eliciting narratives and developing narrative skill. In A. McCabe & C. Peterson (Eds.), *Developing narrative structure*. Hillsdale, NJ: Erlbaum.

McDonald, B. (1982). *Aspects of the American Sign Language predicate system*. Unpublished doctoral dissertation, University of Buffalo.

McNeill, D. (1992). *Hand and mind: What gestures reveal about thought*. Chicago: University of Chicago Press.

McNeill, D. (1998). Speech and gesture integration. In J. M. Iverson & S. Goldin-Meadow (Eds.). *The nature and functions of gesture in children's communications* (pp. 11–28), in the *New Directions for Child Development* series, No. 79. San Francisco: Jossey-Bass.

McNeill, D., & Duncan, S. (2000). Growth points in thinking-for-speaking. In D. McNeill (Ed.), *Speech and gesture: Window into thought and action* (pp. 141–161). New York: Cambridge University Press.

Meadow, K. P. (1968). Early manual communication in relation to the deaf child's intellectual, social, and communicative functioning. *American Annals of the Deaf, 113,* 29–41.

Mehler, J., Jusczyk, P. W., Lambertz, G., Halsted, N., Bertoncini, J., & Amiel-Tison, C. (1988). A precursor of language acquisition in young infants. *Cognition, 29,* 143–178.

Meier, R. (1981). Icons and morphemes: Models of the acquisition of verb agreement in ASL. *Papers and Reports on Child Language Development, 20,* 92–99.

Meier, R. (1982). *Icons, analogues, and morphemes: The acquisition of verb agreement in ASL*. Unpublished doctoral dissertation, University of California, San Diego.

Meier, R. P. (2002). The acquisition of verb agreement in ASL. In G. Morgan & B. Woll (Eds.), *Directions in sign language acquisition* (pp. 115–191). Amsterdam: John Benjamins.

Meier, R. P., & Newport, E. L. (1990). Out of the hands of babes: On a possible sign advantage in language acquisition. *Language, 66,* 1–23.

Meier, R. P., & Willerman, R. (1995). Prelinguistic gesture in deaf and hearing infants. In K. Emmorey & J. Reilly (Eds.), *Language, gesture, and space* (pp. 391–409). Hillsdale, NJ: Erlbaum.

Menyuk, P. (1971). *The acquisition and development of language*. Englewood Cliffs, NJ: Prentice-Hall.

Miller, D. B., Hicinbothom, G., & Blaich, C. F. (1990). Alarm call responsivity of mallard ducklings: Multiple pathways in behavioural development. *Animal Behavior, 39,* 1207–1212.

Miller, P. J. (1996). Instantiating culture through discourse practices: some personal reflections on socialization and how to study it. In R. Jessor, A. Colby, & R. Shweder (Eds.), *Ethnography and human development: Context and meaning in social inquiry*. Chicago: University of Chicago Press.

Miller, P. J. & Hoogstra, L. (1989). How to represent the native child's point of view: Methodological problems in language socialization. Paper presented at the annual meeting of the American Anthropological Association, Washington, DC.

Miller, P. J., Mintz, J., & Fung, H. (1991, October). Creating children's selves: An American and Chinese comparison of mothers' stories about their toddlers. Paper presented at the biennial meeting of the Society for Psychological Anthropology.

Miller, P. J., & Moore, B.B. (1989). Narrative conjunctions of caregiver and child: A comparative perspective on socialization through stories. *Ethos, 17,* 43–64.

Miller, P. J., & Sperry, L. L. (1988). Early talk about the past: the origins of conversational stories about personal experience. *Journal of Child Language, 15,* 293–315.

Miller, P. J., Wiley, A., Fung, H., & Liang, C.H. (1997). Personal storytelling as a medium of socialization in Chinese and American families. *Child Development, 68,* 557–568.

Miller, W. R. (1973). The acquisition of grammatical rules by children. In C. A. Ferguson & D. I. Slobin (Eds.), *Studies in child language development* (pp. 38–391). New York: Holt, Rinehart & Winston.

Mills, A. E. (1985). The aquisition of German. In D. I. Slobin (Ed.), *The cross-linguistic study of language acquisition: Vol. 1. The Data* (pp. 141–254). Hillsdale, NJ: Erlbaum.

Mindel, E. D., & Vernon, McC. (1971). *They grow in silence: The deaf child and his family*. Silver

Springs, MD: National Association of the Deaf.

Mogford, K. (1988). Language development in twins. In D. Bishop & K. Mogford (Eds.), *Language development in exceptional circumstances* (pp. 80–95). New York: Churchill Livingstone.

Mohay, H. (1982). A preliminary description of the communication systems evolved by two deaf children in the absence of a sign language model. *Sign Language Studies, 34,* 73–90.

Moores, D. F. (1974). Nonvocal systems of verbal behavior. In R. L. Schiefelbusch & L. L. Lloyd (Eds), *Language perspectives: Acquisition, retardation, and intervention.* Baltimore: University Park Press.

Moores, D. F. (1982). *Educating the deaf: Psychology, principles, and practices* (2nd ed.). Boston: Houghton Mifflin.

Morford, J. P., & Goldin-Meadow, S. (1997). From here to there and now to then: The development of displaced reference in homesign and English. *Child Development, 68,* 420–435.

Naigles, L. (1990). Children use syntax to learn verb meanings. *Journal of Child Language, 17,* 357–374.

Naigles, L. R., & Hoff-Ginsberg, E. (1998). Why are some verbs learned before other verbs? Effects of input frequency and structure on children's early verb use. *Journal of Child Language, 25,* 95–120.

Namy, L. L., Acredolo, L. P., & Goodwyn, S. W. (2000). Verbal labels and gestural routines in parental communication with young children. *Journal of Nonverbal Behavior, 24,* 105–130.

Nelson, K. (1973). Structure and strategy in learning to talk. *Monographs of the Society for Research in Child Development, 1978, 38* (serial no. 149).

Nelson, K. E. (1977). Facilitating children's syntax acquisition. *Developmental Psychology, 13,* 101–107.

Nelson, K. E., Carskaddon, G., & Bonvillian, J. D. (1973). Syntax acquisition: Impact of experimental variation in adult verbal interaction with the child. *Child Development, 44,* 497–504.

Newport, E. L. (1977). Motherese: The speech of mothers to young children. In N. J. Castellan, D. B. Pisoni, & G. Potts (Eds.), *Cognitive theory, vol. 2* (pp. 177–217). Hillsdale, NJ: Erlbaum.

Newport, E. L. (1981). Constraints on structure: Evidence from American Sign Language and language learning. In W. A. Collins (Ed.), *Minnesota Symposium on Child Psychology* (Vol. 14). Hillsdale, NJ: Erlbaum.

Newport, E. L. (1984). Constraints on learning: Studies in the acquisition of American Sign Language. *Papers and Reports on Child Language Development, 23,* 1–22.

Newport, E.L. (1991). Contrasting conceptions of the critical period for language. In S. Carey & R. Gelman (Eds.), *The epigenesis of mind: Essays on biology and cognition* (pp. 11–130). Hillsdale, NJ: Erlbaum.

Newport, E. L., & Ashbrook, E. F. (1977). The emergence of semantic relations in American Sign Language. *Papers and Reports on Child Language Development, 13,* 16–21.

Newport, E. L., Gleitman, H., & Gleitman, L. R. (1977). Mother, I'd rather do it myself: Some effects and non-effects of maternal speech style. In C. E. Snow & C. A. Ferguson (Eds.), *Talking to children: Language input and acquisition* (pp. 109–149). Cambridge, UK: Cambridge University Press.

Newport, E. L., & Meier, R. P. (1985). The acquisition of American Sign Language. In D. I. Slobin (Ed.), *The cross-linguistic study of language acquisition: Vol. 1. The data.* Hillsdale, NJ: Erlbaum.

Ochs, E. (1982). Ergativity and word order in Samoan child language. *Language, 58,* 646–671.

Ochs, E. (1988). *Culture and language development: Language acquisition and language socialization in a Samoan village.* Cambridge, UK: Cambridge University Press.

Ochs, E., & Capps, L. (1996). Narrating the self. *Annual Review of Anthropology, 25,* 19–43.

Ochs, E., & Schieffelin, B. B. (1984). Language acquisition and socialization: Three developmental stories and their implications. In R. A. Shweder & R. A. LeVine (Eds.), *Culture theory: Essays on mind, self, and emotion* (pp. 276–320). Cambridge, UK: Cambridge University Press.

Ochs, E., & Schieffelin, B. B. (1995). The impact of language socialization on grammatical development. In P. Fletcher & B. MacWhinney (Eds.), *The handbook of child language* (pp. 73–94). Cambridge, MA: Blackwell.

Oller, D. K., & Lynch, M. P. (1992). Infant vocalizations and innovations in infraphonology: Toward a broader theory of development and disorders. In C. A. Ferguson, L. Menn, & C. Stoel-Gammon (Eds.), *Phonological development: Models, research, implications* (pp. 509–538). Timonium, MD: York Press.

Owens, E., & Kessler, D. K. (1989). *Cochlear implants in young deaf children.* Boston: College Hill.

Ozyurek, A., & Kita, S. (1999). Expressing manner and path in English and Turkish: Differences in speech, gesture, and conceptualization. *Proceedings of the Cognitive Science Society, 21,* 507–512.

Padden, C. (1983). *Interaction of morphology and syntax in American Sign Language.* Unpublished doctoral dissertation, Univ. of California at San Diego.

Padden, C., & Humphries, T. (1988). *Deaf in America: Voices from a culture.* Cambridge, MA: Harvard University Press.

Paradise J. L., Dollaghan, C. A., Campbell, T. F., Feldman, H. M., Bernard, B. S., Colborn, D. K., Rockette, H. E., Janosky, J.E., Pitcairn, D. L., Sabo, D. L., Kurs-Lasky, M., & Smith, C. G. (2000). Language, speech sound production, and cognition in 3-year-old children in relation to otitis media in their first 3 years of life. *Pediatrics, 105,* 1119–1130.

Perkins, R. D. (1980). *The evolution of culture and grammar.* Unpublished doctoral dissertation, SUNY at Buffalo.

Petitto, L. A. (1987). On the autonomy of language and gesture: Evidence from the acquisition of personal pronouns in American Sign Language. *Cognition, 27,* 1–52.

Petitto, L. A. (1988). "Language" in the prelinguistic child. In F. S. Kessel (Ed.), *The development of language and language researchers* (pp. 187–221). Hillsdale, NJ: Erlbaum.

Petitto, L. A. (1992). Modularity and constraints in early lexical acquisition: Evidence from children's early language and gesture. In M. Gunnar (Ed.), *Minnesota Symposium on Child Psychology, Vol. 25,* (pp. 25–58). Hillsdale, NJ: Erlbaum.

Petitto, L. (2000). The acquisition of natural signed languages: Lessons in the nature of human language and its biological foundations. In C. Chamberlain, J. P. Morford, & R. Mayberry (Eds.), *Language acquisition by eye* (pp. 41–50). Mahwah, NJ: Erlbaum.

Petitto, L. A., & Marentette, P. F. (1991). Babbling in the manual mode: Evidence for the ontogeny of language. *Science, 251,* 1493–1496.

Phillips, S. B., Goldin-Meadow, S., & Miller, P. (1999). Narrative development without submersion in a native language. *Proceedings of Boston University Conference on Language Development, 23,* 565–574.

Phillips, S. B., Goldin-Meadow, S., & Miller, P. J. (2001). Enacting stories, seeing worlds: Similarities and differences in the cross-cultural narrative development of linguistically isolated deaf children. *Human Development, 43,* 311–336.

Pinker, S. (1984). *Language learnability and language development.* Cambridge, MA: Harvard University Press.

Pinker, S. (1989). *Learnability and cognition: The acquisition of argument structure.* Cambridge, MA: MIT Press.

Pinker, S. (1994). *The language instinct: How the mind creates language.* New York: Morrow.

Plunkett, K. (1995). Connectionist approaches to language acquisition. In P. Fletcher & B. MacWhinney (Eds.), *The handbook of child language* (pp. 36–72). Cambridge: Blackwell.

Polanyi, L. (1985). *Telling the American story: A structural and cultural analysis of American storytelling.* Norwood, NJ: Ablex.

Prasada, S. (2000). Acquiring generic knowledge. *Trends in Cognitive Science, 4,* 66–72.

Pye, C. (1992). The acquisition of K'iche' Maya. In D. I. Slobin (Ed.), *The cross-linguistic study of language acquisition, Vol. 3.* Hillsdale, NJ: Erlbaum.

Quine, W. V. O. (1960). *Word and object.* Cambridge, UK: Cambridge University Press.

Richards, R. (1990). *Language development and individual differences.* Cambridge, UK: Cambridge University Press.

Robins, R. H. (1952). Noun and verb in universal grammar. *Language, 28*(3), 289–298.

Rogoff, B. (1990). *Apprenticeship in thinking: Cognitive development in social context.* New York: Oxford University Press.

Rondal, J. A. (1988). Down's syndrome. In D. Bishop & K. Mogford (Eds.), *Language development in exceptional circumstances* (pp. 165–176). New York: Churchill Livingstone.

Ruben, R. J. (1972). The ear. In H. Barnett & A. Einhorn (Eds.), *Pediatrics* (15th ed., pp. 1881–1892). New York: Appleton-Century-Crofts.

Sachs, J. (1983). Talking about the there and then: The emergence of displaced reference in parent-child discourse. In K. E. Nelson (Ed.), *Children's language, Vol. 4* (pp. 1–28). Hillsdale, NJ: Erlbaum.

Sachs, J., Bard, B., & Johnson, M. L. (1981). Language learning with restricted input: Case studies of two hearing children of deaf parents. *Applied Psycholinguistics, 2,* 33–54.

Samarin, W. J. (1984). Socioprogrammed linguistics. *Behavioral and Brain Sciences, 7,* 206–207.

Sandler, W. (1986). The spreading hand autosegment of American Sign Language. *Sign Language Studies, 50,* 1–28.

Sandler, W. (2003). On the complementarity of signed and spoken language. In Y. Levy & J. Schaeffer (Eds.), *Language competence across populations: On the definition of SLI* (pp. 383–409). Mahwah, NJ: Erlbaum.

Sankoff, G., & Brown, P. (1976). The origins of syntax in discourse: A case study of Tok Pisin relatives. *Language, 52,* 631–666.

Sapir, E. (1921). *Language: An introduction to the study of speech.* New York: Harcourt Brace Jovanovich.

Savage-Rumbaugh, E. S., & Rumbaugh, D. M. (1993). The emergence of language. In K. R. Gibson & T. Ingold (Eds.), *Tools, language and cognition in human evolution* (pp. 86–108). New York: Cambridge University Press.

Schachter, P. (1985). Parts-of-speech systems. In T. Shopen (Ed.), *Language typology and syntactic description: Clause Structure (Vol 1.)* (pp. 3–61). Cambridge, MA: Cambridge University Press.

Schick, B. S. (1987). *The acquisition of classifier predicates in American Sign Language.* Unpublished doctoral dissertation, Purdue University.

Schick, B., & Moeller, M. P. (1992). What is learnable in manually coded English sign systems? *Applied Psycholinguistics, 13,* 313–340.

Schieffelin, B. B. (1985). The acquisition of Kaluli. In D. I. Slobin (Ed.), *A cross-linguistic study of language acquisition, Vol. 1* (pp. 525–593). Hillsdale, NJ: Erlbaum.

Schieffelin, B. B. (1990). *The give and take of everyday life: Language socialization of Kaluli children.* Cambridge, UK: Cambridge University Press.

Schiff-Myers, N. (1988). Hearing children of deaf parents. In D. Bishop & K. Mogford (Eds.), *Language development in exceptional circumstances* (pp. 47–61). New York: Churchill Livingstone.

Schlesinger, H. S. (1978). The acquisition of bimodal language. In I. Schlesinger (Ed.), *Sign language of the deaf: Psychological, linguistic, and sociological perspectives* (pp. 57–93). New York: Academic.

Schlesinger, H. S., & Meadow, K. P. (1972). *Sound and sign.* Berkeley: University of California Press.

Schulman, B. W., Mylander, C., & Goldin-Meadow, S. (2001). Ergative structure at sentence and discourse levels in a self-generated communication system. *Proceedings of Boston University Conference on Language Development, 25,* 815–824.

Seligman, M. E. P., & Hager, J. L. (1972). *Biological boundaries of learning.* New York: Appleton-Century-Crofts.

Senghas, A. (1995). The development of Nicaraguan Sign Language via the language acquisition process. *Proceedings of Boston University Conference on Language Development, 19,* 543–552.

Senghas, A. (2000). The development of early spatial morphology in Nicaraguan Sign Language. *Proceedings of Boston University Conference on Language Development, 24*, 696–707.

Senghas, A., & Coppola, M. (2001). Children creating language: How Nicaraguan Sign Language acquired a spatial grammar. *Psychological Science, 12*, 323–328.

Senghas, A., Coppola, M., Newport, E. L., & Supalla, T. (1997) Argument structure in Nicaraguan Sign Language: The emergence of grammatical devices. *Proceedings of Boston University Conference on Language Development, 21*, 550–561.

Senghas, A., Ozyurek, A., & Kita, S. (2003). Encoding motion events in an emerging sign language: From Nicaraguan gestures to Nicaraguan signs. In A. Baker, B. van den Bogaerde, & O. Crasborn (Eds.), *Crosslinguistic perspectives in sign language research. Selected papers from TISLR 2000.* Hamburg: Signum Press.

Seuren, P. A. M. (1984). The bioprogram hypothesis: Facts and fancy. *Behavioral and Brain Sciences, 7*, 208–209.

Seyfarth, R. M., & Cheney, D. L. (1997). Some general features of vocal development in non-human primates (1997). In C. T. Snowdon & M. Hausberger (Eds.), *Social influences on vocal development.* Cambridge, UK: Cambridge University Press.

Shatz, C. (1992). The developing brain. *Scientific American, 267*, 60–67.

Shatz, M. (1982). On mechanisms of language acquisition: Can features of the communicative environment account for development? In E. Wanner & L. R. Gleitman (Eds.), *Language acquisition: The state of the art* (pp. 102–127). New York: Cambridge University Press.

Shatz, M., & Gelman, R. (1973). The development of communication skills: Modifications in the speech of young children as a function of listener. *Monographs of the Society for Research in Child Development, 38* (Serial No. 152).

Shatz, M., Hoff-Ginsberg, E., & MacIver, D. (1989). Induction and the acquisition of English auxiliaries: The effects of differentially enriched input. *Journal of Child Language, 16*, 121–140.

Silverstein, M. (1976). Hierarchy of features and ergativity. In R. M. W. Dixon (Ed.), *Grammatical categories in Australian languages* (pp. 112–171). Canberra: Australian Institute of Aboriginal Studies.

Singleton, J. L., Goldin-Meadow, S., & McNeill, D. (1995). The cataclysmic break between gesticulation and sign: Evidence against an evolutionary continuum of manual communication. In K. Emmorey & J. Reilly (Eds.), *Language, gesture, and space* (pp. 287–311). Hillsdale, NJ: Erlbaum.

Singleton, J. L., Morford, J. P., & Goldin-Meadow, S. (1993). Once is not enough: Standards of well-formedness in manual communication created over three different timespans. *Language, 69*, 683–715.

Singleton, J. L., & Newport, E. L. (2003). When learners surpass their models: The acquisition of American Sign Language from impoverished input. *Cognitive Psychology*, accepted for publication.

Singleton, J. L., Supalla, S., Litchfield, S., & Schley, S. (1998). From sign to word: Considering modality constraints in ASL/English bilingual education. *Topics in Language Disorders, 18*, 16–29.

Skuse, D. H. (1988). Extreme deprivation in early childhood. In D. Bishop & K. Mogford (Eds.), *Language development in exceptional circumstances* (pp. 29–46). New York: Churchill Livingstone.

Slobin, D. I. (1966). The acquisition of Russian as a native language. In F. Smith & C. Miller (Eds.), *The genesis of language: A psycholinguistic approach.* Cambridge, MA: MIT Press.

Slobin, D. I. (1973). Cognitive prerequisites for the development of grammar. In C. A. Ferguson & D.I. Slobin (Eds.), *Studies of child language development.* New York: Holt, Rinehart & Winston.

Slobin, D. I. (1977). Language change in childhood and history. In J. Macnamara (Ed.), *Language learning and thought* (pp. 185–214). New York: Academic.

Slobin, D. I. (1982). Universal and particular in the acquisition of language. In E. Wanner & L. R. Gleitman (Eds.). *Language acquisition: The state of the art* (pp. 128–179). Cambridge, UK: Cambridge University Press.

Slobin, D. I. (1985a). Introduction: Why study acquisition cross-linguistically? In D. I. Slobin (Ed.), *A cross-linguistic study of language acquisition, Vol. 1* (pp. 3–24). Hillsdale, NJ: Erlbaum.

Slobin, D. I. (1985b). Cross-linguistic evidence for the language-making capacity. In D. I. Slobin (Ed.), *A cross-linguistic study of language acquisition, Vol. 2* (pp. 1157–1256). Hillsdale, NJ: Erlbaum.

Slobin, D. I. (1992). The cross-linguistic endeavor. In D. I. Slobin (Ed.), *A cross-linguistic study of language acquisition, Vol. 3* (pp. 1–13). Hillsdale, NJ: Erlbaum.

Slobin, D. I. (1997a). The universal, the typological, and the particular in acquisition. In D. I. Slobin (Ed.), *A cross-linguistic study of language acquisition, Vol. 5* (pp. 1–39). Hillsdale, NJ: Erlbaum.

Slobin, D. I. (1997b). The origins of grammaticizable notions: Beyond the individual mind. In D. I. Slobin (Ed.), *A cross-linguistic study of language acquisition, Vol. 5* (pp. 265–323). Hillsdale, NJ: Erlbaum.

Smith, C. S. (1970). An experimental approach to children's linguistic competence. In J. R. Hayes (Ed.), *Cognition and the development of language* (pp. 109–135). New York: Wiley.

Smith, D. (1978). Mirror images in Japanese and English. *Language, 54,* 78–122.

Smith, S., & Freedman, D. (1982). Mother-toddler interaction and maternal perception of child development in two ethnic groups: Chinese-American and European-American. Presented at SRCD, Detroit.

Snow, C. (1988). The development of conversations between mothers and babies. In M. B. Franklin & S. S. Barten (Eds.) *Child language: A reader* (pp. 20–35). New York: Oxford University Press.

Snow, C. E. (1972). Mothers' speech to children learning language. *Child Development, 43,* 549–565.

Spelke, E. S., & Newport, E. L. (1998). Nativism, empiricism, and the development of knowledge. In W. Damon (Ed.), *Handbook of child psychology, Vol. 1* (5th ed.) (pp. 275–340). New York: Wiley.

Sperry, D. E., & Sperry, L. L. (1996). Early development of narrative skills. *Cognitive Development, 11,* 443–465.

Stark, R. E. (1986). Prespeech segmental feature development. In P. Fletcher & M. Garman (Eds.), *Language acquisition* (2nd ed.) (pp. 149–173). Cambridge, UK: Cambridge University Press.

Stern, C., & Stern, W. (1907). *Die kindersprache.* Leipzig: Barth.

Stevenson, H. W., Lee, S.-L., Chen, C., Stigler, J. W., Hsu, C.-C., & Kitamura, S. (1990). Contexts of achievement. *Monographs of the Society for Research in Child Development, 55,* No. 221.

Stokoe, W. C. (1960). Sign language structure: An outline of the visual communications systems. *Studies in Linguistics, Occasional Papers, 8.*

Summerfield, A. Q. (1983). Audio-visual speech perception, lipreading, and artificial stimulation. In M. E. Lutman & M. P.Haggard (Eds.), *Hearing science and hearing disorders* (pp. 132–179). New York: Academic.

Supalla, S. (1991). Manually Coded English: The modality question in signed language development. In P. Siple & S. Fischer (Eds.), *Theoretical issues in sign language research: Vol. 2. Acquisition.* Chicago: University of Chicago Press.

Supalla, T. (1982). *Structure and acquisition of verbs of motion and location in American Sign Language.* Unpublished doctoral dissertation, University of California at San Diego.

Supalla, T., & Newport, E. L. (1978). How many seats in a chear? The derivation of nouns and verbs in American Sign Language. In P. Siple (Ed.), *Understanding language through sign language research* (pp. 91–132). New York: Academic.

Supalla, T., Newport, E. L., Singleton, J. L., Supalla, S., Metlay, D., & Coulter, G. (2003). *Test battery for American Sign Language morphology and syntax.* Burtonsville, MD: Linstok Press. In press.

Suty, K. A., & Friel-Patti, S. (1982). Looking beyond Signed English to describe the language of two deaf children. *Sign Language Studies, 35,* 153–168.

Svirsky, M. A., Robbins, A. M., Kirk, K. I., Pisoni, D. B., & Miyamoto, R. T. (2000). Language development in profoundly deaf children with cochlear implants. *Psychological Science, 11,* 153–158.

Swisher, M. V. (1989). The language-learning situation of deaf students. *TESOL Quarterly, 23,* 239–257.

Tager-Flusberg, H. (1994). Dissociations in form and function in the acquisition of language by autistic children. In H. Tager-Flusberg (Ed.), *Constraints on language acquisition: Studies of atypical children* (pp. 175–194). Hillsdale, NJ: Erlbaum.

Talmy, L. (1985). Lexicalization patterns: Semantic structure in lexical forms. In T. Shopen (Ed.), *Language typology and syntactic description: Vol. 3. Grammatical categories and the lexicon* (pp. 57–149). Cambridge, UK: Cambridge University Press.

Talmy, L. (1988). The relation of grammar to cognition. In B. Rudzka-Ostyn (Ed.), *Topics in cognitive linguistics* (pp. 166–205). Philadelphia: John Benjamins.

Tardif, T. (1996). Nouns are not always learned before verbs: Evidence from Mandarin speakers' early vocabulary. *Developmental Psychology, 32,* 492–504.

Tervoort, B. T. (1961). Esoteric symbolism in the communication behavior of young deaf children. *American Annals of the Deaf, 106,* 436–480.

Thal, D., & Tobias, S. (1992). Communicative gestures in children with delayed onset of oral expressive vocabulary. *Journal of Speech and Hearing Research, 34,* 604–612.

Thal, D., Tobias, S., & Morrison, D., (1991). Language and gesture in late talkers: A one year followup. *Journal of Speech and Hearing Research, 34,* 604–612.

Thelen, E., & Ulrich, B. D. (1991). Hidden skills: A dynamic systems analysis of treadmill stepping during the first year. *Monographs of the Society for Research in Child Development,* Serial No. 223, *56.*

Thompson, S. A. (1988). A discourse approach to the cross-linguistic category "adjective." In J. A. Hawkins (Ed.), *Explaining language universals* (pp. 167–185). Cambridge, MA: Blackwell.

Thorpe, W. H. (1957). The learning of song patterns by birds, with especial reference to the song of the Chaffinch Fringilla Coelebs. *Ibis, 100,* 535–570.

Valian, V. (1986). Syntactic categories in the speech of young children. *Developmental Psychology, 22,* 562–579.

Valian, V. (1991). Syntactic subjects in the early speech of American and Italian children. *Cognition, 40,* 21-81.

Valian, V. (1999). Input and language acquisition. In W. C. Ritchie & T. K. Bhatia (Eds.), *Handbook of child language acquisition* (pp. 497–530). New York: Academic.

Vygotsky, L. S. (1934/1962). *Thought and language.* Cambridge, MA: MIT Press.

Vygotsky, L. S. (1978). *Mind in society: The development of higher psychological processes* (M. Cole, V. John-Steiner, S. Scriber, & E. Souberman, Eds.). Cambridge, MA: Harvard University Press.

Waddington, C. H. (1957). *The strategy of the genes.* London: Allen & Unwin.

Wang, X-L., Mylander, C., & Goldin-Meadow, S. (1993). The resilience of language: A comparative study of the self-styled gesture systems of Chinese and American deaf children. In K. Emmorey & J. Reilly (Eds.), *Sign, gesture, and space.* Hillsdale, NJ: Erlbaum.

Werker, J. F., & Tees, R. C. (1984). Cross-language speech perception: Evidence for perceptual reorganization during the first year of life. *Infant Behavior and Development, 7,* 49–63.

Wexler, K. (1999). Maturation and growth of grammar. In W. C. Ritchie & T. K. Bhatia (Eds.), *Handbook of child language acquisition* (pp. 55–109). New York: Academic.

Whorf, B. L. (1956). *Language, thought, and reality: Selected writings of Bejamin Lee Whorf.* Cambridge, MA: MIT Press.

Wilbur, R. (1986). Interaction of linguistic theory and sign language research. In P. Bjarkman & V. Raskin (Eds.), *The real world linguist: Linguistic applications for the 1980's*. Norwood, NJ: Ablex.

Wilbur, R. (1987). *American Sign Language: Linguistic and applied dimensions* (2nd ed.). Boston: Little, Brown.

Williamson, S. G. (1979). *Tamil baby talk: A cross-cultural study.* Unpublished doctoral dissertation, University of Pennsylvania.

Wimsatt, W. C. (1986). Developmental constraints, generative entrenchment, and the innate-acquired distinction. In W. Bechtel (Ed.), *Integrating Scientific Disciplines*. Dordrecht: Martinus Nijhoff.

Young, N. F. (1972). Socialization patterns among the Chinese of Hawaii. *Amerasia Journal, 1*, 31–51.

Zheng, M. (2000). *Language and thought in early development: A comparative study of the expression of motion events in Chinese and American hearing and deaf children.* Unpublished doctoral dissertation, University of Chicago.

Zheng, M., & Goldin-Meadow, S. (1997). Lexical patterns in the expression of motion events in a self-styled gesture system. *Proceedings of Boston University Conference on Language Development, 21*, 730–739.

Zheng, M., & Goldin-Meadow, S. (2002). Thought before language: How deaf and hearing children express motion events across cultures. *Cognition, 85*, 145–175.

AUTHOR INDEX

SUBJECT INDEX